The Science and Pseudoscience
of Children's Mental Health

Recent Titles in Childhood in America

The Science and Pseudoscience of Children's Mental Health

Cutting Edge Research and Treatment

Sharna Olfman, Editor

Childhood in America
Sharna Olfman, Series Editor

 PRAEGER

AN IMPRINT OF ABC-CLIO, LLC
Santa Barbara, California • Denver, Colorado • Oxford, England

Library of Congress Cataloging-in-Publication Data

The science and pseudoscience of children's mental health : cutting edge research and treatment / Sharna Olfman, editor.
    p. cm.—(Childhood in America)
  ISBN 978-1-4408-3083-9 (hardback) ISBN 978-1-4408-3084-6 (ebook)
  I. Olfman, Sharna, editor.   II. Series: Childhood in America.
  [DNLM: 1. Child.   2. Mental Disorders. WS 350]
  RJ499
  618.92'89–dc23   2014045171

ISBN: 978-1-4408-3083-9
EISBN: 978-1-4408-3084-6

19 18 17 16 15   1 2 3 4 5

This book is also available on the World Wide Web as an eBook.

Visit www.abc-clio.com for details.

Praeger
An Imprint of ABC-CLIO, LLC

ABC-CLIO, LLC
130 Cremona Drive, P.O. Box 1911
Santa Barbara, California 93116-1911

This book is printed on acid-free paper ∞

Manufactured in the United States of America

For my mother, Bess Leve

Contents

Acknowledgments

I wish to thank the contributors, all of whom gave so generously of their time and expertise. Chapter 4 was heavily influenced by the work of Philip Landrigan, Philippe Grandjean, and Varda Burstyn. My husband, Daniel Burston, is an "editor's editor," and our ongoing dialogue about children's mental health is reflected in these pages. My children Adam and Gavi are, as always, my inspiration.

PART I

Pseudoscience versus Science

1

A New Paradigm in Children's Mental Health

Sharna Olfman

Over the past two decades, there has been a meteoric rise in the number of children—now estimated to be one in six—diagnosed and treated for a range of psychological disturbances, including attention deficit/hyperactivity disorder (ADHD), autism, mood disorders, and learning disabilities.[1] What is happening? Explanations in the popular media tend to polarize around two viewpoints:

1. Childhood mental illnesses are caused by genetically influenced *chemical imbalances* in the brain. Magic bullet cures will come in the form of drugs that correct these imbalances in much the same way that insulin treats diabetes. Greater awareness and improved diagnostics have led to the spike in incidence rates.
2. We need to *let kids be kids*. Children by definition are inattentive and moody, and we have to let them run and play, and stop pathologizing normal behaviors in order to drug them into silence for the convenience of quiet classrooms and orderly households.

Neither of these perspectives has a monopoly on the truth. Certainly some children are diagnosed unnecessarily because their behavior is inconvenient to the adult world. In *All Work and No Play* and *Childhood Lost*, I described the pathogenic trends in American culture that undermine children's psychological health, such as developmentally insensitive school systems, the disappearance of creative play in early childhood, and screen technologies that remove them from essential developmental tasks and immerse them in violent and sexualized worlds.[2] At the same time, though, many children are struggling with very real symptoms, ranging from impulsivity and learning challenges to panic and rage; they are not merely "quirky" or "willful" kids. But even when we take into account the possibility that clinicians are becoming more adept at recognizing psychopathology, the staggering increase in the number of children who are struggling with psychological disturbances cannot be fully accounted for by a sharper diagnostic lens. Put more simply, these two viewpoints pit nature versus nurture or biology against environment. This is an outmoded dichotomy that has been replaced in serious scientific circles by *epigenetics*, a discipline that explores the interplay of genes and environments that shape brain development and mental health.

THE SCIENCE OF CHILDREN'S MENTAL HEALTH

The *Diagnostic and Statistical Manual of Mental Disorders* (DSM) lists, describes, and codes every psychiatric condition that is recognized by the American Psychiatric Association (APA). The APA considers the manual to be foundational to diagnosis and treatment. Furthermore, almost all mental health professionals in the United States utilize the DSM because the diagnostic codes it contains are required for health insurance reimbursement.

On April 29, 2013, Thomas Insel, director of the National Institute of Mental Health (NIMH)—one of the most influential psychiatrists in the United States—posted a blog on the National Institutes of Health (NIH) Web site in which he wrote very critically of the DSM.[3] The timing of his critique was significant, because it preceded the much-anticipated publication of the fifth edition of the DSM by just a few weeks. In the months leading up to publication, this new edition became a lightning rod for growing dissatisfaction with psychiatric practice, not only from outside of psychiatry but also within its ranks. Following are Insel's comments about the DSM on his NIH blog (emphasis added):

While DSM has been described as a "Bible" for the field, it is, at best, a dictionary, creating a set of labels and defining each. The strength of each of the editions of DSM has been "reliability"—each edition has ensured that clinicians use the same terms in the same ways. *The weakness is its lack of validity.* Unlike our definitions of ischemic heart disease, lymphoma, or AIDS, the DSM diagnoses are based on a consensus about clusters of clinical symptoms, not any objective laboratory measure. In the rest of medicine, *this would be equivalent to creating diagnostic systems based on the nature of chest pain or the quality of fever.* Indeed, symptom-based diagnosis, once common in other areas of medicine, has been largely replaced in the past half century as we have understood that *symptoms alone rarely indicate the best choice of treatment. Patients with mental disorders deserve better.*

Insel goes on to introduce the public to a new NIMH initiative called the Research Domain Criteria (RDoC) project, whose purpose is to

transform diagnosis by incorporating genetics, imaging, cognitive science, and other levels of information to lay the foundation for a new classification system. . . . In this sense, RDoC is a framework for collecting the data needed for a new nosology. But *it is critical to realize that we cannot succeed if we use DSM categories as the "gold standard."* The diagnostic system has to be based on the emerging research data, not on the current symptom-based categories. . . . As two eminent psychiatric geneticists recently concluded, *"At the end of the 19th century, it was logical to use a simple diagnostic approach that offered reasonable prognostic validity. At the beginning of the 21st century, we must set our sights higher."*

And so we have in very clear language an incisive critique of the DSM and of psychiatry as it is currently practiced. Insel's comments have merit, and his sentiments echo those of Allen Frances, the psychiatrist who chaired the DSM-IV task force. Frances vigorously opposed publication of DSM-V, because of the lack of scientific rigor in vetting and creating diagnostic categories.[4] I am in full agreement with Insel that psychiatry and the mental health field are urgently in need of a paradigm shift. As Insel states in his introduction to the RDoC, it will not succeed if it is built upon the edifice of the DSM.

Fever Disorder: Moving beyond Symptoms

If we look at the symptoms that drive the psychiatric diagnoses most commonly given to children, and to adults for that matter, they are generally very broad and do not point to the source of the illness any more than fever does. Lowering a fever can be of vital importance at the acute stage of an illness, but none of us believes that a steady diet of aspirin and cold compresses is in any sense a cure. The same is true of symptoms like hyperactivity and inattention. I often give my undergraduate psychology students the following exercise: generate 10 different reasons that a child might be hyperactive or inattentive. Hands fly up:

- Maybe he's eating a sugary diet.
- His parents are too permissive.
- He spends hours a day playing video games.
- He can't concentrate on his schoolwork because he is being bullied.
- He's got a big imagination.

. . . and so on. My students learn that a wide range of factors—prenatal exposure to stress hormones, drugs such as cocaine and alcohol, and environmental pollutants such as PCBs—are associated with attentional issues, as is neglect and abuse during infancy and childhood. And yet the belief that all children exhibiting hyperactivity or inattentiveness are suffering from the same well-understood, genetically influenced brain disorder, with objective diagnostic criteria and well-established treatment protocols, is widely held by parents and clinicians alike. I would argue that calling depression an illness is a similarly flawed notion, only slightly better than calling it a "weeping" disease. Even psychosis, which generally leads to a diagnosis of schizophrenia, has many root causes. To be clear, like fever, symptoms of depression and psychosis can be devastating and life threatening, at which time symptom relief becomes the top priority. But—in keeping with the NIMH's RDoC agenda—we need to move beyond the idea that everyone who is depressed, or psychotic, or hyperactive has the same disease, any more than we would assume that everyone who has abdominal pain, or headache, or fever does. In so doing, we can begin to address the underlying causes rather than just staunching the wound with a tourniquet.

Nature AND Nurture: Epigenetics

Most serious genetic research is now conducted through the lens of epigenetics: put simply, the understanding that environments, whether they be cellular or social, can activate or silence genes. In chapter 3, using the metaphor of a theater production, Richard Francis explains that the gene is more accurately understood as a member of an ensemble cast rather than as a director. Once we understand that genes, environments ("from neurons to neighborhoods"), and brain development are inextricably linked, there is no turning back. We can no longer categorize genes as "good or bad," but rather as interacting in complex ways with hundreds of other genes, which are activated or deactivated by a complex array of environments.

Experience Expectant Brain Stimulation

An example of an epigenetic process is what developmental psychologists refer to as *experience expectant* brain stimulation.[5] The human brain is born in an extremely immature state, which is why compared with other primates, we are so helpless at birth. Arguably, the two most distinctive features of human evolution are that we became two-legged and large brained. Becoming two-legged necessitated a significant redesign of the pelvis and birth canal, a redesign that does not easily accommodate our large-brained offspring. Hence our prolonged and somewhat complicated births. In order to survive birthing our babies, *all babies are born too soon.*[6] The brain continues to mature at a rapid pace outside of the womb during the first few years of life, and then at a more moderate pace for the next two decades. Once outside the womb, *experience expectant* environmental stimulants—ones that we have evolved to expect through our long evolutionary journey—switch on the appropriate genes at the appropriate times to help orchestrate brain maturation. What are these *experience expectant* stimuli? They are nothing more and nothing less than the stimulation of all the senses through loving interaction with our caregivers, wrapped up in a relationship that psychologists call *attachment*. For this reason, as I discuss in chapter 4, the attachment relationship is essential for healthy brain development, which underlies mental health. These environmental catalysts for gene expression and brain development, which have evolved over the course of millions of years, are infinitely more effective than a *Baby Einstein* video. Conversely, when infants and children are neglected or abused, their emotional trauma, which can last a lifetime, can also be traced to epigenetic processes that undermine brain development.

A Multidisciplinary Lens

Insel stated in his NIH blog that the RDoC program will "transform diagnosis by incorporating genetics, imaging, cognitive science, and other levels of information to lay the foundation for a new classification system." I could not agree more, that any meaningful advances in mental health must take place through a wide multidisciplinary lens. Advances in our understanding of children's mental health have come from several different scientific disciplines, including developmental neuropsychology, functional neurology, environmental health, and developmental behavioral pediatrics, to name a few. We now know, for example, that prenatal exposure to environmental toxicants, depletion of micronutrients, and neglect or abuse in infancy and early childhood can alter gene expression, which in turn undermines brain development and function. We also know that the brain has far more plasticity—the capacity to change and grow in response to environmental stimulation—than we previously imagined, potentiating avenues for restoring mental health. This research moves us beyond merely cataloging symptoms and takes us to the source of children's psychological suffering.

THE PSEUDOSCIENCE OF CHILDREN'S MENTAL HEALTH

On May 13, 2013, just two weeks after posting the blog in which he unveiled the NIMH's new research agenda, distancing it from the

"19th century science" of the DSM, Insel issued a press release along-side president-elect of the APA Jeffrey Lieberman, in which he re-tracted his previous commentary on the DSM, claiming that in fact, the DSM and the NIMH's RDoC research program are not antithetical, but complementary:

> Today, the American Psychiatric Association's (APA) Diagnostic and Statistical Manual of Mental Disorders (DSM), along with the International Classification of Diseases (ICD) represents the best information currently available for clinical diag-nosis of mental disorders. *Patients, families, and insurers can be confident that effective treatments are available and that the DSM is the key resource for delivering the best avail-able care. . . .* DSM-5 and RDoC represent complementary, not competing, frame-works for this goal.[7]

In only two weeks, Insel moved from his position that the DSM "lacks validity," that its "symptom-based diagnosis . . . rarely indicate[s] the best choice of treatment" and therefore that "patients deserve better," to "patients . . . can be confident that effective treatments are available."

How do we make sense of this dramatic about-face? I believe that the earlier blog represents a rare, unvarnished glimpse of the truth from one of psychiatry's most powerful voices about his own disci-pline, whose diagnostic nosology is built on sand rather than science, and whose foundational principles cannot sustain or assist real ad-vances in our understanding of human suffering. This wrinkle in the fabric of the discipline was quickly smoothed over by a consensus statement two weeks later by the two titans of psychiatry: the director of the NIMH and the president-elect of APA.

I could interpret this about-face on the part of Insel in a charitable way: Why alarm millions of patients suffering from mental health is-sues with the inconvenient truth that their diagnoses and treatments are not based in sound science? As Insel states in his original post, the RDoC is in its infancy and may not have anything to offer clinically for a long time to come. I can understand the impulse to maintain pa-tients' faith and optimism, especially if no other treatments are imme-diately available. But at the end of the day, it is patronizing and ethically questionable for clinicians to lie to their patients about the limitations of their understanding and the treatments that they offer, when real science and real treatment options with few (if any) adverse side effects are available. This shameless backpedaling gives higher priority to the reputation of the field of psychiatry than to patient care, in much the same way that partisan politics places party loyalty above the interests of the American public.

The Chemical Imbalance Theory and Drug Therapies

Many psychiatrists, if asked, will admit that the *chemical imbalance theory* of mental illness is simplistic and has little if any evidence to support it. Nonetheless, it is a meme that justifies the treatment of choice in psychiatry: medication.

It is widely believed that psychiatric drugs are rigorously tested and vetted by the Food and Drug Administration (FDA) and that they target well-understood chemical imbalances in the brain. In fact, the FDA only requires that two clinical trials prove that a given drug has a *statistically* greater effect than a placebo, regardless of whether these statistical differences have any clinical significance and of how many other clinical trials for the same drug fail to show a difference. Irving Kirsch's meta-analyses of the research on the efficacy of selective serotonin reuptake inhibitor (SSRI) antidepressants[8] reveal that while antidepressants show a statistically significant difference over placebo pills (whose effectiveness in and of themselves is quite impressive), the difference is so small that it doesn't translate into a therapeutic improvement.[9] Also, this statistical difference is attributable to the fact that antidepressants have a host of side effects, unlike placebo pills. Therefore, most patients in these trials "break blind," meaning that they can guess whether they are on an actual medication or not, which affects their expectations.

One of the biggest controversies surrounding the creation of the fifth edition of the DSM was whether it would include pediatric bipolar disorder as a new category. In the early 2000s there was a 40-fold increase in the number of children diagnosed with this disorder, driven largely by the research of Joseph Biederman, who was considered to be the leading figure in child psychiatry. In 2008 Biederman was investigated for violating conflict of interest policies by accepting more than $1.6 million from Johnson & Johnson and promising a boost in sales of the antipsychotic Risperdal to pediatric patients, as documented in e-mails to Johnson & Johnson executives.[10] One of the grave concerns about including pediatric bipolar disorder in the DSM-5 was that it would have continued to boost prescriptions of antipsychotics, already numbering in the millions, to children. Antipsychotics are known to perturb the nervous and endocrine systems and to cause brain atrophy and increase mortality when used long term.[11] At the same time, there is no research to support their long-term efficacy. Although pediatric bipolar disorder was not included in DSM-5, largely because of its association with Biederman, disruptive mood dysregulation disorder (DMDD) was, despite the fact that it is widely understood to be a code name for childhood bipolar disorder. It is unclear at this early date whether this new diagnostic category will or will not stimulate prescriptions of antipsychotics to minors, but it is certainly not a diagnosis that has a foundation in research.

Beyond the Chemical Imbalance

Diagnostic procedures and treatments outside of the language of chemical imbalances and drug therapies are conveniently placed in a box called "alternative medicine," which for many is a euphemism for "new age" medicine, or junk science. The irony, as Robert Whitaker documents in chapter 2, is that it is the chemical imbalance theory that represents junk science. How has psychiatry—with its history of insulin coma therapy, shock therapy, and today, the wholesale treatment of millions of children with dangerous and ineffective drugs for questionable diagnoses—become the gold standard against which other disciplines and treatment approaches are measured?

The belief in the "chemical imbalance" and the "bad gene" as the cause of children's mental illness lives on as a powerful cultural myth. It is stoked by the pharmaceutical industry, which has identified children as a fertile market for its products, and by the health insurance industry, seeking an easy and cheap solution to complex psychological issues with multifaceted causes. Personal, family, and cultural factors, as well as more compelling biological explanations, are swept under the rug if they don't result in increased drug sales and the promise of a quick fix. We might dismiss this as "business as usual" in corporate America if the stakes weren't so high. As I have described in my last three books—*No Child Left Different*, *Bipolar Children*, and *Drugging Our Children* (with Brent Robbins)—the drug cocktails that millions of children are consuming damage their developing brains and bodies, while the real source of their suffering remains untreated. But this does not negate the value of biological research.[12]

The Science and Pseudoscience of Children's Mental Health exposes the myth of the *chemical imbalance* and the *bad gene* and introduces the science of epigenetics as a compelling conceptual framework for understanding the science of children's mental health. It presents research on the role that the quality of prenatal and early childhood care plays in brain development and mental health from a multidisciplinary, epigenetic perspective. Authors present research that sheds light on the impact of neurotoxicants such as heavy metals and pesticides, as well as the salutary effects of micronutrients. The underpinnings of autism spectrum disorder and concussion syndrome are explored from a functional neurology perspective, which views the brain as a complex, dynamic system with much greater plasticity than we have heretofore understood, opening the door to breakthroughs in diagnosis and treatment.

2

Chemical Imbalances: The Making of a Societal Delusion

Robert Whitaker

In 2010, a study in the *American Journal of Psychiatry* reported that an overwhelming majority of Americans believed that mental illnesses like depression and schizophrenia are caused by chemical imbalances in the brain.[1] That is a belief that tells of a great scientific advance: the biological causes of mental disorders are now known, and psychiatric medications help fix that pathology. Much like "insulin for diabetes," psychiatric drugs help bring brain chemistry back into balance.

This understanding—that psychiatric drugs fix chemical imbalances in the brain—dates back to the late 1960s, and it has reshaped our society in profound ways. It informs us that moods, behavior, and even thoughts are governed by brain chemicals that are largely outside of one's control. In this way, the story of chemical imbalances changes one's sense of the self. It also changes how parents see their children. When children fare poorly in school or display difficult behaviors, parents may quickly reach for the pill bottle—their children may be suffering from a chemical imbalance, which requires treatment with medication. Indeed, it is difficult to think of any other idea over the past three decades that has had as profound an influence on our society as the chemical imbalance theory of mental disorders. It has radically changed our national sense of self and how we view our children.

And here is what is most remarkable about this story: in scientific circles, the chemical imbalance theory of mental disorders basically fell apart during the 1980s. The 2010 *American Journal of Psychiatry* article didn't describe a society well informed about scientific findings; instead, it portrayed a society laboring under the influence of an extraordinary delusion.

BEFORE THE TRANSFORMATION

To understand the rise of the chemical imbalance hypothesis, and how, right from the beginning, it was woven from one part science and one part wishful thinking, it is necessary to revisit the discovery of the drugs that we remember today as the first "antipsychotics" and first "antidepressants." These names indicate drugs that are specific antidotes to schizophrenia and depression, but in fact the drugs were initially introduced into psychiatry because of their side effects. Then, over the course of a few years, psychiatry reconceptualized them as agents that were possible antidotes to these two disorders. Once the drugs were thought of in this way, the chemical imbalance theory of mental disorders was born.

The story of the discovery of chlorpromazine, which is remembered today as the first antipsychotic, begins in the laboratory of a French pharmaceutical firm, Rhone Poulenc. In the 1940s, Rhone Poulenc was testing a class of compounds known as phenothiazines to see if they might be toxic to the microbes that caused malaria, African sleeping sickness, and worm-borne illnesses, and during that process, it was discovered that one of the phenothiazines, promethazine, had antihistaminergic properties. This suggested it might be useful in surgery. In response to a wound, the body releases histamine, and on occasion, this can cause a precipitous drop in blood pressure. Perhaps promethazine could protect against that potentially fatal reaction. In 1949 a surgeon in the French Navy, Henri Laborit, gave it to several of his patients, and he noticed that in addition to protecting against surgical shock, promethazine induced a "euphoric quietude . . . . [P]atients are calm and somnolent."[2]

As Laborit investigated the drug's effects, he came to understand that it "made it possible to disconnect certain brain functions."[3] When he used it in surgery, a patient could stay awake and yet feel no pain or anxiety. This drug had remarkable properties, and Rhone Poulenc immediately sought to develop a stronger version of it. Eventually the company synthesized a compound, chlorpromazine, which when tested in rats, powerfully slowed motor movement and dimmed their emotional responses to the world.

As Laborit told the medical world about this new surgical drug, he noted that it produced a "veritable medicinal lobotomy."[4] This observation suggested it could be of use in psychiatry. In 1949, the Nobel Prize in medicine had been awarded to Portuguese neurologist Egas Moniz for having invented prefrontal lobotomy, a surgery that destroyed the frontal lobes. Although we think of lobotomy as a mutilating surgery, in the 1940s it was hailed as a miracle cure for debilitating anxiety and madness, and thus a chemical that could mimic its effects would be welcomed. The surgery, of course, did produce a noticeable change in being—the patient became lethargic, emotionally disengaged, and childlike—and Laborit was now describing a drug that produced a similar change in being. Two French psychiatrists, Jean Delay and Pierre Deniker, gave it to their patients at St. Anne's Hospital in Paris, which indeed quieted them and made them less engaged. They called the drug a "neuroleptic," meaning it took hold of the nervous system.

In 1954, Smith Kline & French, a pharmaceutical company that is now part of GlaxoSmithKline, introduced chlorpromazine into U.S. psychiatry, marketing it as Thorazine. American psychiatrists dubbed it a "major tranquilizer." There was no sense, at that moment of introduction, that it was an *antipsychotic*. "The drug," reported N. William Winkelman Jr. in the *Journal of the American Medical Association*, "produced an effect similar to frontal lobotomy."[5]

The chemical origins of psychiatry's first antidepressant can be traced back to a metaphorically apt source: rocket fuel. Toward the end of World War II, when Nazi Germany was running out of conventional fuel for its V-2 rockets, its scientists created a novel compound, hydrazine, as a replacement fuel. After the war, the Allied countries grabbed samples of it, becuase their pharmaceutical companies were eager to see if it might have toxic properties against infectious agents. In the next decade, Hoffman-La Roche synthesized a hydrazine derivative, iproniazid, which proved to be effective against the bacillus that caused tuberculosis. Moreover, there were reports that it had a welcome side effect: it stirred many patients from their lethargy. This suggested that it might have use in psychiatry as a drug that could rouse the severely depressed. In 1957, Nathan Kline, a psychiatrist at Rockland State Hospital in New York, reported that if depressed patients were kept on iproniazid for a long period of time (at least five weeks), it worked. The *New York Times* reported: "A side effect of an anti-tuberculosis drug may have led the way to chemical therapy for the unreachable, severely depressed mental patient. Its developers call it an energizer, as opposed to a tranquilizer."[6]

Such were the drugs that kicked off psychiatry's psychopharmacological revolution. The new agents arose from a search for magic bullets that would be useful in infectious medicine, and then they were introduced into psychiatry because of their novel side effects. They arrived as a tranquilizer and as an energizer, names that indicated drugs that perturbed normal functions. However, in fairly quick fashion, these drugs were recast in a new light.

THE RECONCEPTUALIZATION

The 1950s were a heady time for American medicine. In the 1940s, penicillin had revolutionized medicine, for it could miraculously— and quite quickly—kill potentially fatal bacterial infections. Chemists and other researchers had also developed improved anesthetics, sedatives, antihistamines, and anticonvulsants. The polio vaccine arrived in 1955. This was an age of magic bullets, and naturally psychiatry—a field that often felt inferior to the rest of medicine—was eager to have its own wonder drugs.

Chlorpromazine became its first such medication. When Thorazine was introduced in 1954, *Time* reported that "there is no thought that chlorpromazine is any cure for mental illness, but it can have great value if it relaxes patients and makes them accessible to [talk therapy] treatment."[7] But soon psychiatrists were describing the pill in a new way. In 1955, Nathan Kline and several other leading psychiatrists told a U.S. Senate budget committee that thanks to chlorpromazine, "patients who were formerly untreatable within a matter of weeks or months become sane, rational human beings."[8] Newspapers and magazines began describing it as a "wonder drug," with *Time* stating that its arrival marked a medical advance as profound as the "germ-killing sulfas discovered in the 1930s."[9] This was a clear magic-bullet analogy, and together these media reports told of how psychiatry had apparently discovered an antidote to madness.

The official transformation of Thorazine, from neuroleptic to antipsychotic, came in 1963, when the National Institute of Mental Health (NIMH) published the results of a nine-hospital study that compared three neuroleptics to placebo over a six-week period. Nearly 50 percent of the medicated patients improved so dramatically—at least in the eyes of the psychiatrists—that they could now be classified as either "normal" or only "borderline ill." Another 45 percent of the medicated patients improved somewhat. The results were so impressive that the NIMH researchers concluded that these drugs might indeed be curative. "Almost all symptoms and manifestations characteristic of schizophrenic psychoses improved with drug therapy, suggesting that the phenothiazines should be regarded as 'antischizophrenic' in the broad sense. In fact, it is questionable whether the term 'tranquilizer' should be retained."[10]

By this time, the drugs that had arrived as "energizers" had already been recast as antidepressants, and the idea that they reversed a chemical problem in the brain had been floated. During the early 1950s, researchers began to think that the transmission of signals across the tiny gap between neurons in the brain was accomplished chemically (instead of electrically, which had been the prevailing belief). In 1953, researchers isolated serotonin in the brains of animals, and soon they had identified other possible chemical messengers, most notably norepinephrine and dopamine. Then, in 1955, Bernard Brodie, a researcher at the NIMH, reported that reserpine, an herb used to treat mental illness in India, depleted serotonin in the brain. Reserpine also made the laboratory rabbits sluggish, and thus it appeared that lowering serotonin in the brain could affect mood. Next, Arvid Carlsson, a Swedish scientist who had worked in Brodie's lab, announced that reserpine also lowered brain levels of norepinephrine and dopamine. A second drug for depression then came to market, imipramine, and researchers found that if they pretreated rabbits with either iproniazid or imipramine before administering reserpine, the rabbits didn't become lethargic. These drugs seemed to block reserpine's usual effects.[11]

As these research results were announced, newspapers began writing about the possibility that iproniazid and imipramine might, in some manner or another, be fixing something chemically amiss in the brains of depressed patients. In a 1959 article, the *New York Times* described them as antidepressants and reported that they appeared to "reverse psychic states."[12] The two drugs now had antidote status, with psychiatrist Harold Himwich, in an article in *Science,* stating that they "may be compared with the advent of insulin, which counteracts symptoms of diabetes."[13]

In this way, drugs that had been brought to market because of their side effects had morphed into antipsychotics and antidepressants, names that told of drugs that were fixing some unknown pathology. And with the drugs reconceived in this way, psychiatric researchers soon found reason to hypothesize that they might be fixing chemical imbalances in the brain.

THE CHEMICAL IMBALANCE THEORY

The reserpine studies in rabbits raised the possibility that depression might be due to low levels of serotonin, norepinephrine, or dopamine, which the antidepressants might reverse. There were subsequent reports that reserpine induced "depression" in humans, too. During the first half of the 1960s, researchers figured out how antidepressants acted on the brain, and their findings fit with the reserpine studies in a convincing way.

By this point, researchers had come to understand the basic way that neurons communicate. The first neuron, known as the presynaptic neuron, releases a chemical messenger—serotonin, dopamine, or some other molecule—into the tiny gap between neurons, which is called the synaptic cleft, and this chemical messenger fits into receptors on the second neuron. This message may either "excite" the second neuron, causing it to fire, or inhibit it from firing. In order to end this message, the chemical messenger must be quickly removed from the synaptic cleft. This is done in one of two ways. Either an enzyme comes along and metabolizes the chemical messenger, with the metabolites carted off as waste, or the chemical messenger is taken back up by the presynaptic neuron and stored for reuse.

In the early 1960s, researchers discovered how iproniazid and imipramine affected this messaging process. Both hindered the removal of serotonin and norepinephrine from the synaptic cleft, although by different means. Iproniazid inhibited the enzyme that metabolizes serotonin and norepinephrine (which are monoamines), and thus became known as a monoamine oxidase inhibitor. Imipramine, a tricyclic antidepressant, blocked the reuptake of serotonin and norepinephrine from the synaptic cleft into the presynaptic neuron. Both drugs kept serotonin and norepinephrine in the synaptic cleft longer than normal, and thus both could be seen as increasing serotonergic activity.

In 1965, Joseph Schildkraut reviewed this history in a paper published in the *American Journal of Psychiatry* and set forth the chemical imbalance theory of affective disorders:

Those drugs [like reserpine] which cause depletion and inactivation of norepinephrine usually produce sedation or depression, while drugs which increase or potentiate norepinephrine are associated with behavioral stimulant or excitement and generally exert an antidepressant effect in man. From these findings a number of investigators have formulated a hypothesis about the pathophysiology of the affective disorders. This hypothesis, which has been designated the "catecholamine hypothesis of affective disorders," proposes that some, if not all depressions are associated with an absolute or relative deficiency of catecholamines, particularly norepinephrine.[14]

Schildkraut acknowledged that his hypothesis had obvious limitations, starting with the fact that it was "at best a reductionistic oversimplification of a very complex biological state." Even so, the chemical imbalance theory now provided a reason to conceptualize antidepressants as drugs that fixed a chemical imbalance in the brain. Two years later, psychiatric researchers set forth a hypothesis that schizophrenia was caused by too much dopamine in the system, which solidified the notion that the drugs might truly be like "insulin for diabetes."

When patients were treated with Thorazine or the other neuroleptics, they regularly developed Parkinsonian symptoms: twitches, a shuffling gait, and so forth. This suggested that the drugs were hindering the part of the brain that was affected by Parkinson's disease. In the late 1950s, Arvid Carlsson and others suggested that this disease might be related to a deficiency in dopamine. A Viennese scientist, Oleh Hornykicz, then tested this possibility by applying iodine to the brain of a man who had died from Parkinson's disease, as this chemical turns dopamine pink. The basal ganglia, the region of the brain that controls motor movement, was known to be rich in dopamine, but in this instance, no pink discoloration appeared. Parkinson's disease was thus understood to be caused by a dearth of dopaminergic neurons in the basal ganglia, and if antipsychotics caused the same symptoms as the disease did, then it stood to reason that they were hindering dopamine transmission in this region of the brain.

If this were so, might it be possible that schizophrenia was caused by too much dopamine in the brain? Amphetamines, which released dopamine, were known to occasionally induce psychosis, which would be consistent with the idea that psychosis and schizophrenia were caused by dopamine systems that were hyperactive. Thus, or so the reasoning went, drugs that blocked dopamine transmission in the brain might help balance dopamine activity in the brain. In 1967, Dutch scientist Jacques Van Rossum set forth the dopamine hypothesis of schizophrenia: "When the hypothesis of dopamine blockade by neuroleptic agents can be further substantiated, it may have fargoing consequences for the pathophysiology of schizophrenia. Overstimulation of dopamine receptors could then be part of the aetiology" of the disease.[15]

These two hypotheses—that depression was due to low levels of monoamines (serotonin and norepinephrine, in particular), and that schizophrenia was due to too much dopamine activity—served as the foundation for the larger chemical imbalance theory of mental disorders. These two hypotheses were in place by the end of the 1960s, and researchers then began investigating the obvious question: Did people with depression and psychotic disorders actually have such chemical imbalances? Or to put it another way, had psychiatry, by some incredible stroke of good fortune, stumbled upon drugs that fixed pathologies in the brain, which until that point had remained unknown?

PUTTING THE HYPOTHESIS TO THE TEST

Although researchers had no way to directly measure serotonin or dopamine levels in the brains of living patients, they immediately seized upon a novel method for indirectly measuring such neurotransmitter activity. When a neurotransmitter is metabolized by an enzyme, the metabolites show up in the cerebrospinal fluid. Thus, at least in theory, if depressed patients suffered from too little serotonin or norepinephrine, the cerebrospinal fluid of depressed patients should have lower-than-normal levels of metabolites for these two chemicals. Similarly, if people diagnosed with schizophrenia suffered from too much dopamine, then their cerebrospinal fluid should have higher-than-normal levels of dopamine metabolites.

In 1969, Malcolm Bowers at Yale University initiated this research. Serotonin is metabolized into 5-hydroxindole acetic acid (5-HIAA). In a study of eight depressed patients (all of whom had previously been exposed to antidepressants), he announced that their 5-HIAA levels in their cerebrospinal fluid were lower than normal, but not "significantly" so.[16] Two years later, investigators from McGill University reported that they too had failed to find a significant difference in the 5-HIAA levels of depressed patients and normal controls.[17] Then, in 1974, Bowers announced that depressed patients who had not previously been exposed to antidepressants had normal 5-HIAA levels.[18]

The serotonin theory of depression, less than a decade old, didn't appear to be panning out. Two researchers from the University of Pennsylvania, Joseph Mendels and Alan Frazer, also reexamined the reserpine studies, and concluded that when hypertensive patients were given reserpine, only 6 percent of patients became depressed. There were also reports from England of this herb *lifting* the spirits of many patients.[19] Reserpine, in fact, didn't reliably induce depression. The serotonin deficit theory might have died right there, except that in 1975 a report came from Sweden suggesting that there was a subset of depressed patients with low serotonin levels, and this subset of patients was more likely to be suicidal than others.

Marie Asberg and her colleagues at Karolinska Institute in Sweden reported that 20 of 68 depressed patients suffered from low levels of 5-HIAA (compared to the remaining 48). Two of the 20 subsequently committed suicide. They concluded that this was evidence that there might be a "biochemical subgroup of depressive disorders characterized by a disturbance of serotonin turnover."[20]

At that point, the low serotonin theory of depression was hanging by a thread; it wasn't a universal pathology underlying depression, but an abnormality seen in some patients. But even that flimsy thread was woven from a very small number: 20 patients in the Swedish study. In 1984, the NIMH put that "subset" idea to the test. They measured the 5-HIAA levels in a group of depressed patients and hypothesized that those with lower levels in their cerebrospinal fluid, compared to 5-HIAA levels in the rest of the patients, would be the group that responded the best to a drug, amitriptyline, that selectively blocked the reuptake of serotonin from the synaptic cleft. These patients would be having their serotonergic activity renormalized, so to speak. However, as lead investigator James Maas noted, "contrary to expectations, no relationships between cerebrospinal 5-HIAA and response to amitriptyline were found." Those with higher levels of 5-HIAA were just as likely to respond as those with lower levels. The NIMH investigators then drew the obvious conclusion: "Elevations or decrements in the functioning of serotonergic systems per se are not likely to be associated with depression."[21]

That report was published 20 years after Schildkraut first floated his hypothesis that a chemical imbalance in the brain was the cause of depression. The hypothesis was investigated and found to be invalid. The biological cause of depression remained unknown, and thus there was no evidence supporting the idea that antidepressants fixed a chemical imbalance in the brain. After that 1984 report, investigators continued to study serotonergic function in the brains of depressed patients (and the function of norepinephrine and other monoamines), but they never found that low levels of serotonin or any of the other neurotransmitters were to blame for depression. In his 2000 textbook *Essential Psychopharmacology*, psychiatrist Stephen Stahl summed up this research: "[T]here is no clear and convincing evidence that monoamine deficiency accounts for depression; that is, there is no 'real' monoamine deficit."[22] Finally, Eric Nestler, a scientist famous for his investigations into the biology of mental disorders, detailed in a 2010 paper how the many types of investigation into this theory had all come to naught:

"After more than a decade of PET studies positioned aptly to quantitatively measure receptor and transporter numbers and occupancy, monoamine depletion studies (which transiently and experimentally reduce brain monoamine levels), as well as genetic association analyses examining polymorphisms in monoaminergic genes, there is little evidence to implicate true deficits in serotonergic, noradrenergic, or dopaminergic neurotransmission in the pathophysiology of depression. This is not surprising, as there is no *a priori* reason that the mechanism of action of a treatment is the opposite of disease pathophysiology.[23]

From a scientific standpoint, the low-serotonin theory of depression had been thoroughly investigated, and now was officially dead and buried.

Investigations into the dopamine hyperactivity theory of schizophrenia have followed a somewhat similar path, although even today there are at least a handful of investigators still studying whether there might be something amiss in the dopamine function of schizophrenia patients, or at least in certain subsets of patients. However, the idea that schizophrenia is due to a simple excess of dopamine activity, which is then put back into balance by an antipsychotic, was put to rest by the early 1990s.

In the early 1970s, Solomon Snyder at Johns Hopkins Medical School and other researchers reported that there were two distinct types of dopamine receptors in the brain, which were dubbed D1 and D2. In 1975, Snyder reported that antipsychotics, at a therapeutic dose, blocked 70–90 percent of the D2 receptors. This provided evidence that neuroleptics hindered dopaminergic function in a profound way, and thus provided a confirmation of the evidence used to launch the dopamine hypothesis of schizophrenia. However, even as Snyder was announcing his findings, Malcolm Bowers was reporting that the level of dopamine metabolites in the cerebrospinal fluid of unmedicated patients was quite normal.[24] His findings were then confirmed by Robert Post at the NIMH.[25]

It was clear that the presynaptic neurons in unmedicated schizophrenia patients were not producing too much dopamine. Researchers then turned their attention to a second possibility: perhaps people with schizophrenia had too many dopamine receptors. If so, this would make their brains extra-sensitive to dopamine released into the synaptic cleft. This, in fact, was the precise abnormality Van Rossum speculated might be the cause of schizophrenia, and in 1978, Philip Seeman, from the University of Toronto, announced that at autopsy he had found precisely this pathology. The brains of 20 schizophrenia patients had 70 percent or more D2 receptors than normal. However, in his paper, Seeman cautioned that all of these patients had been on antipsychotics before their deaths. "Although these results are apparently compatible with the dopamine hypothesis of schizophrenia in general," Seeman wrote, the increase in D2 receptors might "have resulted from the long-term administration of neuroleptics."[26]

Subsequent research found that to be the case. When neuroleptics were given to rats, it caused an increase in their D2 receptors.[27] This was evidence that the brain was trying to compensate for the presence of the drug. The drug blocked dopamine activity in the brain, and the brain, in an effort to maintain normal dopaminergic function, tried to increase its sensitivity to the chemical. In 1982, Angus MacKay reported that this increase in D2 receptors was only seen at autopsy in "patients [in] whom neuroleptic medication had been maintained until the time of death, indicating that they were entirely iatrogenic [drug caused]."[28] Finally, investigators in France, Sweden, and Finland used positron emission topography to study D2 receptor levels in living patients, and they too found that in schizophrenia patients who had never been exposed to antipsychotics, there were no significant differences from normal controls.[29]

At that point, the simple chemical imbalance theory of schizophrenia—that schizophrenia is due to too much dopamine activity, which is then put back into balance by neuroleptics—had fallen apart. As Pierre Deniker observed in 1990, "the dopaminergic theory of schizophrenia retains little credibility for psychiatrists."[30] However, researchers have continued to investigate dopaminergic function in psychotic patients and in animal models of psychosis, and now and then they announce an abnormality of dopaminergic function of some type, in perhaps one area of the brain and not another. But none of this research is thought to have resurrected the simple dopamine hyperactivity theory of schizophrenia, with this pathology then fixed by antipsychotic medication. In a 2002 book, *Molecular Neuropharmacology*, Stephen Hyman, a neuroscientist who directed the NIMH during the 1990s, summed up the body of evidence in this way: "There is no compelling evidence that a lesion in the dopamine system is a primary cause of schizophrenia."[31]

A PUBLIC DELUDED

Given this history of science, the obvious question is: Why then did the public come to believe that depression, schizophrenia, and other mental disorders were known to be due to chemical imbalances, which were then fixed by psychiatric drugs? The answer, of course, is that this was the story told to the public by the pharmaceutical companies in their advertisements for SSRIs (selective serotonin reuptake inhibitors) antidepressants and other psychiatric medications; the story told by many patient advocacy groups, such as the National Alliance for the Mentally Ill (NAMI); and the story told by leaders of the American Psychiatric Association (and in forums run by the APA). Even today, in 2014, it is possible to find such claims on patient advocacy Web sites, which the APA cites as reliable resources.

For instance, the Balanced Mind Parent Network, which has a scientific advisory board composed of more than 20 academic psychiatrists, tells visitors that "depression is a medical illness caused by a chemical imbalance . . . . [A]ntidepressant medications work to restore proper chemical balance in the brain."[32] The Depression and Bipolar Support Alliance (DBSA) tells the public the same thing: "Depression is caused by a chemical imbalance in the brain."[33] It too has a scientific advisory board comprised of well-known academic psychiatrists. Perhaps no organization has done more to promote this idea than NAMI, which has made the chemical imbalance story its signature statement for more than two decades. Its Web site informs the public that "scientists believe that if there is a chemical imbalance in these neurotransmitters (norepinephrine, serotonin, dopamine), then clinical states of depression result . . . .

[R]esearch has shown that imbalance in neurotransmitters like serotonin, dopamine and norepinephrine can be corrected with antidepressants."[34] NAMI's scientific advisory board is populated by many of the most prominent psychiatrists in the country, including Nancy Andreasen, former editor-in-chief of the *American Journal of Psychiatry*, and Jeffrey Lieberman, chair of the psychiatry department at Columbia University, who was the APA's president in 2013.

Thus, at least in many information channels, the American public is still being told a false story, one belied by science, and so the delusion persists. However, many within psychiatry are now publicly acknowledging that the chemical imbalance story never panned out. In a 2011 blog, Thomas Insel, director of the NIMH, wrote that "earlier notions of mental disorders as chemical imbalances are beginning to look antiquated."[35] Psychiatrists on a National Public Radio show in 2012 echoed this conclusion: "Chemical imbalance is sort of last-century thinking," explained Joseph Coyle, editor-in-chief of *Archives of General Psychiatry*. "It's much more complicated than that. . . . It's really an outmoded way of thinking."[36] But the most complete renunciation of the theory may have been penned by Ronald Pies, editor-in-chief emeritus of *Psychiatric Times*, a publication of the American Psychiatric Association. In a piece titled "Psychiatry's New Brain-Mind and the Legend of the 'Chemical Imbalance'," Pies put the blame for this scientific delusion squarely on the shoulders of others:

I am not one who easily loses his temper, but I confess to experiencing markedly increased limbic activity whenever I hear someone proclaim, "Psychiatrists think all mental disorders are due to a chemical imbalance!" In the past 30 years, I don't believe I have ever heard a knowledgeable, well-trained psychiatrist make such a preposterous claim, except perhaps to mock it. On the other hand, the "chemical imbalance" trope has been tossed around a great deal by opponents of psychiatry, who mendaciously attribute the phrase to psychiatrists themselves. And, yes—the "chemical imbalance" image has been vigorously promoted by some pharmaceutical companies, often to the detriment of our patients' understanding. In truth, the "chemical imbalance" notion was always a kind of urban legend—never a theory seriously propounded by well-informed psychiatrists.[37]

That was the moment when the APA officially washed its hands of the entire affair. Science had told one story, the public had been informed of another, and if the public wanted to know why this was so, they could look for someone other than psychiatry to blame. Well-informed psychiatrists had long known that a hypothesis, born in the 1960s, had not panned out.

3

Epigenetics and Children's Mental Health

Richard C. Francis

How is it that our environment can affect our genes? That idea seems incongruous. This seeming incongruity reflects a basic misperception about how genes influence human development, a misperception popularized not only in the media, but by many geneticists as well. Recognizing the role of environment in regulating gene behavior unleashes enormous potential for understanding children's mental health and developing interventions ranging from diet to relationships, which in turn alter gene expression. The standard belief—which focuses on identifying the "ADHD" gene or gene sequence, for example, with a view to intervening at the level of the gene, without any consideration of the role of environment—is shortsighted and fundamentally flawed.

The problem with the old paradigm begins with certain foundational metaphors that shape our conception of DNA, most fundamentally, that of instruction. DNA has come to be conceived as the instructor of development by virtue of encoding the program or recipe by which the developmental process is executed. I refer to this conception of DNA's role in development as the "executive gene." Epigenetics is not compatible with the executive gene. From an epigenetic perspective, genes are as much instructed as instructors.

I have used the metaphor of a theatrical production to distinguish the executive gene view from that of an epigenetically informed view of genes as they function in the cell (microcosm) and development (macrocosm).[1] From the perspective of the executive gene, DNA functions as the director of the theatrical production, proteins as the actors, and all other biochemicals as the stage hands. From an epigenetic perspective, in contrast, DNA, proteins, and everything else interact more as an ensemble cast. The executive function lies at the level of the cell. This is important to bear in mind for what follows.

The executive gene view seems most compelling when DNA is viewed abstractly, as an information bearer. It becomes much less compelling when the biochemical nature of DNA is emphasized. The abstract gene is one dimensional, a code-bearing sequence. The material gene, however, is a three-dimensional biochemical. It is in these extra dimensions that epigenetic processes occur. The twisting and folding of DNA, for example, greatly affects gene activity. In part, epigenetic processes regulate gene activity through their shape-shifting effects. Once we abandon the perspective of the executive gene, it is not at all surprising that our environment—the food we eat, the chemicals to which we are exposed, and our social interactions—influences the behavior of our genes. Developmental biologists recognized this long before the advent of epigenetics. But epigenetics has markedly increased awareness of environment and gene influence.

When considering how our environment affects our genes, it helps to think about the gene's environment in a nested way. The most fundamental environment for a gene is the cellular environment. It is here, ultimately, that gene regulation lies. But the cellular environment is influenced by a cell's interaction with other cells, whether directly—that is, with adjacent cells (particularly important in understanding cancer)—or more indirectly, with more distant cells via the endocrine or nervous system or both. These cell-cell interactions are what our external environment most directly affects, and they determine the intracellular environment in which a gene functions.

WHAT IS EPIGENETIC GENE REGULATION?

Epigenetics is the study of long-term alterations in gene activity, or what biologists refer to as gene expression. It is the persistence of epigenetic influences on gene regulation that distinguishes it from garden-variety gene regulation. Garden-variety gene regulation occurs over minutes or hours, for example when your eyes accommodate to changes in light level, or your blood pressure responds to the unexpected appearance of someone you dislike. These sorts of alterations are reversible over small time scales. Epigenetic alterations are also reversible, but they can last a lifetime, and sometimes beyond.

Technically, what makes an alteration in gene activity epigenetic, as opposed to garden variety, is that it survives cell division or "mitosis."

That is, the epigenetic mark is passed from a mother cell to the daughter cell and subsequent descendants in a cell lineage. It is this cellular level inheritance that makes epigenetic alterations special. Given these cellular ancestor-descendant relationships, the earlier in development an epigenetic alteration occurs, the more pervasive are its developmental effects. Indeed, the most fundamental epigenetic alterations are those that affect the fate of stem cells. The process of cellular differentiation—the cellular alterations that, over a number of cell generations, cause stem cells to become skin cells or neurons (brain cells) or white blood cells, as the case may by—is a highly ordered epigenetic process. All of the 200 plus cell types in the human body are genetically identical; it is only epigenetic differences that distinguish skin cells from neurons.

TYPES OF EPIGENETIC PROCESSES

For convenience, in this discussion I divide epigenetic processes into three categories based on biochemical criteria: DNA methylation, chromatin remodeling, and RNA-mediated control of gene expression. I begin with DNA methylation, which is especially well documented.

DNA methylation involves the addition of a methyl group (a carbon atom with three hydrogen atoms attached = CH^3) to a DNA molecule. Methyl groups don't attach just anywhere on the DNA molecule; they attach specifically between a cytosine (C) base and a guanine (G) base. Since the cytosine and guanine bases are connected by a phosphate bond, the site of attachment is usually written as CpG. Generally, the addition of a methyl group at or near a gene's regulatory elements will tend to inhibit gene activity and reduce gene expression. Demethylation has the opposite effect. Methylation and demethylation are a matter of degree, not all or nothing. The more methylated a gene is, the less active it is in protein synthesis.

Chromatin remodeling involves several distinct processes, all of which affect the binding of histones to DNA. In cells, DNA is inextricably bound to histone proteins of various sorts. The combination of DNA and histones is called chromatin. So intimate is the relationship between DNA and histones that it took a long while and ingenious experimentation to figure out that DNA, not histones, is the hereditary material. Once this was demonstrated, histones were completely ignored. Epigenetics has brought histones back to the fore. Indeed there is now talk of a histone code. In general, the more tightly bound the histones to the DNA the less active a gene in that vicinity will be. The boundedness of histones to DNA varies greatly across the genome, and on a smaller scale, over the length of a particular chromosome.

Several distinct biochemical processes influence how tightly bound the histones and DNA will be, all through modifications of the histones. Among the more pervasive of these biochemical processes are methylation, acetylation, phosphorylation, and ubiquitination. The best studied are methylation and acetylation of the amino acid lysine on the histones H3 and H4. Methylation of lysine can have either repressive or activational effects on nearby genes, depending on the precise position of the lysine residue.[2] Lysine acetylation tends to promote transcription, whereas deacetylation tends to inhibit gene activity.

RNA-mediated processes are coming increasingly to the fore as an important component of epigenetic gene regulation but are the least understood. One class of RNAs, called micro-RNAs (miRNAs), stands out epigenetically. As their name implies, miRNAs are quite small, only 17–25 nucleotides, but they pack a punch. About 2,000 miRNAs have been discovered to date, each of which regulates the expression of up to 100 genes, primarily by targeting their messenger RNAs (mRNA). Generally miRNAs reduce gene expression by causing the premature breakdown of mRNAs, before they can be translated into proteins.

EPIGENETICS IN THE INTRAUTERINE ENVIRONMENT

Epigenetic processes begin before fertilization, during the manufacture of sperm and eggs, but here I begin with what goes on in the womb. It has long been known that the intrauterine environment has life-altering consequences; recent epigenetic research helps us understand why. One particularly important study, which commenced long before the advent of epigenetics, will serve as the entrée into this subject.

Nutrition

Toward the end of World War II, the Germans imposed a food embargo on Holland, which resulted in a serious famine, the last to occur in Western Europe. Conditions were particularly dire in Western Holland during the winter of 1944–1945, when the average daily diet consisted of only 1,000 calories, less than half of the minimum required for good health. Many died. Many more suffered, including those who experienced the famine in their mothers' wombs. Low birth weight was common, of course, but other adverse effects were less predictable and only became manifest later in life. One of the adverse effects seemed paradoxical: obesity. It seems that some satiety, or calorie-monitoring, mechanism was altered by the experience—in the womb—of food, particularly protein, deprivation. Obesity was first noticed in the 1960s in 18-year-olds undergoing medical examinations for compulsory military service.[3] This cohort was carefully monitored over the years, to the present day. As the cohort aged, obesity rates continued to increase. Other effects of in utero exposure to the famine were also noted, including elevated rates of diabetes and heart problems, as well as mental health issues, including schizophrenia, mood disorders, and antisocial personality disorder.[4]

In recent years researchers have looked for epigenetic signals in the Dutch famine cohort. Though the results remain preliminary, there is suggestive evidence that the famine did indeed have epigenetic effects, one of which is methylation of the insulin-like growth factor IGF2, which plays an important role in embryonic development.[5] The Dutch famine study highlights the importance of fetal nutrition for adult onset diseases. Research along these lines is rapidly proliferating, to the point where it has been assigned a label: nutritional epigenetics.[6] Much nutritional epigenetic research is conducted on animal models, especially mice and rats. It is clear from these studies that many, if not most, instances of heart disease and diabetes began with epigenetic alterations of the fetus.[7] There is also evidence of a significant in utero nutritional influence on neurocognitive pathologies, such as autism,[8] mediated by epigenetic processes. For example, folic acid— a methyl donor—deficiencies seem to increase the likelihood of autism spectrum disorder due to insufficient methylation of a subset of genes active in neurodevelopment.

Environmental Toxicants

As David Crews and Andrea Gore have emphasized, we live in an increasingly contaminated world.[9] Since the Industrial Revolution, we humans have created over 80,000 unprecedented chemicals, that is, chemicals that never before existed in nature. Many of these chemicals, unfortunately, have proven toxic to us and other living things. Some of them adversely affect the fetal environment. The adverse effects of exposure to these chemicals results from epigenetic alterations.[10]

Among the more problematic of these man-made chemicals are those known as endocrine disruptors, so called because in mimicking hormones, they wreak havoc on the endocrine system. Those that mimic estradiol are particularly dangerous, including polychlorinated biphenyls (PCBs) and bisphenol A (BPA; used in the production of plastics, including water bottles). A number of agricultural pesticides are also endocrine disruptors, including atrazine and the fungicide vinclozolin.

The potential danger of endocrine disruptors was first noticed in fish and amphibians, aquatic animals that live in habitats where endocrine disruptors tend to be concentrated. Fish and amphibians are also particularly sensitive to endocrine disruptors because their sexual development is largely under environmental control.[11] In mammals, the effects of endocrine disruptors are less dramatic, but are troubling nonetheless. Male mammals, including human males, are particularly sensitive to endocrine disruptors, through their effect on imprinted genes.

Imprinted genes are genes that are under normal conditions differentially expressed in males and females. That is, the allele is active in one sex and turned off in the other, through an epigenetic process in the germ cells (sperm and ova). If the imprinting process is disturbed by endocrine disruptors, all manner of developmental problems occur, including prostate cancer, kidney disease, and abnormal testis development.[12] In many cases the problems don't become manifest until adulthood. One of the best models for investigating the effects of endocrine disruptors in mammals is that of rats exposed to vinclozolin. Male rats exposed in utero to vinclozolin have defective sperm and markedly reduced fertility as adults.[13] I return to this model later in this chapter.

Stress

Many researchers believe that the in utero epigenetic effects of food deprivation—as in the Dutch famine—are mediated by alterations in the stress response. In essence, from this point of view, any stressor, whether starvation, poverty, or an adverse social environment, is ultimately manifested by alterations of the stress response. I think this is a bit simplistic, but it is certainly the case that the stress response influences virtually every organ and tissue type in our bodies. It is also true that we should be wary of prenatal exposure to glucocorticoids, which are related to the stress hormone cortisol.

Unfortunately, glucocorticoids are routinely administered to late term fetuses, to promote organ maturation. Studies on guinea pigs—which like humans but unlike rats have long pregnancies—indicate that these exogenous glucocorticoids permanently alter the stress response[14] in ways that render the male guinea pigs hypersensitive to stress as adults. Moreover, when pregnant females are subjected to environmental stresses during the period of rapid fetal brain growth, the male offspring have an elevated stress response.[15] The cause of the sex-specific effects of these manipulations remains unknown but is worth further investigation, given the male bias for symptoms related to conditions such as ADHD and autism spectrum disorder. Given the epigenetic potency of glucocorticoids, the precautionary principle should be adhered to, and fetal exposure to exogenous glucocorticoids should be minimized. A well-functioning stress response is an important foundation of mental health. It is therefore important to exercise extreme care in applying any chemical treatment that may adversely affect the stress response.

EPIGENETICS FROM INFANCY TO CHILDHOOD

Humans are unique among primates in our protracted period of dependency during early development. Neural development is not completed until well after the teenage years. As such, we humans are particularly vulnerable to the long-term consequences of adverse environments in early life, beginning in infancy. But our knowledge of these effects and their causes is largely indirect and retrospective, simply because, for obvious ethical reasons, controlled experiments cannot be performed on humans. Animal models are of some help in this regard, especially laboratory rats and, to a lesser extent, nonhuman primates.

Maternal Neglect

Michael Meaney and his collaborators have conducted some particularly compelling experiments concerning the effects of parenting in rats. Like humans and other mammals, rats are tactile creatures, and touch of various sorts is crucial for a sense of psychological well-being, beginning at birth. In rats, licking is the relevant form of tactile stimulation, the more the better. As you would expect, rat mothers vary in the amount of licking they deliver to their pups. Moreover, some genetic strains of lab rats lick a lot, and some lick very little. This has proved very useful in Meaney's experiments.[16]

Pups reared by poor lickers, in other words inattentive mothers, tend to have an overactive stress response as adults, while pups reared by good lickers, or attentive mothers, tend to have a more normal stress response.[17] When pups from the poor-licking genetic strain are cross-fostered with mothers from the good-licking line, their stress response resembles that of typical pups from the high-licking line.[18] Clearly it is the experience of being licked, not a genetic difference in the stress response, that causes the over-amped stress response in mice from the poor-licking line. The fact that these effects of early experience are so long-lasting led Meaney to look for epigenetic signatures.

The stress response evolved long ago, before the advent of mammals; it is vertebrate-wide. There are three basic components: the hypothalamus (a part of the limbic system in the brain) and the pituitary and adrenal glands, which together comprise the hypothalamic-pituitary-adrenal (HPG for short) axis. The stress hormone cortisol is secreted by the adrenal glands, but it is ultimately regulated, through positive and negative feedback loops, at the level of the pituitary and ultimately the hypothalamus. More important than cortisol levels—which can fluctuate wildly over short time scales—are the levels of cortisol (or glucocorticoid) receptors. Cortisol itself has no effect unless it binds to the proper receptor.

Meaney discovered that glucocorticoid receptor (GR) levels were especially altered in the hippocampus in accordance with how the rat pups were nurtured.[19] Further research revealed that the different levels of GR in well- and poorly mothered rats was in part the result of epigenetic (methylation) differences in the GR gene. The pronounced response of the GR receptors in the hippocampus is in keeping with what we know about the effects of stress on this structure, so vital for learning and memory. Those who suffer from post-traumatic stress disorder (PTSD) experience hippocampal atrophy, as do those with Cushing's syndrome, a disorder of chronically elevated cortisol levels.

Like human mothers, mother rats undergo a suite of hormonal changes prior to and just after giving birth. Oxytocin levels rise, as do the levels of estrogen and estrogen receptors. Estrogen receptor levels seem to be particularly important for maternal behavior. Levels of this receptor are reduced in the female offspring of poor lickers relative to good lickers, one consequence of which is that these females do not respond normally to the elevated estrogen levels they experience when they give birth.[20] This dampened response to elevated estrogen levels is caused by reduced binding of oxytocin in the hypothalamus, which is crucial for maternal behavior. Oxytocin promotes social—or affiliative—behavior, so any reduction in oxytocin activity tends to make rats—and other mammals—less inclined toward prosocial interactions. Actually, as with cortisol and estrogen, it is the level of the receptor, in this case the oxytocin receptor, that is paramount. It appears that estrogen receptors (when bound with estrogen) bind directly to the control panel of the oxytocin receptor gene, promoting transcription. The reduced expression of the estrogen receptor gene—and hence reduced oxytocin receptor levels—that occurs in female pups of poor lickers persists into adulthood, which makes it more likely that they will be less-devoted lickers when they become mothers. In this way, the effects of inadequate maternal care are perpetuated for another generation.

The long-term effects of lick deprivation on estrogen receptor expression are due to epigenetic alterations of the estrogen receptor gene.[21] In pups raised by poor lickers this gene is methylated to a greater degree than that of pups raised by good lickers. Hence, the expression of this gene is inhibited in offspring of poor lickers relative to the offspring of good lickers. Female offspring of poor lickers experience an epigenetic double deficit with regard to their own mothering. First, their stress response is elevated as a result of epigenetic alterations affecting the expression of the GR gene in the hippocampus. The presence of neonates is stressful in and of itself; so afflicted mothers tend to be distractible and unsolicitous in the presence of their own young. Second, epigenetic alterations of the estrogen receptor gene in the hypothalamus, and the consequent reduction in oxytocin receptor expression, renders such mothers less likely to lick their offspring even in unstressful conditions.

TRANSGENERATIONAL EPIGENETIC EFFECTS

Meaney's experiments demonstrate how some epigenetic effects can be perpetuated beyond an individual lifetime. Poor mothering tends to perpetuate itself in a vicious cycle; conversely, high-quality mothering tends to perpetuate itself in a virtuous cycle, from one generation to the next. This sort of social inheritance occurs in primates as well. In Harry Harlow's notorious studies, rhesus monkeys completely deprived of maternal care during the first three months exhibited a number of pathologies in brain and behavior, not least in the stress response.[22] Steven Soumi investigated what happened when the deprived female monkeys themselves became mothers. Not surprisingly, the motherless mothers were not good mothers themselves, often abandoning their offspring entirely.[23]

Social Inheritance

The results of Meaney's experiments represent a phenomenon we can call *social inheritance*. Victor Denenberg was a pioneer in this area,[24] but when Denenberg first characterized social inheritance, it remained at the descriptive level. Meaney has provided a mechanism, an epigenetic mechanism, for social inheritance that may apply broadly to other mammals, including us. Human children who are subjected to poor parenting, ranging from neglect to psychological and physical abuse, suffer reduced mental health, and as in rats and monkeys, a hyperactive stress response.[25] Moreover, there is evidence of epigenetic alterations of the GR gene in the hippocampus, similar to that observed in rats.

But parenting that falls within the normal range can also have lifelong effects on adult behavior, much of it mediated by the stress response. One commonly used measure of maternal care is the parent bonding instrument (PBI). Counterintuitively, low scores for maternal care are often associated with high levels of maternal control, a combination referred to as "affectionless control," which is a risk factor for depression, anxiety, antisocial personality disorder, obsessive-compulsive disorder, drug abuse, and a reactive stress response.[26] On the other hand, high PBI scores are associated with high self-esteem, low anxiety, and a dampened stress response.

The suite of behavioral responses of a mother to her offspring is called "maternal style." The spectrum of maternal styles runs from abuse to neglect to affectionless control to affectionate noncontrolling. Maternal style within the normal range can be transmitted transgenerationally in humans, as in rats. In contrast to rats—and most other mammals—though, fathers also play an important role in parenting. There have been relatively few studies on the effects of paternal style on the stress response of children or adults. One intriguing recent study did report a correlation between reported levels of parental—not just maternal—care and the levels of corticotrophin-releasing hormone, the master stress hormone manufactured in the hypothalamus.

TRUE EPIGENETIC INHERITANCE

The examples of social inheritance described here can be considered transgenerational epigenetic effects, but they do not rise to the level of true epigenetic inheritance. For epigenetic inheritance to occur, the epigenetic mark itself must be transmitted from parent to offspring. An epigenetic alteration in brain cells cannot be transmitted directly to the offspring, nor can epigenetic alterations to liver cells, blood cells, or any of the other 200 plus cell types in the human body. (The same is true for any standard genetic mutation.) The only cells that can be transmitted from parent to offspring are the germ cells (sperm and ova). So only epigenetic alterations (called epimutations) to these special cells are potentially heritable in the way that DNA mutations are.

True epigenetic inheritance in mammals remains somewhat controversial, though it is a well-established fact in plants and many invertebrate animals.[27] One of the first demonstrations of epigenetic inheritance in a mammal comes from experiments on mice with a mutation in the agouti gene called viable yellow, which causes a change from the normal agouti coloration (called pseudo-agouti) to yellow. This mutation is called viable yellow to distinguish it from a similar yellowing mutation that is lethal. The viable yellow mutation actually results in a spectrum of color phenotypes, from normal coloration (called pseudo-agouti) to all yellow, even in genetically identical mice, depending on random differences in the degree of methylation of the agouti gene. Despite this random component to the methylation of this gene, it is noteworthy that viable yellow mice tend to give birth to yellow mice, while pseudo-agouti viable yellow mice tend to produce pseudo-agouti offspring and grand-offspring.[28] There is no such influence of the male parent, however.

Superficially, this maternal effect resembles that of mothering in Meaney's rats, but in this case, the maternal effect occurs much earlier, before pregnancy, in fact. When the fertilized eggs of yellow mothers are transplanted to black or pseudo-agouti mothers, the offspring tend to be yellow at birth.[29] So there is no effect of the intrauterine environment. Instead, the methylation pattern, which determines coat coloration in genetically identical mice, has been directly transmitted from mother to pup.

In another set of experiments it was demonstrated that environmental factors could alter the pattern of epigenetic inheritance. Folic acid is a known methyl donor, hence capable of altering the methylation process. When viable yellow mothers are fed a diet high in folic acid, the spectrum of coat colors in their offspring is shifted toward the pseudo agouti end.[30] Moreover, when the offspring that experienced folic acid supplementation in utero themselves become mothers, the color spectrum shift is sustained in their offspring. The transmission of the diet-induced change to the grand-offspring occurred even though these second-generation mothers received no further methyl supplementation. So here we have a case in which partly random and partly environmentally induced epigenetic alterations are inherited.

Other cases of true epigenetic inheritance in mammals have also been documented. Of particular note is the Axin gene, which when methylated results in a kinked tail. The methylation pattern and hence kinked tail can be inherited from both mother and father.[31] There is now enough evidence of true epigenetic inheritance in mammals, including humans, to warrant concern over transgenerational effects of toxins, including cigarette smoke, and adverse environmental conditions characteristic of poverty. The mental health implications of true epigenetic inheritance are certainly worthy of research.

GENOMIC IMPRINTING

I alluded to imprinting in my discussion of the vinclozolin exposed rats. Here I expand on this epigenetic phenomenon a bit in relation to the broader topic of transgenerational epigenetic effects. Recall that imprinting results in the deactivation of a gene in one sex. Such unisexual gene expression in an important subset of genes is crucial for normal development in all mammals. Imprinting failures cause many cancers, as well as a host of other ailments.[32] Indeed, imprinted genes are overrepresented in pathologies of many kinds, partly because the imprinting process is vulnerable to impairments of various sorts, one category of which, as we have seen, is endocrine disruptors. There are actually two distinct stages in the imprinting process at which things can go wrong. The first stage is the manufacture of sperm and ova. It was long thought that all epigenetic marks inherited from the parents are eliminated at this stage, creating an epigenetic blank slate. After this global demethylation, gamete (sperm or ova) specific marks are restored to the subset of imprinted genes. So, under normal conditions, the only methylation marks in sperm and egg, prior to fertilization, are on imprinted genes. If the epigenetic marks are not restored in a sex-appropriate way, things go awry developmentally. The second stage in which things can go awry is just after fertilization, when there is another round of global demethylation—this one, however, sparing the imprinted genes. If the imprinted genes are not spared, developmental problems again arise. This stage of imprinting has proven to be a particular problem in cloning mammals and even in assisted reproductive technologies (ARTs).[33]

Most biologists don't consider imprinting itself to be a form of epigenetic inheritance, because the epigenetic mark is not transmitted from one generation to the next, but rather reconstructed during each round of sperm and egg production. Yet there are cases of epigenetic inheritance of defects in imprinted genes. The best documented evidence comes from the vinclozolin exposed rat model described previously. Recall that male rats exposed to vinclozolin experience a suite of pathologies, not least, defective sperm. Michael Skinner and his associates have shown that the male offspring of the vinclozolin exposed males also have defective sperm, as do their male offspring, on through four generations, even without subsequent vinclozolin exposure.[34] The effects of vinclozolin exposure on a male rat while in the womb are visited upon not only his sons and grandsons, but his great-grandsons as well.

The implications of Skinner's studies are truly scary, given the number of toxins to which we are exposed. The transgenerational effects of many prescription drugs, licit or illicit, should also be a source of concern. Smoking is now known to have effects on the smoker's offspring who don't smoke. Again, as in vinclozolin exposure the effect is especially pronounced in the male offspring. It seems to involve disregulation of miRNAs in sperm cells.[35]

EPIGENETICS AND THE PRECAUTIONARY PRINCIPLE

Unlike genetic mutations, epimutations are reversible. This is especially good news for ailments like cancer, many of which have an epigenetic etiology. New epigenetic treatments are on the horizon, which may more specifically target the cancer cells, with less broadly toxic consequences for noncancer cells. For other conditions, though, conservatism is in order. For example, though it is tempting to epigenetically engineer treatments to reverse conditions ranging from PTSD to autism, we are nowhere near being able to do so in a responsible way.

Meaney's rats are instructive in this regard. Meaney and his coworkers were able to epigenetically rescue individuals subject to poor mothering through a chemical intervention, a proof, in principle, of such an epigenetic therapy.[36] But Meaney was just as effective in rescuing such pups by simply exposing them to well-mothered and hence well-adjusted peers after weaning.[37] And if we extrapolate to interventions for human infants who are being raised by negligent or abusive parents, providing parents with the support and guidance they need has incalculable long-term benefits. Given that we should expect side effects from any chemical intervention, it seems obvious that socialization is the way to go here. The precautionary principle also applies to the growing list of pathologies with a significant epigenetic component, including, among the more topical, autism, asthma, rheumatoid arthritis, and ADHD. With more knowledge of the etiology of these conditions, it will be possible to intervene in prophylactic ways. To the extent that this could occur through environmental manipulations, that is all to the good. Pharmaceutical epigenetics is another matter entirely, rife with potential side effects born of our limited knowledge. These dangers apply not only to prophylactic measures, but also to treatments for those who have these conditions. ADHD is worth considering in this regard.

The first obstacle for any pharmaceutical intervention in ADHD is that it is actually, both etiologically and symptomatically, a heterogeneous condition. Currently, forms of ADHD are defined largely by how they respond to pharmaceuticals such as methylphenidate (commonly marketed as Ritalin), which is putting the cart before the horse. There is no doubt that methylphenidate reduces hyperactivity, but it is a drug that potentially has adverse effects on the developing brain during a period of crucial structuring of neuronal circuits. Ritalin has known epigenetic side effects in neurodevelopment in rats.[38] There is increasing awareness of the epigenetic side effects of pharmaceuticals generally, an area of study that is rapidly expanding.

PROMISE AND PERILS OF EPIGENETICS

Many diseases and pathologies formerly thought to be primarily genetic are now known to have a significant, sometimes paramount, epigenetic component. Cancer research, for example, has taken a decidedly epigenetic turn. This is good news, because epimutations are potentially reversible. Moreover, epigenetically caused conditions are potentially treatable through simple environmental manipulations, from diet to social interactions. Mutations are not amenable to such therapies.

But there is always the temptation to take pharmaceutical shortcuts. Potential profits from pharmaceutical epigenetic treatments are enormous. For some conditions, including many cancers, such epigenetic treatments represent a significant advance over prior genocentric approaches. But for many other conditions, such as autism spectrum disorder and ADHD (also a spectrum of disorders), the benefits of epigenetically targeted pharmaceutical interventions are less apparent. Indeed, given our current state of knowledge, potentially adverse side effects should council caution.

PART II
The Science of Children's Mental Health

4

The Impact of Toxic Chemicals on Children's Mental Health

Sharna Olfman

For centuries we have been taught that the womb is a pristine environment that safeguards the developing fetus, and that breast milk is the purest form of nourishment a mother can offer her newborn.[1] However, neither the uterus nor breast milk serves as an impenetrable fortress to the outside world. In fact, the fetus and infant are *more* exposed and vulnerable to the dangers of industrial pollutants than at any other point in the life cycle.[2] A 2004 study spearheaded by the Environmental Working Group found 287 toxic chemicals in the umbilical cord blood of 10 newborns selected randomly from hospitals across the United States, including pesticides, stain removers, wood preservatives, heavy metals, and industrial lubricants. Two hundred and seventeen of these were brain toxins.[3]

In her book *Having Faith*, ecologist Sandra Steingraber recalls a presentation she gave in 2001 at a United Nations conference about persistent organic pollutants (POPs). At the start of her talk, she circulated a jar of fluid among the participants that she described as "the most contaminated human food on the planet."[4] It contained her own breast milk.[5] Many toxic chemicals biomagnify, meaning that they become increasingly concentrated as they make their way up the food chain, and the *breast-feeding infant is at the pinnacle of the food chain*. (The long-term implications of this planetary process were first brought to our attention by Rachel Carson with regard to DDT.) "On average" states Steingraber, "in industrialized countries, breastfed infants ingest each day fifty times more PCBs per pound of body weight than do their parents. The same is true for dioxins."[6] In fact, the most efficient way for a woman to detoxify her own body from industrial pollutants is to get pregnant and start offloading her body burden of chemicals onto the fetus, then continue the process by breast-feeding her infant, whose toxic load will soon be higher than her own.[7] As Varda Burstyn points out in *Childhood Lost*, research has shown that the breast milk of Inuit women, who live as far away as humanly possible from industrial production sites, has concentrations of toxins comparable to those of women living in the Great Lakes area, where industrial activity is very high.[8] It wasn't always this way. In all likelihood, the placenta sufficed as a barrier against many naturally occurring toxins in the preindustrial era.[9] But it is no match for the onslaught of tens of thousands of chemical pollutants that industry, with limited government oversight, releases into the air that children breathe, the water they drink, and the soil in which their food grows.

As I write this, I am vacationing near an old growth forest. I feel intoxicated by the sweet smell of the air, the grandeur of the trees, and the music of bird song as I walk along the forest trails. Regardless of what my senses tell me, no one alive today can know what unadulterated air smells like or what unpolluted water and food tastes like, because these essential elements of life have been so radically altered. Even the most pristine corners of the globe and the most sacred spaces of women's bodies are awash in man-made toxicants, which cannot be held at bay by nature preserves or gated communities. They circulate across the planet on air currents, cross oceans, contaminate groundwater, and biomagnify up the food chain. And they remain in our ecosystems long after they are no longer being manufactured.

The lion's share of media coverage about industrial chemicals to date has focused on their more obvious and immediate harms: massive exposures from industrial spills causing death or grave illness and more moderate exposures that are cancer causing. However, two of the world's experts on lead and mercury toxicity, Philip Landrigan and Philippe Grandjean, caution us that far lower doses of these chemicals, which are often judged safe for adults by regulatory bodies such as the U.S. Environmental Protection Agency (EPA), can cause irreparable harm to the complex and intricately timed development of the fetal and infant brain.[10] Children who were exposed to developmental neurotoxicants (chemicals that harm brain development) prenatally or during infancy may not manifest symptoms until they are of school age, when they struggle to control their impulses, pay attention, understand math concepts, socialize with their peers, or regulate their moods. Because of the time delay, it is easier to deny the causal relationship between chemical exposures and behavioral disorders. If the consequences were immediate and dramatic, as with babies born with missing limbs after prenatal exposure to thalidomide (a drug marketed by Vick Chemical Company for morning sickness to Canadian and European women in the late 1950s), action to ban developmental neurotoxicants from the industrial chemical arsenal would be swift.[11] Instead, routine exposures continue unabated, contributing significantly to the meteoric rise in children's psychological disturbances, including learning and attentional challenges, autism spectrum disorders, mood dysregulation, and poor impulse control—estimated to affect as many as one in six children.[12] The U.S. National Research Council concluded that 3 percent of developmental disabilities are the direct consequence of neurotoxic environmental exposures, and that another 25 percent are epigenetic, meaning that toxic chemicals are negatively impacting genes that help to program the brain.[13]

THE UNIQUE VULNERABILITY OF THE FETUS AND INFANT TO NEUROTOXICANTS

In the following passage, Landrigan and Grandjean describe the complexity of human brain development and its unique vulnerability to toxic chemicals:

The developing human brain is inherently much more susceptible to injury than the adult brain. The brain begins as a small strip of cells along the back of the embryo that develops, over the next nine months, into a complex organ of billions of precisely located, highly interconnected, specialized cells. Optimal brain development requires that neurons move along precise pathways from their points of origin to their assigned locations, establish connections with other cells both nearby and distant, and learn to communicate with other cells via such connections. All of these processes must take place within a tightly controlled time frame in which each developmental stage must be reached on schedule and in the correct sequence.

Because of the extraordinary complexity of human brain development, windows of unique susceptibility to toxic interference arise that have no counterpart in the mature brain or in any other organ. If a developmental process in the brain is halted or inhibited, there is little potential for later repair and the consequences can therefore be permanent. During fetal development, the placenta offers some protection against chemical exposures, but it is not an effective barrier against many environmental pollutants. For example, many metals easily cross the placenta, and the concentration of mercury in umbilical cord blood is often substantially higher than in maternal blood. The blood-brain barrier which protects the adult brain from many toxic chemicals, is not completely formed until about six months after birth.

The human brain continues to develop after birth, and the period of heightened vulnerability therefore extends over many months, through infancy and into early childhood. Although most brain cells have been formed by the time of birth, growth of glial cells and myelination of axons continues for several years.[14]

In summary, brain development takes two decades to complete. During that time there are *sensitive periods of development* when specific areas of the brain are undergoing rapid maturation. During these sensitive periods, very low levels of exposure to neurotoxicants can be devastating to the particular brain function that is in rapid formation. The full impact of the exposure will not be evident until the affected region reaches full maturity, years later. In addition, stem cells destined to become brain cells that are exposed to neurotoxic chemicals can catalyze epigenetic changes that adversely impact brain development.

There are other compelling reasons why children are uniquely vulnerable to neurotoxicants throughout prenatal and early childhood development. In *No Child Left Different*, Burstyn and coauthor David Fenton enumerate them as follows:

- Fetuses are physically unable to process or defend against toxicants because their nervous, respiratory, reproductive, and immune systems are immature, *and* they are in the process of dynamic change.

- In their first year, babies spend hours close to the ground, where they may be exposed to toxicants in dust, soil, and carpets as well as to pesticide vapors in low-lying layers of air on lawns and porches. For the first few years of children's lives, even after they learn to walk, stature and play patterns keep them much closer to the ground—where toxicants are concentrated.

- Children have higher metabolic rates than adults. Their cells are multiplying and their organ systems are developing at a very rapid rate.

- Children absorb nutrients and toxicants from the gut at different rates. Children need more calcium than adults, for example. But when lead is present, they will absorb it in preference to calcium. So adults will absorb an average of 10 percent of ingested lead, but a toddler will absorb closer to 50 percent.

- A lot of hand to mouth exposure is a normal part of childhood and provides another route for exposure to such toxicants as lead in paint dust and pesticide residues.

- Children breathe more rapidly and respire more air per unit of body weight than do adults, and they often spend more time outdoors. Tiny particulates of air pollution penetrate the blood/brain barrier (also weaker in children) and affect the brain as well as the lungs and the circulatory system.

- Children eat more fruits and vegetables and drink more liquids in proportion to their body weight than do adults. Consequently, their potential exposure to ingested toxicants such as lead, pesticides, and nitrates is greater. Consider that the average infant's daily consumption of six ounces of formula or breast milk per kilogram of body weight is equivalent to an adult male drinking fifty eight-ounce glasses of milk a day. This average one-year-old eats two to seven times more grapes, bananas, pears, carrots, and broccoli proportionally than does an adult.[15]

A GLOBAL SILENT PANDEMIC OF NEURODEVELOPMENTAL TOXICITY

In February 2014 Landrigan and Grandjean published a follow-up to their groundbreaking 2006 article in the *Lancet* that shone an urgently needed spotlight on the damaging effects of industrial chemicals on the developing brain. Their report documents that 11 industrial chemicals are proven developmental neurotoxicants, meaning that they interfere with the process of development of the brain: lead, mercury, arsenic, manganese, fluoride, polychlorinated biphenyls (PCBs), dichlorodiphenyltrichloroethane (DDT), toluene (a solvent), chlorpyrifos (an organophosphate pesticide), tetrachoroethylene (known as PERC, which is commonly used as a dry cleaning fluid), and polybrominated diphenyl ethers (or PBDE flame retardants). An additional 214 chemicals are known to harm the adult brain, and it is a virtual certainty that they are even more toxic to the developing brain at lower dosages. Landrigan and Grandjean have targeted another 1,000 or so chemicals that in all likelihood are neurotoxic based on evidence from animal studies and what is known about their chemical makeup and the biology of brain development. And this doesn't even scratch the surface of the more than 80,000 chemicals that are used commercially in the United States, less than 20 percent of which have been tested for safety, not to mention consideration of the cumulative and synergistic effects of multiple exposures.[16]

These data impel us to ask why our regulatory bodies—the EPA and the Food and Drug Administration (FDA) are not keeping us out of harm's way. In 1977 the U.S. Congress passed the Toxic Substance Control Act, which mandates testing of new industrial chemicals, but according to Grandjean, this law has no teeth. The obligatory research is designed and funded by the industries in question, creating a significant conflict of interest, and results are often not released to the public or even to the EPA. Furthermore, tests for developmental brain toxicity are not required, even though the Organisation for Economic Co-operation and Development (OECD) has developed excellent assessment protocols, which have been in place since 1999. Also, the EPA "grandfathered in" (exempted from regulation) 62,000 chemicals that were already in commercial use. As a result, about 92 percent of the most commonly produced chemicals today are allowed for use without any testing. These untested chemicals include fully half of the 3,000 high-volume production chemicals that are produced in excess of 50,000 kg per year.[17]

The FDA is equally lax in regulating food containers and packaging materials. Since the Toxic Substance Control Act was passed, the EPA has only limited production of five groups of chemicals, and the FDA has only banned 9 chemicals out of 10,000 ingredients.[18] Most of the neurotoxicants that have been identified so far are not exotic or rare. They are the pesticides that are sprayed on our lawns, produce, homes, and schools; the lead in our water pipes; the mercury in cans of tuna fish; and the solvents and phthalates in our cleaning and beauty products, such as shampoo and nail polish. Landrigan and Grandjean have labeled children's exposures to neurotoxic chemicals as nothing less than a "global, silent pandemic of neurodevelopmental toxicity."[19] In almost every case, safe alternatives already exist and are readily available on the market. Given that solutions are at hand, it is vital that we understand the roadblocks that have prevented us—parents, educators, health professionals, business leaders, and lawmakers—from effectively protecting children from these harms. Grandjean and Landrigan point to two factors that are working synergistically to forestall immediate action: (1) the conservatism of traditional scientific protocols, which (2) dovetail perfectly with corporate agendas.

SLOW SCIENCE VERSUS THE PRECAUTIONARY PRINCIPLE

In chapter 2, Robert Whitaker demonstrates that the "chemical imbalance" theory of mental illness has virtually no scientific support in spite of decades of research. In contrast, the developmental neurotoxicity of an ever-widening array of poorly regulated industrial chemicals is now well established. And yet this information is largely ignored by the mental health community. To be fair, some clinicians may be aware that exposures to chemicals such as heavy metals and pesticides can harm children's brains, but as a rule, they don't know where to direct their patients for testing, how to advise them to protect themselves from exposure, or where to seek help if they have been heavily exposed. And so they resort to the tools that are already in their toolkit: the stimulants, antidepressants, anticonvulsants, (rebranded as mood stabilizers), and antipsychotics that are themselves potent neurotoxicants.[20] One explanation is that the pharmaceutical industry funds the lion's share of medical research and therefore sets its agenda, which more often than not keeps drug sales humming. By contrast, identifying and removing developmental neurotoxicants often works against corporate interests. While this is true as far as it goes, there is more to this than meets the eye.

Another reason environmental health experts face an uphill battle is that there is an inherent conflict between traditional scientific protocols and those that keep members of society safe. For example, research has established that 11 industrial chemicals are developmental neurotoxicants, meaning that they damage the developing brain of the fetus and young child. Each of these chemicals was first discovered to be toxic to adults at far higher doses. This is not surprising, because for reasons already discussed, the developing brain is significantly more vulnerable than the mature brain. Therefore, it follows logically that a chemical that is toxic to an adult brain will not only be toxic to a developing brain, but will cause harm at a lower dose. Two hundred and fourteen additional industrial chemicals have been proven to be toxic to the adult brain. It is a virtual certainty that these chemicals will be even more harmful (and at lower doses) to the fetal or infant brain. And yet scientific protocol demands explicit proof. Here, science and ethics part ways. It was this very "reasoning" that kept lead in paint and gasoline for decades, in spite of compelling evidence of its harms. Traditional scientific methods buttressed the self-serving desires of the industries that were profiting from its use.[21]

The "gold standard" of scientific research is the *randomized controlled trial*. If this research design was used to determine whether a chemical, already shown to be harmful to the adult brain, was a developmental neurotoxin, a representative sample of pregnant women and infants would be selected, and these research subjects would be randomly assigned to control and experimental groups. We would then expose the fetuses and infants in the experimental group to chemicals already proven to be toxic to the brains of adults in order to prove beyond a reasonable doubt that they are toxic to the immature brain. As Grandjean points out, such research would never be condoned by an institutional review board (IRB)[22] because *we already know* that these chemicals are unsafe, and it would be correctly judged as highly unethical. Yet ironically, *we are carrying out these very experiments* on generations of children, worldwide, whose brains and bodies are exposed daily to neurotoxic chemicals in their food, toys, furnishings, personal care products, and so on. And so we are locked in a bizarre and macabre cultural charade in which our children are held hostage by scientific conventions.[23]

Prospective epidemiological birth cohort studies that don't introduce new toxins, but follow children who are already exposed to the chemicals in question over several years beginning prenatally, can yield meaningful results without the ethical roadblocks, and research of this description is currently being carried out, the most extensive of which is the National Children's Study under the auspices of the National Institute of Child Health and Human Development (NICHD). This ambitious study, a decade in the making, is following 100,000 children across the United States from before birth until the age of 21 on a daily basis to test the effects of a wide range of industrial chemicals.[24] A study of this scope will provide the incontrovertible evidence that industry and regulatory bodies demand before they will take protective measures. But two decades is a long time to wait when we know with certainty in many cases, and where there is excellent probability in other cases, that chemicals to which children are routinely exposed are harming their brains. Not only are we continuing to subject children to these poisons for many years to come, but long after their use is discontinued, they will persist in our air, water, and food supplies.

For these very reasons, several regulatory bodies in the European Union have begun to implement the *precautionary principle*, which turns the mandate of conventional research on its head. Whereas the mandate of traditional research is to prove that these chemicals are unsafe beyond a shadow of a doubt, the precautionary principle requires that chemicals *must be proven safe* for humans and for our planet before they can be adopted for use in industry.[25]

PERSISTENT ORGANIC POLLUTANTS: A LASTING LEGACY

Persistent organic pollutants (POP) are a class of toxic chemicals that are particularly insidious because they can penetrate the placenta and the blood-brain barrier, accumulate in fat stores, biomagnify, and travel across the planet on air and water currents. Most of them are neurotoxicants, and some are endocrine (hormone) disruptors. Because hormones in turn help to regulate the development of the brain, this is another way in which brain development is impacted. The term is sometimes used very narrowly to refer to manufactured chemicals such as PCBs and DDT, but any chemical that shares the qualities listed above qualifies as a POP, including those that occur in nature, such as lead and mercury.[26]

The Dirty Dozen

The UN Environment Program's Stockholm Convention on POPs was signed into law in 2001 and became effective in 2004, with the goal of eliminating or restricting the production of "the dirty dozen," the term used to describe 12 heavily manufactured and highly toxic persistent chemicals, including PCBs and DDT.[27]

DDT was used during World War II to fight malaria and typhus. After the war it was widely adopted as a pesticide. The harms caused by DDT were a central theme in Rachel Carson's visionary work *Silent Spring* (1962), which first alerted the general public to the devastation wrought by industrial chemicals on ecosystems and human health.[28]

Although the Stockholm Convention instituted a worldwide ban on its use as a pesticide, it continues to be used to help fight malaria, even though its use leads to pesticide-resistant mosquito populations.[29]

Because of their highly effective insulating and fireproofing abilities, PCBs were used prodigiously in the United States and around the world for several decades. The Monsanto Chemical Corporation had a near monopoly on the manufacture of PCBs in the United States from the late 1930s until they were banned in 1979. They were produced in a factory in Anniston, Alabama. The toxic waste was released into a nearby creek, and millions of pounds of PCBs were dumped into open landfills. Monsanto's in-house scientists were well aware of how virulently toxic PCBs were almost from the start and actively suppressed their findings. Hundreds of Monsanto documents about the dangers of PCB exposure, with labels such as "confidential" and "read and destroy," were subsequently uncovered.[30] In the mid-1940s General Electric began to use PCBs in its capacitors in its New York plant. As a consequence, a 200-mile stretch of the Hudson River spanning from New York City to Hudson Falls became heavily polluted. In 1984 the EPA named it the largest chemical waste dump to date. Because they are persistent, DDT and PCBs continue to circulate the globe, accumulate in our food, and become stored in our fat, and they are passed along to fetuses and infants through the placenta and breast milk. After six months of breast-feeding, a woman will pass half of her body burden of PCBs to her infant.[31] Research has established that PCBs and DDT damage children's developing brains, undermining short-term memory, attention, and impulse control, and they are associated with lower IQ and reading scores.[32]

Other POPs recognized by the Stockholm Convention include brominated flame retardants used to fireproof textiles and electrical equipment (one of the original "dirty dozen," which I discuss later in the chapter) and perflourinated compounds, which are used in clothing, carpeting, furniture, and food packaging such as pizza boxes and fast-food containers, to make them stain and stick resistant (one of nine POPs more recently recognized by the convention). In addition, they can be found in fire-fighting foams, paints, and hardwood floor protectants. It is worth noting that the United States is one of a handful of signatories of the convention that has not yet ratified it.

Pesticides

While the UN's Stockholm Convention was a great leap forward in recognizing and addressing the harms caused by POPs, the pesticides that were banned have generally been replaced by other, equally toxic chemicals. Most pesticides in use today target the nervous or endocrine system. Although it is unpleasant to imagine that we have much in common with insects, in fact, the neurochemistry of the insect and human brain is very similar. So it follows that what is toxic to the termite nervous system for example, is toxic to humans as well. According to the EPA, the United States consumes 22 percent of the world market of pesticides, which in 2007 was 857 million pounds, or about three pounds per U.S. citizen annually.[33]

A Rose by Any Other Name . . .

The rose symbolizes love and beauty and is de rigueur at weddings, anniversaries, on Valentine's Day, and on virtually any other occasion that spells romance. Roses are imported heavily from the Ecuadorean Andes, where the climate is perfectly suited to their growth. But even in the Andes, the "perfect" rose does not grow naturally; it is cultivated with the heavy use of pesticides. Rosebushes for commercial use are sprayed daily with multiple pesticides, some of which are banned for use in the United States, but nonetheless are sometimes manufactured here and then exported. We then reimport them on the flowers and produce we buy. Because much of the pruning and cutting in the rose industry is performed by women, Grandjean decided to study children in Tabacundo, a town in the Ecuadorean Andes whose mothers worked in the rose industry throughout their pregnancies. He then compared them with children who had not been exposed prenatally. Grandjean found that while none of the mothers had experienced symptoms from pesticide exposure, the children on average *were two years behind* in spatial ability and muscular coordination. His findings are in keeping with the established pattern. Toxic exposures that do not have an apparent impact on the mature brain can be devastating to the developing brain.[34]

Organophosphates

Organophosphates are a class of pesticides originally produced in Germany in the 1940s that are still used worldwide. While organophosphates are not POPs, they are extremely toxic to the brain, because they obstruct cholinesterase, an enzyme that breaks down the neurotransmitter (brain chemical) acetylcholine, which enables nerves to signal muscles.[35] According to Dana Boyd Barr, a scientist at Emory University, organophosphates work in the same way as nerve gases such as Sarin, a notorious nerve agent that was classified as a weapon of mass destruction in 1991 by a UN Security Council Resolution.

While high-level exposure to organophosphates is lethal, chronic low-level exposure, deemed safe in the United States, can significantly impact the brains of fetuses, infants, and young children. The EPA has asked manufacturers to *voluntarily* reduce the use of organophosphates in products designed for residential use, but they can still be found in a handful of products designed for garden and home use, and they are used heavily in agriculture.[36]

Chlorpyrifos is an organophosphate that was registered in 1965 by Dow Chemical and marketed under the trade names Dursban, Lorsban, and Renoban. For several decades it was the most widely used household pesticide in the United States. In 1995 Dow Chemical was fined $732,000 for not disclosing 249 poisoning incident reports to the EPA. In 2001, in anticipation of more stringent EPA regulations, Dow stopped marketing chlorpyrifos for use in American homes, although it continues to sell Dursban for residential use in developing countries. In 2003 Dow paid $2 million dollars to the state of New York to settle a lawsuit filed by the attorney general over Dow's illegal advertising of Dursban as "safe." For a corporate giant like Dow Chemical, with sales nearing $60 billion, lawsuits like these are merely part of the cost of doing business, but they underscore the fact that the manufacturers of these chemicals are well aware of their dangers.[37]

Grandjean and Landrigan earmark chlorpyrifos as an established developmental neurotoxin in their 2014 *Lancet* article. Researchers have found that children exposed to chlorpyrifos evidenced thinning of the frontal and parietal regions of the cortex (the most evolved part of the brain) after prenatal exposures at levels that are not deemed hazardous. This suggests that exposure during fetal development prevented brain cells from successfully migrating to their correct locations in the cortex, and/or that brain cell multiplication or survival was diminished. More generally, organophosphate pesticides are associated with small head circumference, which suggests that brain development was slowed down in utero.[38] In spite of the research, chlorpyrifos remains in use, as do 39 other organophosphate pesticides in the United States, with at least 73 million pounds used in agricultural and residential settings annually.[39] Although all of the organophosphate pesticides have the same basic chemical properties and impact the nervous system in similar ways, the protocols of science and regulatory law require that each of these pesticides be tested individually to prove over and over again what is already a virtual certainty: they harm the developing brain. Ethical standards as embodied in the precautionary principle to protect children from harm are once again trumped by the "logic" of scientific principles and the pursuit of profit.

NATURAL CHEMICALS PUT TO UNNATURAL USES: LEAD, MERCURY, ARSENIC, FLUORIDE, AND MANGANESE

Lead: A Cautionary Tale

The uphill battle to ban the use of lead encapsulates many of the challenges that environmental health experts continue to face. As Landrigan and Grandjean point out in their *Lancet* review, it has been known since Roman times that overexposure to lead can cause life-threatening illness. The first report of an epidemic of lead poisoning in children was reported a century ago, in connection with children ingesting lead paint chips while playing on verandas with leaded paint. It was widely known that lead is a brain toxin by the early 20th century, because it was proposed for use as a weapon in World War I. Until the mid-20th century, however, the belief persisted that lead toxicity was akin to an illness, and that once the victim recovered from the most acute symptoms, there were no residual effects. More subtle but significant effects of lead toxicity were not connected to the initial exposure. The argument went that because lead is a natural element, exposure is innocuous at low levels. Similar arguments were made about mercury and arsenic. But there was nothing natural about the lead levels of the average American by the mid-20th century. It was in fact a hundredfold higher than that of our ancestors, as determined by studying untainted skeletons.[40]

In 1924 a young scientist named Robert Kehoe was hired by General Motors (GM) to determine the safety of leaded gasoline. He was then appointed medical director for the Ethyl Gasoline Corporation, which produced TEL, the lead-infused compound added to gasoline in the United States. He was also named director of the Kettering Laboratory in 1930, with funding from the lead industries. For 40 years he was the "chief apologist" for the lead, gas, and automotive industry and was handsomely rewarded for playing this role. In 1924, the same year that Kehoe was hired by GM, 32 of 49 factory workers at the Standard Oil Refinery who were in contact with TEL were hospitalized, and 5 died. Among the survivors, many sustained symptoms ranging from memory loss and poor coordination to episodes of rage, convulsion, and delirium. When confronted about the safety of lead following several poisoning incidents among factory workers, Kehoe's stock response was that the industry would recommend the removal of lead from gasoline if he had "indisputable proof" that lead was harmful, and this came to be known as the "show me" rule, which set the stage for the burden of proof to fall on the public as opposed to industries and governments.[41]

Two decades later, the proof that Kehoe claimed to be looking for materialized. In 1943 two Boston pediatricians named Randolph Byers and Elisabeth Lord studied 20 children after they were released from the hospital for lead poisoning. They discovered that long after they had recovered from the acute phase of lead poisoning, 19 of the 20 children had severe learning or behavioral problems, and only 5 had normal IQs. Byers surmised that lead toxicity damages brain development, and therefore far lower exposures would be hazardous to children even if they hadn't shown acute signs of lead poisoning initially. Their research was reported in *Time* magazine. Industry leaders first tried to bribe Byers into silence, but when that strategy failed, they threatened to sue him. Byers and Lord's research was also spun through "blame the victim" strategies. Because a majority of children who suffered from lead poisoning came from poor neighborhoods, where they were more likely to be exposed to peeling leaded paint, the argument went that they had negligent mothers who taught them poor health habits, and this allegedly explained their excessive exposures, bad behavior, and low IQs. Herbert Needleman, one of the most prolific researchers on the impact of lead on children's brains and behavior, who judiciously maintained his autonomy from corporate interests, was accused of fraud by the lead industry and remained under investigation for close to a decade. Although his name was cleared and his research is exemplary, he lost years of productive work while fighting various lawsuits.[42]

During the 1970s a critical mass of research confirmed that lead causes a range of neurobehavioral symptoms, including deficits in concentration, memory, and thinking, and places children at higher risk for school failure and delinquent behavior. More recent research using brain imaging of young adults who had elevated lead levels in childhood reveals dose-related decreases in brain volume. In the early 1970s leaded gasoline began to be phased out, but by then it was no longer considered to be a viable additive because of changes in the design of catalytic converters, which made it easy for the gasoline and automobile industries to appear to be good corporate citizens. Due in large part to the efforts of Philip Landrigan, lead-based paint was finally banned in the United States in 1978 (although it wasn't until after 1992 that paint products were entirely free of trace amounts of lead). In 1991 the EPA finally passed the Reduction of Lead in Drinking Water Act, but remarkably, it was not until January 2014 that "lead free" was redefined as "not more than a weighted average of 0.25% lead with reference to pipes, pipe fittings, plumbing fittings, and fixtures."[43] The legacy of lead will continue to burden our children in the peeling paints of older homes and schools; in decaying water pipes; and in the unregulated cosmetics industry, where lead is commonly used as an ingredient in lipstick. If a school was built before 1978, it is likely to contain paint having a lead content in excess of .06 percent. Even one lead paint chip can poison a child. As lead paint deteriorates, it can release lead dust. At present the United States has 700,000 miles of aging pipes, some more than 100 years old, many made of lead. On a positive note, the average blood level of lead in the United States has fallen by more than 80 percent since 1976, due to the ban on leaded gasoline, leaded paint, and lead-soldered food cans. The bad news is that we know that blood lead levels once thought to be safe are hazardous, especially to children. Based on the most recent findings about lead exposure, Grandjean and Landrigan conclude that *no safe level of exposure to lead exists.*[44]

Mercury: The Same Old Story

It would be some consolation if the battle to limit the commercial use of lead were an aberration, but Grandjean, who has been at the forefront of mercury research for decades, encountered identical roadblocks in his efforts to help usher in regulations to limit mercury toxicity. In spite of what was already apparent through methylmercury[45] poisonings of workers in British laboratories in the 1880s, it wasn't until 2009 that a meeting of UN member countries finally carved out an agreement to try to curb mercury pollution worldwide, which finally took effect in 2013. This agreement was named the Minamata Convention, after a nightmarish epidemic of mercury poisoning that occurred in 1955 in Minamata, a fishing village in Japan, because a plastics factory was dumping methylmercury poisoned wastewater into Minamata Bay, where local residents fished. The worst impact was on the fetuses of mothers who consumed the poisoned fish while pregnant. Typically, the mothers were far less affected and exhibited more specific and localized symptoms. Infants born in Minamata that year who managed to survive had severe and pervasive brain damage, causing spasticity, blindness, and profound mental retardation. Although a scientist working for the plastics factory quickly established the link between methylmercury poisoning and the resulting symptoms, the research was suppressed and denied for decades, even though equally compelling research continued to pile up. More recent longitudinal research by Grandjean and others is focusing on the neurodevelopmental impact of mercury exposure on the fetus and young child at very low doses, among populations whose diet is heavy in seafood and freshwater fish. These studies have established that even with low dose exposure, the children who were first exposed prenatally are exhibiting lowered IQ scores, alterations in mood, as well as dose-related deficits in memory, attention, language, and visuospatial perception.[46]

As is the case with lead, international efforts to regulate mercury emissions are a far cry from eliminating excess mercury from our environment. Mercury continues to be released from coal-fired power plants and many other sources and to be transformed into methylmercury: an extremely toxic compound that is readily bioaccumulated in large fish.[47] Until 2003, more than 11 tons of mercury were used in the manufacture of car ignition switches each year. While the car is operating the mercury poses no harm, but when it is being junked, mercury is released into the atmosphere. Mercury can also be found in fluorescent lightbulbs, batteries, light switches, and "silver" dental fillings. Mercury is a component of thimerosal, a compound widely used as a preservative and antiseptic in eye drops, nasal sprays, contact lens cleaners, and childhood and flu vaccines.[48]

According to the Centers for Disease Control and Prevention, one in 12 women of childbearing age has a mercury blood level in the danger range, and as Burstyn points out in *Childhood Lost*, the body stores mercury in tissues, so blood samples would significantly underestimate the actual concentration. The EPA estimates that as many as three million American children have elevated levels of mercury in their blood, and about seven million women and children regularly eat fish that is tainted with unsafe levels of mercury.[49]

Arsenic in the Water

Arsenic is another natural element that is highly toxic that is being found in unnaturally high concentrations in our environment. It has long been established as a neurotoxicant in adults, but research that established it as a brain toxin in children came from another poisoning incident in Japan (also in 1955), involving a popular powdered milk (produced by the Morinaga company), which was used to supplement or replace breast milk. It was contaminated with arsenic, and more than 100 infants died. A majority of the children who survived were tested in adolescence and compared to children who had been fully breastfed, and to those whose milk had been supplemented, but not with the tainted milk. The exposed children exhibited a tenfold increase in mental retardation, poor academic performance, emotional disturbances, and irregular electroencephalograms (brain wave patterns). More recent research in the United States and other countries has established dose-related effects on IQ with exposure to arsenic.[50]

Arsenic is released into the atmosphere through industrial emissions from coal-burning power plants and from mining, smelting, pesticides, and fertilizers. It was used heavily in the United States as a wood preservative until 2004, and it is still found in paints, dyes, drugs, soaps, and semiconductors. It is also used as a herbicide/fungicide called MSMA. It is approved as a dietary supplement for chickens to kill intestinal parasites that are common in fowl raised on factory farms. Arsenic turns up in heavy concentrations in groundwater and well water. In 2001 the EPA significantly reduced allowable concentrations of arsenic based on a decade of research overseen by the National Academy of Sciences, but the George W. Bush administration overturned this rule, ostensibly because there was insufficient science to support it.[51]

Fluoride

Fluoride, a naturally occurring compound, has a stellar reputation because of its role in reducing cavities. As recently as October 1999, the Centers for Disease Control and Prevention (CDC) described fluoridation as one of the top 10 public health achievements of the 20th century. However, the most compelling research suggests that while topical application of fluoride (in toothpaste, for example) can protect against cavities, *it needn't be ingested*. Nonetheless, approximately 70 percent of America's drinking water is fluoridated. The safety of *ingesting* fluoride has long been a topic of concern. In the 1940s and 1950s fluoride was routinely prescribed to treat hyperthyroidism, which indicates that it has been known for several decades that fluoride impacts the functioning of the thyroid gland. In 2012 a meta-analysis of 27 studies by Grandjean and his colleagues at the Harvard School of Public Health alongside colleagues from the China Medical University in Shenyang established fluoride as a developmental neurotoxin that negatively impacts intellectual development as measured on IQ tests. Fluoride exposure has also been linked to ADHD and Alzheimer's disease. These findings are supported by members of the National Research Council and the National Academy of Sciences.[52]

Most dentists believe that fluoride is added to our drinking water in the form of pharmaceutical grade sodium fluoride. In fact, more than 90 percent of the fluoride in our drinking water is unfiltered industrial grade hexafluorosilicic acid, formed by combining two toxic waste products from the phosphate fertilizer industry: hydrofluorosilisic acid and silicon tetrafluoride. By law, hexafluorosilicic acid cannot be dumped into the air or into seas or rivers, but the EPA allows it to be diluted down with our public drinking water. On June 27, 2000, Dr. J. William Hirzy, then senior vice president of the EPA union representing scientists at the EPA headquarters in Washington, D.C., testified at a congressional hearing on the Safe Drinking Water Act on behalf of the union, requesting a moratorium on fluoridation of drinking water. He made special mention of the practice of taking a known pollutant and removing it from the air and other natural bodies of water, then adding it directly to our drinking water. This untreated pollutant often contains other toxins, including heavy metals such as lead. Other sources of fluoride include processed foods and beverages made with fluoridated water, including infant formula and dairy products, pesticides, bottled teas, pharmaceuticals, Teflon pans, and mechanically deboned chicken. The Obama administration is working to lower fluoride levels in public water supplies, but this may be another case of "too little, too late." By contrast, 97 percent of western European countries do not fluoridate their water, and their tooth decay measures have shown similar rates of decline. Countries that have elected not to fluoridate their water because they deem the practice unsafe include Denmark, Finland, France, Germany, and 90 percent of the United Kingdom.[53]

Manganese

Manganese is a natural element and an essential nutrient that is found in a wide variety of foods, including nuts, legumes, seeds, tea, whole grains, and leafy green vegetables. Nonetheless, with overexposure it becomes neurotoxic. Manganese is especially problematic when it finds its way into our drinking water, because it becomes more bioavailable, meaning that it is more readily absorbed by the body. Manganese is used in the production of metal, especially "stainless steel" products. Ironically, just as lead was being phased out of gasoline, in 1995 the EPA was forced by a federal judge to grant a waiver to the Ethyl Corporation allowing production and sale of methylcyclopentadienyl manganese tricarbonyl (MMT), so in essence, one brain toxin was substituted for another. Research has established an association between manganese exposure and reduced mathematics achievement scores, hyperactivity, lowered intelligence, and impaired motor skills. When manganese and lead are ingested together, lead effects become more pronounced.[54]

SOLVENTS

After pesticides, the second largest group of developmental neurotoxicants is solvents such as toluene, more than 40 of which have been identified as harmful. Solvents are used in dry cleaning, nail polish and nail polish removers, glue, spot removers, detergents, perfumes, and paint thinners. They are fat soluble and capable of passing through the placenta and blood-brain barrier to the fetal brain. In addition to ubiquitous household exposures, women are frequently surrounded by solvents in workplaces such as hospitals, beauty salons, or as domestic workers, to name a few. Research in France and the United States that studied the children of mothers who were exposed to solvents at work revealed dose-related risks for hyperactivity and aggression and increased likelihood of psychiatric diagnoses. Other research has documented that solvents impact children's sensory, motor, and cognitive abilities, including attention and impulse control commonly associated with ADHD.[55]

FLAME RETARDANTS

Chemical compounds called polybrominated diphenyl ethers (PBDEs, one of the original "dirty dozen POPs") have a similar chemical makeup to PCBs and until very recently were widely used as flame retardants. They can be found in a multitude of products, including foam padding used in baby products, polyurethane foam in upholstered furniture and bedding, electronics, wire insulation, communication and building cables, stadium seats, lamp sockets, kitchen hoods, pipes, electrical equipment, building and construction panels, and cars.[56] Because PBDEs are not chemically bound to the products in which they are used, they wind up in dust and indoor air, which we then breathe or ingest. They have also entered the food chain and have been found in meat, fish, eggs, dairy products, fruits, and infant formulas. Studies show that babies born in the United States have the highest average concentrations of flame retardant chemicals in their bodies in the world. Research has established PBDEs as a developmental neurotoxin, which causes hormonal disruption and lowered IQ.[57]

There are three commercial PBDE products: pentaBDE, octaBDE, and decaBDE. Production of pentaBDE and octaBDE in the United States ceased at the end of 2004, and decaBDE was banned as of December 31, 2013. However, because they were banned so recently, they are still "living" in our homes, and because they are POPs, they will remain in our ecosystems for decades to come.

PHTHALATES AND BISPHENOL A

Phthalates and bisphenol A are hormone disruptors found in plastics, cosmetics, and many other consumer products. Because of the well-established role of hormones in helping to organize brain development, they can also be considered neurotoxins.[58] Phthalates are used in cosmetics and personal care products, including perfume, hair spray, soap, shampoo, nail polish, and skin moisturizers. They are also found in flexible plastic and vinyl toys, shower curtains, wallpaper, vinyl miniblinds, food packaging, plastic wrap, wood finishes, detergents, adhesives, plastic plumbing pipes, lubricants, medical tubing and fluid bags, solvents, insecticides, medical devices, building materials, and vinyl flooring. In other words, they are everywhere.[59] Until 1999 phthalates had been used to make pacifiers, soft rattles, and teethers, but at the request of the U.S. Consumer Product Safety Commission, U.S. manufacturers stopped using them. As of January 1, 2012, Congress has permanently banned three types of phthalates—DEHP, DBP, and BBP— in any amount greater than .1 percent in children's toys and child-care articles designed to facilitate sleep or feeding of children ages three and younger or to help children ages three and younger with sucking or teething. Congress also temporarily banned three additional phthalates, DINP, DIDP, and DnOP, used for the same purposes. However, it is still legal to use phthalates in products such as backpacks and lunch boxes, not to mention in all of the applications listed earlier.[60]

Bisphenol A was originally used as a synthetic estrogen. It is a key component of polycarbonate plastic, a hard plastic used to make numerous products, including reusable water bottles, compact discs, beverage containers, auto parts, toys, eyeglasses, and the plastic lining of food cans; as a dental sealant; and in thermal paper used in cash registers and credit card terminals. Our most significant exposure to BPA is currently from eating canned foods and drinking canned beverages. Once BPA is in our bodies, it imitates hormones such as estrogen. It has been linked to early puberty and depression in adolescent girls.[61]

THE IMPACT OF CHEMICAL TOXICANTS ON CHILDREN'S MENTAL HEALTH

As Landrigan and Grandjean report in their 2014 *Lancet* article: "A recent study compared the estimated total IQ losses from major pediatric causes and showed that the magnitude of losses attributable to lead, pesticides, and other neurotoxicants was in the same range as or even greater than, the losses associated with medical events such as preterm birth, traumatic brain injury, brain tumors, and congenital heart disease."[62]

It is difficult to tease out the effects of individual toxicants, because children are rarely exposed to one at a time. But researchers have established some links between certain chemicals and specific childhood syndromes. Neurological deficits in childhood that have been directly linked to chemical exposures include lowered concentration and information processing power; reduction in the ability to handle stress, leading to increases in frustration and volatility; increases in depression; a greater predisposition to violence, addiction, and criminal behavior; and lowered IQ scores. A five-point drop in average population IQ is estimated to reduce by half the number of gifted children (IQ over 130) and increase by half the number with borderline IQ (below 80). Symptoms of ADHD have been linked to prenatal exposures to manganese, organophosphates, and phthalates. Autism spectrum disorder is associated with exposure to phthalates and air pollution caused by the automotive industry. Lead exposure is associated with antisocial, criminal, and violent behavior; lowered IQ; shortened attention span; increased impulsivity; lowered motor coordination; and impaired memory and language skills.[63]

STEPS WE CAN TAKE TO PROTECT CHILDREN FROM DEVELOPMENTAL NEUROTOXICANTS

Developmental neurotoxicants are everywhere: in the air we breathe, the food we eat, the water we drink. They are in toys, personal care products, furniture, homes and schools, lawns and playgrounds, and hundreds of other products and places we use and visit every day. They are in our groundwater, streams, rivers, lakes, oceans, and the farthest reaches of the planet. They are in our bodies, brains, and breast milk. While (for the most part) we can elect not to take pharmaceuticals that we believe to be harmful to ourselves or our children, industrial toxicants are inescapable.

For most parents, the thought that they cannot protect their children from harm or intervene effectively when they have been harmed is extremely distressing. The urge to deny or downplay threats to ourselves or our loved ones that we think we have no control over is powerful and pervasive. But as comforting as minimizing and denial may be in the short term, the long-term consequence of denial is an intensification of the problem. The integrity of children's minds all around the world is endangered by toxic chemicals, and we need to move beyond complacency and self-deception to protect children today, as well as future generations.

What Can Parents and Professionals Do?

Many Americans equate freedom of the marketplace with freedom of expression, but *children's* rights are trampled on when they are the unwitting victims of neurotoxic exposures resulting from unregulated and unscrupulous business practices. Protecting children's brains from toxic chemicals requires "top down" solutions, involving legislative and international agreements. In order for that to happen, American regulatory bodies—the EPA and FDA—will need to operate with greater authority, unencumbered by conflicts of interest. I return to this topic later. First I address some of the steps that parents, teachers, and mental health professionals can take to protect the children under their care from undue harm.

Action Steps

In order to avoid additional toxic chemical burdens (beyond those already present in our ecosystem), here are a few general principles that caregivers can adopt, in line with Burstyn's recommendations in *No Child Left Different*:

- Eat organic when possible to avoid additional exposures to pesticides and products fed to poultry and cows, such as antibiotics, growth hormones, and arsenic.
- Eat low on the food chain (vegetarian) when possible, because larger animals bioaccumulate more toxins.
- Try not to live near industrial sites or factory farms.
- Use environmentally friendly household cleaners, paints, and products.
- Avoid PVC (polyvinyl chloride) plastic toys, bibs, mattress covers, bottles, plastic wraps, etc. PVC is indicated by the number 3 or the letters PVC beside the triple arrow recycling symbol. PVCs contain phthalates, which are hormone disruptors.
- Avoid hard plastics, indicated by the number 6, often found in products such as opaque plastic spoons and forks, and Styrofoam coffee cups. These plastics contain styrene, a neurotoxicant.
- Avoid products containing bisphenol A, a hormone disruptor found in hard plastics, indicated by the number 7. Until recently bisphenol A was in most baby bottles, and it is still used in clear plastic silverware that is not manufactured specifically for children, as well as water and sports bottles, and in the lining of food cans. As pointed out on the Healthy Child Healthy World Web site (see next page), the number 7 is now also used to indicate greener plastics, so you need to read labels with extra care.
- If you need to treat pests in your backyard or home, seek out professionals who practice integrated pest management and encourage your children's school and school district to do the same.
- Don't let your dentist place silver-mercury fillings in your children's teeth, and have mercury fillings that are already in place removed.
- Purchase a water filtration system. A relatively inexpensive choice is a pitcher with a block charcoal filtration system.[64]

Beyond these basic recommendations, there are many excellent resources available for parents, teachers, mental health professionals, and pediatricians. Healthy Child Healthy World (www.healthychild .org) is a nonprofit organization created to help parents protect their children from industrial chemicals. Its advisory board includes environmental luminaries Theo Colborn and Philippe Grandjean, among others, and it boasts a very well organized Web site that is full of practical information and advice for parents. Whether they are planning or expecting their first child or already have several, parents will find the following books reader friendly, with very specific directives for choosing foods and products and improving their environment: *Raising Healthy Children in a Toxic World*, by Philip Landrigan; *Only One Chance: How Environmental Pollution Impairs Brain Development—and How to Protect the Brains of the Next Generation*, by Philippe Grandjean; *The Complete Organic Pregnancy*, by Deirdre Dolan and Alexandra Zissu; *Healthy Child Healthy World*, by Christopher Gavigan (with a foreword by Meryl Streep); and *Raising Baby Green*, by Alan Greene, Jeanette Pavini, and Theresa Foy DiGeronimo. Other books of interest to parents are *Disconnect: The Truth About Cell Phone Radiation*, by Devra Davis; and *Not Just a Pretty Face: The Ugly Side of the Beauty Industry*, by Stacy Malkan.

Prenatal groups, parenting groups, and book clubs can be readily organized (with or without expert leadership) with the resources listed in this section. Meetings can be built around specific books or themes, such as toxic-free cleaning products in the home. The Healthy Child Healthy World Web site lists five readily available natural ingredients—white vinegar, lemon juice, baking soda, washing soda, and borax—that can be combined to make any product necessary to keep your home sanitary and clean, and the recipes for various cleaning applications are also provided. (This is an example of how nontoxic choices can sometimes be more cost effective.) Other meetings might focus on toys made from natural and toxic free materials or integrated pest management practices that avoid or minimize the use of toxic pesticides. And so on . . . .

Once you begin adopting healthier practices, you may find that you're no longer comfortable knowing that your children are playing on neighbors' lawns, in public parks, and on school playgrounds that are treated with pesticides, and you may decide that collective action in your community is imperative. You could then join (or form) a green gardening club to see if you can interest and educate your neighbors and community in these issues, and as a group, attend meetings in your local borough or county to request that local ordinances promote greener practices in public spaces. The Green Schools Initiative (www .greenschools.net) was founded in 2004 by parent environmentalists. The Web site provides resources, ideas, and action steps that can be taken to PTA or school board meetings so that individual parents don't feel that they have to reinvent the wheel, but can learn from successful initiatives to make schools or school districts freer of developmental neurotoxicants in their playgrounds, play materials, building materials, and cleaning products. You might also investigate the extent to which your state and federal representatives prioritize regulating environmental toxicants, participate in or initiate e-mail campaigns to share your own priorities, and vote your priorities in the next election.

Health Professionals and Educators

The impact of toxic exposures on the developing brain are rarely integrated into the training curriculum for mental health professionals or pediatricians. Clinicians can find excellent materials for their own edification or to share with their patients through the Physicians for Responsibility Web site (http://www.psr.org/chapters/boston/), including a downloadable Pediatric Environmental Health Toolkit (http://www.psr.org/resources/pediatric-toolkit.html). In May 2000 the Greater Boston chapter of the Physicians for Responsibility published *In Harm's Way: Toxic Threats to Child Development*, which is replete with important research and information; it can be downloaded from http://www.psr.org/chapters/boston/resources/in-harms -way-materials-download.html. In addition, the Boston chapter offers fact sheets and PowerPoint presentations for health professionals based on the findings from *In Harm's Way*. The Children's Environmental Health Network (http://www.cehn.org) also has pediatric environmental health training resources as well as fact sheets about eco-healthy child care. Other informative resources include Theo Colborne's book *Our Stolen Future*; Varda Burstyn's Web site The Chemical Edge (www.thechemicaledge.com); the Environmental Working Group's site (www.ewg.org), which rates the eco-safety of a wide range of consumer products; and its sister Web site (http://www.ewg.org/skindeep/), with its focus on the safety of beauty products. Clinicians who teach in mental health or medical training programs need to lobby for inclusion of environmental health instruction as part of their core curriculum. Children often spend more hours each day in school than in their own homes. The public school system has a mandate to keep children safe and to create optimal learning environments. There is no merit in increasing the amount of time that children spend in school in an effort to improve their standardized test scores when their physical environments are chock-full of chemicals that diminish their ability to concentrate, learn, and rein in their impulses. Teachers can organize around these concerns.

Prevention is clearly the best approach, but what happens when it doesn't suffice? For example, consider children living near industrial sites where the water and air quality are toxic, or who live in poverty, in apartments with peeling leaded paint. Still other children may be more genetically vulnerable to toxic exposures. Children who are exhibiting symptoms of neurotoxicity in the form of impulsivity, poor concentration, autistic symptoms, learning challenges, and so forth require more than preventive measures. They need treatment. Approaches to treatment are addressed in other chapters by Melillo and Leisman, Galluci, Kaplan, and Rucklidge. Parents and health professionals can seek out specialists who are knowledgeable about detoxification programs that focus on diet, nutritional supplements to help rebuild their brains, and pharmaceutical chelation to pull heavy metals form the body. Unfortunately, such treatments are often not covered by health insurance policies, so often only a small percentage of children, whose parents can afford to pay out of pocket for medical expenses and travel to special clinics, can take full advantage of these treatments. For this reason, individual and grassroots efforts need to be supplemented by legislative initiatives to create and pass laws that are aligned with the *precautionary principle*: laws that ensure that industry does not manufacture chemicals or dump waste products in bodies of water or landfills unless they have been proven to be safe for developing minds and bodies. We also need to work toward health insurance reforms so that environmental illnesses are recognized and their treatments are covered. Too often, children who exhibit symptoms of hyperactivity, poor concentration, impulsivity, or moodiness are labeled as ADHD, depressed, or bipolar and given medications, when the real issue is developmental neurotoxicity.

Top-Down Strategies

Grandjean and Landrigan, the leading experts on the subject of development neurotoxicity, have developed a proposal for addressing this global threat. Following is their strategy, as presented in their 2014 *Lancet* article. The three pillars of their proposed strategy are

- legally mandated testing of existing industrial chemicals and pesticides already in commerce, with prioritization of those with the most widespread use and incorporation of new assessment technologies;
- legally mandated premarket evaluation of new chemicals before they enter markets, with use of precautionary approaches for chemical testing that recognize the unique vulnerability of the developing brain; and
- the formation of a new clearinghouse for neurotoxicity as a parallel to the International Agency for Research on Cancer. This new agency will assess industrial chemicals for developmental neurotoxicity with a precautionary approach that

emphasizes prevention and does not require absolute proof of toxicity. It will facilitate and coordinate epidemiological and toxicological studies and will lead the urgently needed global programs for prevention.

These new approaches must reverse the dangerous presumption that new chemicals and technologies are safe until proven otherwise. They must also overcome the existing requirement to produce absolute proof of toxicity before action can be started to protect children against neurotoxic substances. Precautionary interpretation of data about developmental neurotoxicity should take into account the very large individual and societal costs that result from failure to act on available documentation to prevent disease in children. Academic research has often favored skepticism and required extensive replication before acceptance of a hypothesis, thereby adding to the inertia in toxicology and environmental health research and the consequent disregard of many other potential neurotoxicants. In addition, the strength of evidence that is needed to constitute "proof" should be analyzed in a societal perspective, so that the implications of ignoring a developmental neurotoxicant and of failing to act on the basis of available data are also taken into account. Finally, we emphasize that the total number of neurotoxic substances now recognized almost certainly represents an underestimate of the true number of developmental neurotoxicants that have been released into the global environment. Our very great concern is that children worldwide are being exposed to unrecognized toxic chemicals that are silently eroding intelligence, disrupting behaviors, truncating future achievements, and damaging societies, perhaps most seriously in developing countries. A new framework of action is needed.[65]

5

Functional Brain Imbalance and Autism Spectrum Disorder

Robert Melillo and Gerry Leisman

Three decades ago autism was diagnosed in 1 in 10,000 children.[1] Today it is diagnosed in 1 in 68 children, and in 1 in 42 boys.[2] While some researchers have suggested that these statistics are an artifact of improved diagnosis and changes in diagnostic criteria, as explained in *Autism: The Scientific Truth About Preventing, Diagnosing and Treating Autism Spectrum Disorders and What Parents Can Do Now*, fully 50 to 60 percent are new cases that never existed before.[3] This qualifies as an epidemic. As a point of comparison, polio was declared an epidemic when it was diagnosed in 1 in 2,700 children.[4] We believe that epigenetic factors that stimulate uneven maturation of the brain are driving this epidemic.

Our research indicates that many children diagnosed with autism spectrum disorder, attention deficit/hyperactivity disorder, obsessive compulsive disorder, Tourette's syndrome, and even schizophrenia have a significant imbalance in the rate of development of the left and right hemispheres of their brains.[5] In the case of autism, the right hemisphere typically shows immature physical and functional development, whereas the left hemisphere is often advanced in its development and function. We see this reflected in the neurologic exam, cognitive testing, and health history. This imbalance affects the full spectrum of autistic symptoms, including immune, gut, and autonomic issues. The more severe the autistic symptoms, the greater the imbalance.[6]

There are many well-documented environmental factors that elevate the risk of a parent having a child with autism. Most of these factors affect the individual before conception or during the prenatal period, and in many cases they are avoidable or reversible. In the case of children who have been diagnosed with autism or other developmental disorders and exhibit signs of functional brain imbalance, treatments that address these imbalances and alleviate or eliminate their symptoms are available.[7] In this chapter we explore the nature of the brain, the causes and consequences of functional brain imbalances, and approaches to prevention and treatment. First we introduce a case study that illustrates our approach to assessment and treatment of children with functional brain imbalances.

SEAN: A CASE STUDY

Sean was a 12-year-old student in sixth grade when his parents brought him to our center. At three years of age, he had been diagnosed with an autism spectrum disorder. His parents were especially concerned about the fact that Sean was a very anxious child with poor social skills and no friends to speak of. Although his speech was delayed as a toddler, at age 12 he was articulate but spoke with almost no vocal inflection. Both his fine motor and gross motor skills were weak, he had poor muscle tone, and he had been diagnosed with dyspraxia. Sean had been developmentally delayed in many of his motor milestones; he crawled in an unusual way and for only a very short time, and he rolled over late and only to one side. He did not walk independently until he was 17 months old, and at 12 years he still had a very awkward gait and poor coordination. Sean had almost no history of illness (he never got colds), but he did have eczema and a number of food sensitivities, as confirmed by IgG blood testing. He was an extremely picky eater; he was very sensitive to soft, creamy types of foods, preferring hard, crunchy foods. He never commented on smell; when he was tested, it was discovered that his sense of smell was almost completely absent. He was constipated and would often go for days without moving his bowels.

Sean did not have clear hand dominance; he wrote with his left hand but would eat with his right hand. He was extremely intelligent. His combined IQ was 130, with a 145 verbal IQ and a 115 performance IQ. He had an almost photographic memory. He was very good at basic math calculations, and he was hyperlexic, having started to read spontaneously at around three and a half years of age. In spite of his superior intelligence, Sean needed academic support in certain subjects at school, and he had been assigned an IEP. Although he was an advanced reader, Sean did not enjoy "chapter" books, and he struggled with reading comprehension and extrapolating the main idea of a story. He preferred factual books about dinosaurs and trains. He was in fact obsessed with dinosaurs and could go on for long periods of time discussing them in detail. Sean had perfect pitch and was an exceptional musician. He preferred classical music to popular music. He was hypersensitive to high-pitched sounds and hated loud noises. Sean did not like to be touched and expressed very little emotion or affection. He had a number of "stims" or tics, such as flapping his hands. Although the stims had decreased with age, they were more apparent when he was excited or upset. Sean made very little eye contact. He could not read social signals or facial expressions very well, and he was hyperactive and compulsive. When he was frustrated he could have anger outbursts; otherwise he showed very little emotion. He felt very little pain when he was injured and almost never cried.

Sean's developmental history was fairly typical of autism spectrum disorder, in that he had a clear unevenness of skills. His verbal IQ marked him as a genius, but his motor and nonverbal communication skills were severely delayed. He had several sensory issues, with some hypersensitivities and some hyposensitivities. He also had autonomic, gut, and immune issues. Behavioral scales filled out by his parents indicated that he met the criteria for Asperger's, ADHD, and autism.

Sean's Test Results

Upon assessment we found that Sean was *mixed dominant*; he had a dominant right hand, mixed foot dominance, left eye dominance, and mixed ear dominance. This type of mixed dominance is a by-product of a brain that has not fully matured. Another indicator that his brain was developmentally immature is that he had retained a number of primitive reflexes, including the Moro reflex, asymmetric tonic neck reflex, symmetric tonic neck reflex, rooting reflex only on the left side, and the Babinski reflex, also only on the left foot. These primitive or infantile reflexes are usually gone by four to six months, and at most by one year. The asymmetry in his primitive reflexes showed that there was an asymmetry to his brain development. In Sean's case, his right hemisphere was developmentally delayed, and his left hemisphere was advanced in its development. His delayed motor milestones, slight language delay, and unevenness of skills are consistent with his asymmetrical brain development. His brain imbalance was also reflected in measurements of his autonomic nervous system; his blood pressure was elevated in his right arm compared to the left, his pulse rate and respiratory rate were much faster than would be expected for his age, and his right pupil was significantly larger than his left. Taken together, these measurements showed a global increase in sympathetic tone, which was greater on the right side of his body than on the left, consistent with a decrease in right hemisphere activity. A number of other neurological signs were asymmetrical, such as deep tendon reflexes reflective of muscle tone, vestibular and optokinetic reflexes, and muscle strength testing. Sean had a postural tilt of his head to the right. He had mixed dominance in his core stability, and his gross muscle strength was very low for his age. On the interactive metronome his timing was very poor, and his movements were uncoordinated and asymmetrical, with one side being faster than the other. Vestibular testing clearly showed an imbalance of this system, as did his eye muscle tone and his auditory processing and visual processing. His sense of smell was almost completely absent, as he missed almost every smell on the brief smell identification test. He was clearly advanced in most of his left brain skills, as seen in his verbal IQ scores. Academic achievement testing also demonstrated this gross unevenness of cognitive skills. Although he was in sixth grade, his reading and spelling skills were at a 12.9 grade or 19-year-old level, as were his decoding and math operations. These academic subjects are predominantly left brain skills, and on average his left brain academic scores were around eighth or ninth grade. Sean's listening comprehension was at sixth grade level, his reading comprehension was at third grade level, and his oral expression was at fourth grade level. His math reasoning and written expression were also well below his grade and age level. These represent primarily right hemisphere academic skills. Most of his right brain academic skills were on average around second or third grade. His most and least advanced academic skills spanned 10 years.

In summary, Sean exhibited the functional brain imbalance that is so often found in children diagnosed with autism. The right hemisphere of Sean's brain was developmentally delayed, and his left hemisphere development was accelerated. This was also reflected in the functioning of his autonomic system. His sympathetic (fight or flight) tone was unusually high, and the parasympathetic (rest and digest) was low. The sensory systems were affected as well. Sean, as is typical with this type of brain imbalance, was hypersensitive to high frequency sounds but lacking in sensitivity to low frequency sounds and hypersensitive to light touch but less sensitive to touch on the left side of his body (which is connected to the right side of his brain). He had exceptional ability to notice visual detail, but could not see the "big picture" and was verbally gifted with weak nonverbal communication. This pattern of subjective complaints and symptoms, along with objective testing, is consistent with a majority of children who are properly diagnosed with autism. His MRI scans were unremarkable, and blood tests other than those indicating food sensitivities were normal. All of his autistic symptoms, including immune, gut and autonomic symptoms, can be traced to this brain imbalance. The key to helping Sean was to identify and quantify all of his neurological weaknesses and stimulate them until they began to match his areas of strength. Achieving balance in the brain and nervous system is key to minimizing or eliminating symptoms. We describe the program that was designed for Sean and the outcome at the end of this chapter.

THE DYNAMIC BRAIN

The 1990s was declared the "Decade of the Brain" by then President Bill Clinton, resulting in an explosion of brain research. At that time we saw the development of more dynamic ways of measuring brain function, including fMRI, SPECT, PET, magnetoencephalograpy, and other techniques that allowed us to examine brain function in real time with significantly better spatial resolution. This window into the living brain helped us to appreciate that it was far more complex and dynamic than we had previously thought. Most of what was known about the brain until these recent technological advances in functional brain imaging was based on lesion studies, in which specific symptoms were related to discrete lesions.[8] This, along with split-brain research from the1960s, allowed us to understand that the brain was asymmetrical in its functions.[9] Little was known, however, about the nature of hemispheric interaction in normal function and about brain dysfunction in the absence of focal observable lesions.

Early investigators started mapping normal brain function based on the study of lesions in the neurologically impaired. Paul Broca was one of the early pioneers in this type of research. In the late 1800s he established that a lesion in a particular area of the left frontal lobe would reproducibly result in a form of motor aphasia (loss of speech). Broca extrapolated that this region of the brain, which came to be known as Broca's area, controlled speech production.[10] It became apparent that different areas of the brain were specialized for various functions. This was even more clearly established through the "split-brain" research conducted by Phillip Vogel, Joseph Bogen, and Roger Sperry in California in the 1960s. They discovered that severing the corpus callosum, or the white matter that connected the left and right hemispheres of the brain, produced significant deficits, collectively referred to as a disconnection syndrome.[11]

In 1965 Norman Geschwind revolutionized clinical neurology when he published "Disconnection Syndromes in Animals and Man," in which he stated that disconnecting regions of the brain led to deficits that were as severe as trauma caused by lesions in specific regions of the brain.[12] In other words, in order for the brain to function, different regions had to actively communicate with each other.

Most psychiatric and neurological disorders do not involve lesions in the brain's gray *or* white matter, but we still can identify soft neurological signs and obvious neurological symptoms that are often accompanied by physical, immunological, and autonomic changes. With the advent of new technologies, functional rather than physical neurological deficits associated with cognitive ability, executive function, attention, verbal and nonverbal communication, emotional regulation, social skills, motor functions, perception, and processing of sensory stimuli can now be measured. With attention turned to brain functions rather than brain lesions, researchers began noting that many individuals demonstrating neurological and psychological disorders had uneven brain development. But these observations have been overshadowed by the undue focus on the *chemical imbalance theory*, which states that psychiatric disturbance is caused by too much or too little of a particular neurotransmitter (brain chemical).[13] As there is no real way to measure the levels of chemicals in a living, functioning brain without perturbing the brain in ways that would themselves alter the levels of chemicals we would be measuring, this is an example of the Heisenberg uncertainty principle[14] in which measurement would itself alter the subject of that measurement. We have no idea what "normal" levels of neurotransmitters like serotonin, dopamine, and norepinephrine are. The notion that these neurotransmitter levels are static and are or should be balanced among different areas of the brain is inaccurate.[15] Chemical receptor sites are not distributed evenly in the brain; rather, they are concentrated more in certain areas than in others, and there are different levels in the two hemispheres. The brain is not some "bag of chemicals" trying to achieve an equi-molar concentration gradient.

Functional versus Chemical Brain Imbalances

In spite of the ongoing popularity of the chemical imbalance theory in the media, researchers are turning their attention to functional rather than chemical deficits in the brain. Neurotransmitters and their receptors are produced by the (neuron) nerve cell in response to activation. Neurotransmitter levels are therefore more likely to reflect how actively a neural pathway is used. In other words, less neuronal activity results in a decreased need for neurotransmitters and decreased production. If a deficit or surfeit of a particular brain chemical does exist, it is more likely a reflection of the nature and intensity of environmental stimulation, rather than the capacity of the nerve cell to produce neurotransmitters. Artificially increasing the availability of neurotransmitters through certain drugs may "trick" the neurons into believing that there is increased activation and temporarily reduce symptoms. However, since it is not actual activation, there are no long-term improvements in the deficits being treated by these agents.[16]

The extent to which products of a specific gene are expressed in the brain is a matter of the demands placed on the neuronal or glial cells (cells that support neurons) by external stimulation. The environment, which is both physical and social, is the primary source of these external stimuli. This information is then converted into synaptic signals, which are in turn transduced into intracellular second messengers and ultimately into altered cytoplasmic and nuclear signals that determine which genes are turned on or kept off by regulating transcription. Therefore, the degree to which our genotype is reflected in our functional form or phenotype comes under environmental influence. The effects of the environment are likely to be cumulative and perhaps vary with the stages of development, and these influences on early brain function may not be apparent until much later in life.

In summary, the phenotypical expression of the genotype is dependent on synaptic activity, which is dependent on receptor activity, which is dependent on environmental stimuli. Alteration of gene expression can result from alterations in environmental stimuli. Therefore, a purely biochemical approach to such a complex system does not make sense. These sentiments are reflected in the following statement by cognitive psychologists Liotti and Tucker (1995). "The idea that a psychiatric disorder can be traced to a neurochemical abnormality is simplistic, and may lead to a functional understanding only as the neuromodulator systems are seen within the context of the parts they play in the brain's multileveled motivational circuitry."

Functional Connectivity in the Brain

Many elements in addition to neurotransmitters affect brain function. Cytokines, hormones, and other chemicals also play a role, and at this point we have little understanding of how they all work together. Synaptic transmission via neurotransmitters may in fact function as the brain's "pacemakers," with neural communication taking place primarily through "electrotonic coupling" in which shared membrane contacts enable nearly simultaneous activity and activation of a large population of neurons and their postsynaptic connections. This enables synchronization and coordination of large cortical and subcortical networks in the brain and sets the baseline tone of brain activity, providing the context in which more specific content or information can be coordinated.

The thalamus is the main relay station in the brain for almost all sensory input and motor activation.[17] Different nuclei (compact clusters of neurons) within the thalamus transmit different types of information.[18] The *relay* or specific nuclei send specific sensory and motor information to discrete areas of the cortex. The *medial geniculate* nucleus sends information about sound to the temporal lobe for primary processing. The *lateral geniculate* sends visual signals to the occipital lobe, and so forth. The *association* nuclei, such as the *pulvinar* and *medial dorsal*, are connected to the association cortex (areas that integrate information within particular sensory modalities and between sensory areas). Nonspecific or *intra-laminar* nuclei send pulsatile oscillations to widespread areas of the cortex. Electrotonic coupling takes place within these nuclei, which then have widespread connections to a given hemisphere or to the entire cortex.[19]

Thalamic cells can exist in two different states of activation. They can be in a burst mode, in which they will fire periodically, or they can fire continuously.[20] Typically when they are hyperpolarized or inhibited, they fire in burst mode, and when they are depolarized they fire continuously. The *midline intra-laminar* nuclei, however, are always in this burst mode, and they can speed up or slow down the oscillations they create in the cortex depending on whether they are hyperpolarized or depolarized. These oscillations are what we read on EEG recordings, and we know that they can exist at various frequencies. The highest frequencies are called gamma oscillations, which are greater than 30 hertz. These gamma oscillations are believed to be what creates consciousness and enables cognitive binding. These fast cortical waves act as glue that allows multiple areas of the cortex to coordinate and integrate information in space and time. Like a symphony orchestra, the brain needs to be able to coordinate and connect different distant areas of the brain simultaneously to create one perception of the world around us at any given moment. This occurs by combining information from specific thalamic nuclei and cortical areas, integrating them in the association areas of the brain and thalamus, and then coordinating and combining them together through these gamma oscillations that coordinate all of these areas to fire simultaneously. It is this timing that synchronizes these various areas of the brain into one conscious perception of our environment. Without these underlying oscillations there would be no glue to hold this information together, and the world would seem fragmented and disconnected.

Functional Disconnectivity in the Brain

The thalamus is divided into two halves. The right half sends information to the right cerebral hemisphere, and the left half sends information to the left hemisphere of the brain.[21] The speed of oscillations or bursts in the right thalamus can be very different from the speed of oscillations in the left, resulting in asynchronous firing of the entire left and right hemispheres.[22] This asynchrony or dysrhythmia, if large enough, could prevent information in the right hemisphere being coordinated and synchronized in time and space with information in the left hemisphere. This is referred to as functional disconnection syndrome, and it appears to be a central issue in many childhood neurological disorders, including autism spectrum disorder, ADHD, OCD, Tourette's, and schizophrenia.[23] This is more in keeping with how the brain actually functions than the chemical imbalance theory, but many clinicians and researchers do not make use of this information, in part because of the difficulty in documenting disrupted functional connectivity. Disordered temporal coherence in the brain can be measured to a certain degree with sophisticated imaging like quantitative EEG or magnetoencephalograpy, but these techniques may be too slow to pick up more subtle dysrhythmias. Functional disconnectivities take place in nanoseconds, which at this time makes them virtually impossible to measure or image. For example, fMRI scans possess a temporal resolution in the two-second time range and are therefore unable to detect areas of desynchronization.

THE ASYMMETRICAL BRAIN

Functional disconnections are well documented and can occur between any two areas of the brain, between or within hemispheres. Our research, as well as that of others using the most advanced functional imaging, has shown poor temporal coherence, reduced and unbalanced functional activity and connectivity, as well as a variety of neuropsychological, immune, autonomic, motor, and sensory functional imbalances in children diagnosed with autism, dyslexia, and ADHD. It appears that most functional disconnections are a result of developmental imbalances between the hemispheres.

If two brain regions mature at significantly different rates, they may become incompatible with one another and therefore unable to integrate information synchronously. This may present clinically as "unevenness of skills" or a functional imbalance. Areas that are more mature and more developed will naturally perform at a higher functional level than areas that are relatively immature and underdeveloped. In fact, almost all functional neurological disorders, especially those that are known to involve developmental issues, present with this unevenness of skills. In most neurobehavioral childhood disorders, like autism, ADHD, and dyslexia, we often see individuals whose brains function at or well above their age and grade level on certain tasks and well below their age and grade level on others.[24] Furthermore, the degree of unevenness of skills correlates with the level of impairment. The most extreme example of this is savant syndrome in autism. Brain imbalances resulting from functional disconnections that arise while the brain is developing appear to be at the root of many neurological disorders.

Neuropsychologist Donald Hebb introduced the concept of functional connectivity in 1948[25] with his oft-quoted phrase "cells that fire together, wire together." In other words, nerve cells that are active at the same time will become interconnected. Therefore, functional connectivity implies both physical connection—which we can see and measure through the formation of synapses—and temporal connection, which is harder to image and measure. In all likelihood, the temporal connection starts first. Cells start to fire in a synchronous fashion and then begin to build physical connections with each other to help facilitate coordination or in essence increase their "bandwidth." In many children with neurobehavioral disorders, we see areas within their brains that are "hyperconnected" along with areas that are "underconnected." None of these areas in and of themselves look abnormal. However, when we examine the brain as a whole, we see differences in the functional efficiency of different regions, reflecting differences in developmental trajectories that in turn correlate with their functional strengths and weaknesses.

Developmental Dyslexia and Disconnectivities

In 1982 neurologist Norman Geschwind, one of the pioneers in disconnection syndrome research, reflected on his observations of individuals diagnosed with dyslexia:

[I]t has become increasingly clear in recent years that dyslexics themselves are frequently endowed with high talents in many areas. All of you who spent many painstaking hours treating patients can point proudly to former students who have been outstanding figures in this society who are or were dyslexic. I need only point out the names of Thomas Edison and Albert Einstein to make clear that dyslexics do not merely succeed in making marginal adjustments in some instances, but they rank among those who have created the very fabric of our modern world. . . . I would suggest to you that this is no accident . . . . Many dyslexics have superior talents in certain areas of nonverbal skill, such as art, architecture, engineering, and athletics. . . . [I]f certain changes on the left side of the brain lead to superiority of other regions, particularly on the right side of the brain, then there would be little disadvantage to the carrier of such changes in an illiterate society; their talents would make them highly successful citizens. . . . [T]he more we know about the intimate processes that lead to these brain changes, the more we are likely to be able to face these dilemmas intelligently. I am convinced there is a satisfactory solution, since the evidence is all around us.[26]

Geschwind observed that throughout most of human history we were illiterate, and therefore it is not surprising that not everyone's brains adapt readily to reading but nonetheless excel in other ways. In the early 1980s Geschwind autopsied the brains of seven dyslexic subjects and noted a physical difference in their brains. The temporal planum in the left hemisphere, which is generally larger in all humans than the right planum, and which is thought to be associated with verbal ability, was smaller in dyslexics on the left and larger on the right. This reverse asymmetry also seemed to correlate with unevenness of skills in these individuals. Each of the subjects had poor verbal and reading skills, but they all possessed exceptional nonverbal and visual-spatial skills. This physical imbalance of the hemispheres was mirrored by a functional imbalance in skill. Geschwind referred to this unevenness of skill and anatomic imbalance as "pathology of superiority." He attributed it to what he referred to as the "testosterone hypothesis," in which abnormal levels of testosterone in the mother during prenatal development somehow resulted in abnormal development of the brain. We see these same phenomena in ADHD and autism, but with the reverse asymmetry. In ADHD and autism we observe advanced or more mature skills related to the left hemisphere, with developmental delays in skills associated with the right hemisphere.

In summary, it has been known for some time that most neurobehavioral disorders in children and adults do not show obvious pathologies in the brain. This lack of overt evidence has led to different theories to explain the clinical observations, the most common of which is that there exists a chemical imbalance in the brain, although there is little evidence to support this theory. Diagnosed individuals, however, often show a functional brain imbalance. There is no damage to gray matter structures, but differences in white matter development have been noted, with areas of hyper-connectivity along with areas of hypo-connectivity, albeit without damage to white matter, which fits well with a disconnection syndrome.[27] One of the most notable differences in white matter often observed in the brains of individuals with neurobehavioral disorders is the comparatively small corpus callosum, in all likelihood affecting interhemispheric communication.[28] But this in and of itself does not explain why one side of the brain would be more delayed in development than the other side. Current thinking is that the timing of hemispheric development is a critical factor in the manifestation of childhood neurobehavioral disorders.

CRITICAL PERIODS FOR RIGHT AND LEFT BRAIN DEVELOPMENT

The left and right halves of the brain do not develop at the same rate or at the same time.[29] Throughout the course of a child's development, beginning prenatally, brain development occurs more intensively in one hemisphere than the other. The timing of hemispheric maturation plays a large role in determining what type of specialized abilities and processing each hemisphere will be best suited for. Researchers have established *critical periods* or windows of opportunity during which development of particular regions of the brain must occur for optimal development.[30] Prenatal and postnatal exposure to hormones and environmental stimulation during critical periods of brain development shape the relative efficiencies of each hemisphere. Nonetheless, it is important to remember that no ability is exclusively represented on one side of the brain or the other. Each side has the capacity to process all types of information.

The critical period for right hemisphere development in humans begins prenatally and continues through to the end of the child's second year. (The critical period for the left hemisphere begins after the second year.)[31] It is during this period of rapid development that the right side of the brain is *most susceptible* to negative environmental influences. Any environmental exposure that negatively impacts the prenatal, perinatal, or postnatal development through the child's second year could impact right hemisphere development. Children diagnosed with neurobehavioral disorders whose symptoms reflect right hemisphere disabilities, such as ADHD, autism, and Asperger's, are more likely to have had negative environmental exposures during the first two years of life, or more probably in the womb.[32] A recent study published in the *New England Journal of Medicine* confirmed previous research that autism often starts in the womb during the first or second trimester, during right-brain development.[33]

The right hemisphere is the nonverbal side of the brain. It is holistic; in other words, it is good at seeing the "big picture." It develops an internalized map of the body and enables us to feel and move our bodies through space. It is because the right half of the brain develops first that it specializes in the skills that are critical during infancy and early childhood.[34] During prenatal development, the brain is not exposed to much light. In consequence, the right hemisphere is visually focused on outlines, movement, and shades of grey. It does not see detailed images, but rather blurry images, and it is sensitive to movement. Newborns therefore do not see very well. They see only the shape or outline of the mother, and they don't perceive color well. They rely heavily on their peripheral vision, which is sensitive to motion. It is of developmental value for infants to direct their attention to movement.[35]

Similarly, the fetus hears sounds after they have vibrated through the mother's body and the amniotic fluid. By the time the sound reaches the fetus, it is low and muffled.[36] Newborns do not need to and cannot understand words, so they do not need the details of sounds right away. They hear their mother's breathing, her heartbeat, and muffled voices. But infants are sensitive to sounds that convey emotions, such as anger and excitement. They are responsive to their parents' voices and can tell the difference between them. They respond to their mother's coos and are soothed by the sound of her breathing and heartbeat. Throughout life, the right brain is superior in interpreting nonverbal aspects of language. It is attuned to the intonation, pitch, and emotionality of a person's voice.[37]

Fetuses and newborns can only move the big muscles of their bodies: the muscles of the trunk, head, mouth, and eyes. They can move their arms and legs, but with very little control. These are the muscles that are most important during early development, and they are controlled by the right side of the brain.[38] It would not make sense to divert much energy to the development of finger and toe movements during early infancy, because this kind of muscle control is not yet necessary. These skills will develop later, when the focus of brain development shifts to the left hemisphere. The right brain develops first through experience-expectant stimulation that builds the very skills that are necessary for infants' optimal functioning. This early development will lay the foundation for all of the skills that the right side of the brain will specialize in for the rest of the child's life.

WHY MALE BRAINS ARE DISPROPORTIONATELY VULNERABLE TO AUTISM SPECTRUM DISORDERS

Male and female brains do have some developmental differences, primarily due to hormone concentrations during prenatal and postnatal development.[39] Relative exposure to testosterone and estrogen will partly determine if the brain develops male or female characteristics. Male brains tend to have more disproportionate hemispheres than female brains. The right side of the male brain is significantly bigger than the left side, especially toward the front of the brain. Female brains tend to be more symmetrical or balanced. They also have a much larger corpus callosum between the two halves of the brain, and therefore the left and right hemispheres can function in a coordinated way more easily. Female brains also tend to be slightly larger toward the back of the left hemisphere. Males tend to have an advantage in right-brain abilities. Females are better at left-brain skills, but seem to have better conscious access to both hemispheres. Many of the disabilities we discuss in this chapter are right hemisphere disabilities. It is no coincidence that these disabilities are more common in males, who rely more heavily on their right brains.[40]

Four out of five children diagnosed with autism are males. There is also a higher incidence of boys than girls diagnosed with ADHD. Negative environmental exposures during the right brain's critical period of development, beginning prenatally and extending through the first two years of life, will more adversely impact boys, who are more dependent on right hemisphere abilities. Also, boys are more susceptible to negative environmental factors than girls, especially in the womb. This seems to have some evolutionary significance. Studies with rats have shown that during times when food supplies are scarce and diet depends more heavily on carbohydrates rather than proteins, there is a greater percentage of female offspring. However, when food supplies are plentiful and there are adequate supplies of protein, there is a greater percentage of male offspring. This dietary change seems to affect the prenatal environment and will favor one gender over the other.[41]

Research with animals and humans also suggests that when mothers are significantly stressed prenatally, male offspring will be more negatively affected by exposure to stress hormones, and their brains are less likely to develop strong male characteristics. As a result, the right hemisphere does not grow as large relative to the left hemisphere as it normally would.[42] Female infants do not seem to be as adversely affected by maternal stress.[43] So, reduced food (protein) supply, or an increase in stress hormones released by the mother prenatally, and exposure to environmental toxins seem to affect male offspring to a much greater extent than females. Since right hemisphere development is more dependent on stimulation from early movement and spatial exploration, reduced physical activity during infancy will also affect the development of the right hemisphere. Reduced physical movement, as in delayed crawling or walking, or sedentary behavior, will have a greater effect on males than on females. While this helps us to understand why we see a disproportionate numbers of boys diagnosed with neurobehavioral disorders, it doesn't fully explain the timing of the autism epidemic that we have witnessed over the past three decades.[44]

THE AUTISM EPIDEMIC: AN EPIGENETIC PERSPECTIVE

The best way to understand the explosion of new cases of autism is through an epigenetic lens. There are many well-known, well-documented environmental risk factors that increase the likelihood that either a father or a mother will have a child with autism. Most of these risk factors take effect either before conception or during the pregnancy, and many are avoidable or reversible. So awareness can significantly lower the chances that a child will be born with autism. Some of these environmental risk factors are SSRI antidepressants, valproic acid (Depakote), mercury, pesticides such as organophosphates, pollution, unchecked hypertension, diabetes or obesity during pregnancy, maternal and paternal age, psychological and emotional stress, inflammation, and autoimmunity disorders.[45] As previously discussed, tens of thousands of man-made chemicals have been released into our environment in recent decades, many of which are established neurotoxicants. It is not that females are unaffected by these stressors; we are seeing a steep rise in cases of autism in girls, too. However, since females can use both sides of their brains in a more coordinated way than males because of the greater connectivity between their left and right hemispheres, they compensate in stressful environments, in the same way that someone who is ambidextrous will be less impacted than someone who is right handed should he or she lose dexterity in the right hand.

AUTISM SPECTRUM DISORDER: A LEFT-RIGHT BRAIN IMBALANCE

Autism has for a long time been known to be associated with more than just cognitive and behavioral symptoms. Motor, sensory autonomic, dietary, and immunological symptoms are also part of the picture.[46] When Leo Kanner first identified autism in 11 patients in his seminal paper in 1943, he noted not only many of the behavioral symptoms of autism, but also dietary, bowel, immunological, and digestive as well as motor and sensory issues in every case. However, until recently most physicians believed that the physical symptoms associated with autism were either coincidental and unrelated or at best not clearly understood.[47] Autism spectrum disorders, however, can best be understood in the context of functional disconnections of the brain in which brain regions are less optimized in their communication abilities with each other, resulting in less integration of behavioral and physical functions to various degrees. By reviewing the various functions of the left and right hemispheres, the range of behavioral and physical challenges autistic children face begins to form a more cohesive picture.

Specializations of the Left Hemisphere

Anything involving verbal language is within the purview of the left hemisphere, including reading, writing, speaking, and understanding verbal language. The left hemisphere is better at noticing details and breaking things and events down into their component parts for close examination. Understanding the literal meaning of a word, reading the individual word in the sentence, and reading the individual sentence in the story are likewise left-brain functions. The left brain is better at looking at the parts as opposed to the whole. It controls fine-motor skills that involve moving small muscles rapidly in sequence, as in tying shoelaces, playing the piano, or speaking. When we speak we rapidly activate a number of small muscles in a very specific sequence to produce words. The left hemisphere is also adept at processing the sounds of individual words, which are made up of rapidly changing sounds. Children diagnosed with dyslexia (reading disability), which is primarily a left-brain deficit, may have difficulty perceiving all of the rapidly changing sounds of distinct words. In other words, they may lack phonemic awareness if their left hemisphere is processing sounds at a slower than normal speed. If they cannot perceive the sounds, they will not be able to match the sounds with the appropriate letters. The left hemisphere is specialized to perceive high frequency sounds that change rapidly. Visually, the left hemisphere perceives highly detailed input, and this takes longer to process, so the brain needs to compensate for these different speed requirements to bind vision and hearing together. When children cannot process visual stimuli fast enough, or if their visual and auditory processing is out of sync, they will struggle to read.

The left hemisphere is the conscious side of the brain. Whenever we are doing something of which we are aware, the left brain is more involved. When, for example, we make a conscious effort to read, learn, perform math problems, or remember, the left brain is responsible. This type of memory is called declarative or explicit memory. When we talk to ourselves, the left brain is involved. Females tend to have better language skills than males. The left side of the brain is also better at basic math operations and remembering numbers in a sequence. The left brain is good at pattern recognition skills, such as figuring out what comes next in a sequence. Pattern recognition plays an important role in language development. Learning to play a musical instrument involves the left hemisphere, because it involves both pattern recognition ability and fine motor skills. The left brain loves computer and video games because they also rely on pattern recognitions skills. It is systematic and logical. Because of this, the left brain subserves pattern and has a preference for the same routine. It is more linear or logical in its thinking and prefers examining one stimulus at a time and in order. The left brain prefers science and math and other logical pursuits. It is investigative. It underlies verbal intelligence and is more easily measured by traditional IQ tests.

Behaviorally, the left brain controls what we call approach behavior: it wants to approach a situation to study all the details and figure out a pattern and remember that pattern. These attitudes are associated with positive emotions such as happiness, fun, or curiosity. The left brain is not cautious. Depression is thought to result from decreased activity in the left side of the brain.[48] Children who are shy or depressed have less approach behavior and tend to be more withdrawn, sad, and less motivated to initiate action.[49] The left brain is the gas pedal of the brain. It initiates a thought, an action, or a word. It gets us started, whereas the right side of the brain is the brake. It stops the action or thought or movement or word so that we can stop and move on to the next thing. Obsessive tendencies and hyperactivity, impulsivity, or tics as in Tourette's syndrome can be associated with decreased activity of the right-parietal and prefontal regions and their ability to inhibit stimulation.[50] This is known as perserverative behavior.

The left hemisphere also controls part of the immune system. It activates the immune system to fight off infections and toxins. It also stimulates the growth and development of immune tissue, called lymphoid tissue, which houses white blood cells and other immune-mediated chemicals. It activates the immune system to produce antibodies to fight off foreign invaders. So if a child is sick and has an infection, the left hemisphere will mobilize the immune system to fight off that infection. If the left brain is hypoactive relative to the right, the child may be prone to chronic infections like ear infections. The left brain also helps regulate some of the body's automatic functions, like the heartbeat. It keeps the heart beating in a pattern and helps to regulate one of the pacemakers of the heart. If the left brain is slower or weaker, the heart's rhythms may be abnormal or arrhythmic. Following is a summary of normal functions of the left hemisphere and symptoms that can arise when it is underactivated.[51]

Functions of the Left Hemisphere

- Verbal communication, reading, mathematical calculation, musical ability
- Approach behavior, desire or motivation to do things, social motivation
- Attention to details and facts (local coherence)
- Pattern recognition skills (computer skills are a good fit with the left-brain)
- Seeking sameness
- Immune activation
- Fine motor skills
- Processing of high-frequency sound and light

Symptoms Associated with Left Hemisphere Underactivation:
Dyslexia/Processing and Language Disorders

- Poor reading
- Delayed speech
- Poor auditory processing
- Poor object identification
- Poor verbal communication skills
- Depression
- Poor math operations
- Graphomotor problems
- Cross laterality
- Autonomic dysregulation
- Decreased immune response
- Missing small details
- Poor motivation
- Abnormal heart rhythm

Specializations of the Right Hemisphere

The right hemisphere specializes in nonverbal communication, which includes the ability to read someone's body posture, facial expression, or tone of voice and understand what that person is thinking or feeling. This ability has also been referred to as "theory of mind," the ability to empathize with another person. Nonverbal communication is the foundation of socialization, so the right brain is the social brain. Nonverbal ability is also the foundation of verbal communication, so if a child does not develop nonverbal communication, he or she will be delayed or may never develop proper verbal communication. The right side of the brain is more emotionally literate. It enables us to feel our own emotions and to read other people's emotions. Nonverbal communication and emotional literacy develop very early, because the right hemisphere develops first.[52]

Most people describe emotions as an internal feeling, a change inside their bodies. We know that when we experience an emotion, it is accompanied by physiological changes. Our heart rate intensifies, as does blood pressure, and we release certain chemicals. We may sweat. However, these physiological changes are exactly the same for each emotion, so how do we learn to distinguish among sadness, anger, excitement, and happiness? This process starts early, at about the third month of life, as we start to communicate nonverbally with our parents, especially our mothers. We begin to mimic facial and body movements and are affected by our caregiver's tone of voice. This results in certain changes in our bodies that in turn trigger changes in our stomachs and intestines. Soon we come to recognize that these different patterns of muscular contractions linked to these physiological changes are associated with certain feelings that we call emotions. Some muscular contractions like facial movements seem to be genetically programmed and are universal. No matter what language we speak, we can all look at a picture of someone with a particular facial expression and recognize the emotion that the person is expressing.

The ability to feel our own emotions is located in the right brain in the insula cortex, where we perceive the internal sensations from our gut, heart, and lungs, and the parietal lobe, which has a sensory map of the whole body. Together these two regions of the right brain give us a complete picture of our bodies' movements and reactions, which we come to recognize as emotions.[53] Once we are able to read our own emotions, we start to develop the ability to read these same emotions in other people. We do this using a special network of cells in the brain called mirror neurons. These mirror neurons allow us to notice the muscular contractions, body posture, and facial expressions in others. We then "mirror" those movements in our own brains. We literally perform a virtual reality simulation of the movements and postures of the other person in our minds.[54] In this way, we have a window into what the other person is feeling and thinking. This is how the right brain enables us to experience empathy. Learning to read our own and other people's emotions, to empathize with them, takes place outside of conscious awareness. This nonverbal ability to read our own and other people's feelings is the foundation of socialization. We learn the rules of socialization, first at home from our parents and siblings and later on the playground or in the classroom. We learn that if another child backs away or if an adult frowns, this is bad, and if an adult smiles and nods approval, this is good. We all naturally have a drive for social acceptance by other humans, so we are reinforced to continue doing the right thing and avoid doing the wrong thing.

The right brain is the "cautious brain" that keeps us safe. Before the curious left brain can approach something, the right brain has to give it permission and indicate that it is safe to continue. If not, we avoid the situation. This can generate more negative emotions, like fear or anger. It tells us whether to fight or run away. Because the right brain needs to determine whether a new environment or situation is good or bad, it needs to see the big picture quickly. The right brain visually sees the whole scene all at once. It is not concerned with detail. The right brain "sees the forest" and the left brain "sees the trees." Because the right brain is nonverbal, it learns subconsciously or subliminally. We do not realize we are learning something new, but that does not make it less important. This type of learning is called procedural or implicit memory. The right brain likes new or novel situations or locations.[55] It hates to do the same thing over and over, and it gets bored easily by routines. The right brain is also very attuned to the sense of smell and taste. It tells us if something is alright to eat or should be avoided, or whether a person should be avoided because he or she "smells bad."[56] The insula cortex is responsible for these decisions, and its dysfunction may affect appetite. We may avoid foods because we cannot smell or taste them adequately.[57]

The right side of the brain is also responsible for spatial skills. It allows us to feel our bodies in space. It helps us to understand directions and to control the muscles of posture and gait. It controls our balance and proprioception, the ability to know where one's body is in relationship to its other parts and to other people.[58] The right hemisphere is primarily responsible for receiving information from the inner ear, or vestibular sensations.[59] Children with right hemisphere deficits do not feel their bodies well. They tend to be clumsy and have poor muscle tone, especially of the big postural muscles. They have delayed and poor gross motor abilities. They also tend to have poor balance and coordination, and they trip and fall. The most common finding in a child with right hemisphere delay is abnormal posture and gait and low muscle tone.[60] This is most common in children with autism. We know that children with autism do not feel their bodies, as is readily observed in the way that they move. They are clumsy.[61]

A number of individuals who have grown up autistic have written books about their experiences. Temple Grandin (1992), who has written several books, describes how she felt disconnected from her body; she did not feel that her body was whole, but rather broken up into separate pieces. Others describe how they did not feel "grounded." Jean Ayres (1979) called this feeling *gravitational insecurity*. Others have said that they did not even realize they had a body at all. This is not only important from a movement standpoint, but also because feeling our own body movements is how we are able to experience our emotions. Children who do not feel their bodies never learn to link body movements with physiological reactions and thus experience emotions. If they cannot feel their bodies and label emotions, then they cannot activate mirror neurons and "read" the emotions of others. Nonverbal communication becomes difficult, as does socialization. They will behave socially inappropriately, invading other people's space. Others will think of them as "weird" and will avoid contact with them. Eye contact will be difficult or absent, because for most humans emotional information is heavily dependent on the sense of vision.

Whereas the left brain is optimized for reading words, the right brain "reads" people and situations. Children with right hemisphere deficits cannot read people and situations, but are often good at reading words. Some autistic children can teach themselves to read at extremely early ages (hyperlexia).[62] However, as they get older, because they are poor at big picture skills, they have great difficulty with reading comprehension. They are skilled in word reading, spelling, and vocabulary, but poor at the main idea or inference. They are not good at pragmatic skills like humor. They always miss the joke or the gist of the story. They can memorize the details of the story, but cannot tell the meaning. The same thing is true for math skills. Children with right-brain deficits are good at basic math operations, but poor at math reasoning skills involving word problems.

The right hemisphere also helps to control and inhibit the immune system. It prevents the immune system from overreacting.[63] If the right hemisphere is weak, one may suffer from autoimmune disorders, be overly sensitive to the environment, and demonstrate allergic reactions to common environmental elements, problems commonly seen in autistic children. Because the right side of the brain is cautious and sensory, it is associated with the control of impulsivity. It allows us to inhibit socially inappropriate behaviors. Children with right hemisphere deficits demonstrate poor attention and are impulsive. They also tend to be compulsive. The right hemisphere also controls most of our automatic reactions, especially digestion. It controls the pacemaker in the heart that regulates the rate of the heartbeat. So a child with a right hemisphere weakness will have a more rapid heart rate and poor digestion.

Functions of the Right Hemisphere

- Nonverbal communication, math reasoning, reading comprehension, spatial perception, attention, impulse control, bodily awareness, proprioception
- Seeing the big picture (global coherence)
- Facial recognition
- Social skills
- Withdrawal behavior; stopping any activity that could be dangerous
- Novelty seeking
- Immune suppression
- Processing of low-frequency sound and light
- Gross motor control, eyes, posture, movement of big muscles, rhythm

Symptoms Associated with Right Hemisphere Underactivation: Autism/Asperger's/ADHD/Tourette's/OCD

- Poor spatial orientation
- Inappropriate social behavior

- Missing the big picture
- Inability to reflect on own mental processes
- Poor nonverbal communication skills
- Poor attention
- Impulsivity
- preservative behavior and movements
- Poor reading comprehension and pragmatic skills
- Overactive immune response (autoimmunity)
- Poor gross motor skills and development
- Poor math reasoning
- Anxiety

NEUROIMMUNE ISSUES AND AUTISM SPECTRUM DISORDER

Many individuals with autism or other neurological symptoms, whether they are developmental or a result of a traumatic brain injury, also present with immunological symptoms. It is clear that chemicals that play a role in the immune system, like cytokines, inflammatory chemicals, and hormones, have a significant effect on brain function, but what is much less appreciated and perhaps actually much more important is the role that the brain plays in immune, autonomic, and endocrine regulation and dysregulation. The brain plays a major role in balancing the sympathetic and parasympathetic branches of the autonomic nervous system, which in turn helps to regulate the immune system. In a previous paper we discussed how the biomedical and immunological issues that are typically associated with autism could be explained by an imbalance in the left and right hemispheres and a subsequent imbalance in the sympathetic and parasympathetic nervous systems.[64] If the brain is underdeveloped on either side, the sympathetic nervous system tone will be higher, and this will affect—through the release of epinephrine and norepinephrine as well as cortisol—digestive, hormonal, and immune responses, which will ultimately impact the whole body and the brain.

The two hemispheres of the brain have been well documented as playing opposing roles in the regulation of the immune system.[65] The left hemisphere—consistent with its behavioral role of approach, intention, and activation—increases the activation of T cells, B cells, and natural killer cells, increasing the immune response. The right hemisphere—consistent with its behavioral roles of withdrawal and inhibition—promotes immune suppression and assists the immune system in recognizing self from other. Decreased right-brain activity combined with increased left hemispheric activation can result in an overactive immune response, autoimmunity, and oversensitivity of antibodies, leading to molecular mimicry. This issue is most apparent in a disorder known as PANDAS or PANS (pediatric autoimmune neuropsychiatric disorders).[66] This condition is one of the clearest examples of the two-way role that the brain and immune system can play in neurological disorders. Many if not all of the children with PANS present with symptoms typical of a right hemisphere delay. In fact, the primary symptoms that constitute a positive diagnosis of PANS are ADHD, OCD, and Tourette's, which are all right-hemisphere-associated syndromes. However, the diagnosis also requires a history of an acute or even chronic infection immediately preceding the manifestation of symptoms.

According to Madeleine Cunningham (2012), the primary hyperkinetic symptoms of ADHD, OCD, Tourette's, and tics, are a result of molecular mimicry, in which the immune system develops antibodies against an infectious agent but also develops antibodies against D1 or D2 receptors in the basal ganglia. Hyperkinetic disorders involve the basal ganglia to one degree or another, and at the core of any of these issues is an imbalance between the direct and indirect pathways in the basal ganglia.[67] The D1 receptor initiates direct pathway activation, and the D2 receptor initiates indirect pathway activation. There is normally a delicate balance between these two pathways; the direct pathway increases movement, motivation, saccadic eye movements, executive function, and socialization based on which of the five prefrontal loops becomes active. The indirect pathway inhibits or dampens those same loops and functions to eliminate unwanted activation. In normal human behavior, these two pathways and all of these functions are being activated and inhibited in a limitless combination, and together all of these loops are associated with much of human behavior. If one of these pathways dominates, it can result in either hypokinetic disorders—in which there is too much direct activation or too little indirect activation, leading to disorders such as Parkinson's, depression, and bradykinesia—or hyperkinetic disorders such as ADHD, OCD, tics, or mania.

There are many causes for the imbalance of activation of the direct and indirect pathways, including strokes, brain injury, genetics, and infections, that can lead to damage of various structures and receptors, which in turn produce an imbalance in these pathways, resulting in one dominating over the other. But in most cases of both hyperkinetic and hypokinetic disorders, there is no obvious infection, pathology, injury, genetic, or biochemical cause. And yet the symptoms of this imbalance are quite apparent. Functional imbalance involving the brain and the nervous system is the most comprehensive explanation for the array of seemingly dissociated symptoms seen in these conditions, and there are abundant data to justify such conclusions. The two cerebral hemispheres, along with different networks like the nigrostriatal pathway, which promotes activity in the direct pathway, and the mesolimbic and meso-cortical pathways, can bias these systems. The neocortex also has a direct influence on the basal ganglia, as it does on all systems of the body. The right hemisphere also activates the indirect pathway. Through the hyperdirect pathway, the right inferior frontal lobe has direct connections to the subthalamic nucleus of Luys, which is the area of the basal ganglia that is primarily involved with activating the indirect pathway. Therefore, like a brake in a car, the right hemisphere inhibits the direct pathway and activates the indirect pathway. When the right hemisphere is not activated or the left hemisphere is more active, the emphasis will be on the direct pathway. This is an elegant way in which the brain can exert top-down control over the basal ganglia, the thalamus, and all human behaviors as well as gate its own activity.[68]

CONCLUSION

Many theories about autism spectrum disorders, ADHD, OCD, tics, and schizophrenia involve the dopaminergic pathways and other neurotransmitter systems like GABA, glutamate, and so forth. Some theorists have speculated that a deficiency in GABA, glutamate, or dopamine may cause imbalances in the direct and indirect pathways. However, both the direct and indirect pathways utilize GABA, glutamate, and dopamine, so a chemical imbalance or even a receptor imbalance would not result in an imbalance between the direct and indirect pathways. This once again demonstrates that the chemical imbalance theory does not make much sense and is based on a fundamental misunderstanding of the nervous system. These considerations are of critical importance when considering treatment options. Drugs, hormones, and nutritional and dietary interventions may all play a role and be useful in treatment, but they are all nonspecific interventions that do not address the primary underlying problem and may create unwanted and dangerous side effects because they are nonspecific. Biomedical interventions like vitamins, minerals, amino acids, and dietary modifications may help reduce symptoms and inflammation and may be less dangerous, but at their core, there use is the same as prescription medication: they are being used to alter biochemistry. Of course there are certainly infections; autoimmune, genetic, and metabolic disorders; toxicity; and true micronutrient vitamin and mineral deficiencies that can cause a wide variety of symptoms that can look like or exacerbate ADHD and ASD, and these issues may occur independently or without an actual neurological imbalance. This is where neurological examination, lab and genetic testing, and developmental history are critical to make a differential diagnosis. However, biochemical imbalances and deficiencies are almost never the primary cause of most illnesses, especially neurobehavioral disorders in children and adults. Functional treatments that target specific networks in the brain using specific motor, sensory, cognitive, or behavioral modalities specific to a given network are the only treatments that can effectively and specifically target the primary problem. In the case of functional disconnectivities and hemispheric imbalances, these treatments must be targeted toward the underactive networks and/or hemisphere to attempt to restore balance to this system.

SEAN: TREATMENT AND OUTCOME

Sean was placed on a right hemisphere program that targeted his specific weaknesses. He was seen three times a week for 12 weeks for an hour each time at a brain balance center, and given an individualized program of motor training and sensory stimulation along with specific processing exercises. He was also given specific neuroacademic training and cognitive skills training targeting the particular weaknesses in the right hemisphere that were identified in standardized testing. He was assigned primitive reflex inhibitory exercises and placed on an elimination diet that excluded wheat, eggs, dairy, yeast, citrus, and soy. We limited his screen time and increased his physical activity at home. We targeted visual, auditory, smell, tactile, vestibular balance, proprioception, timing, and rhythm sensory motor activities, all directed toward the right hemisphere with the goal of matching his functional and chronological age. He was reevaluated after 12 weeks, and the changes in him were remarkable but consistent with the outcomes we have come to expect. His parents and teachers filled out follow-up behavioral scales, and according to their results, he no longer fit the behavioral scale criteria for Asperger's and autism, although he still showed some symptoms of ADHD. His academic achievement scores increased dramatically in both left and right hemisphere scores, but especially in right hemisphere academics. His listening comprehension was now at a 12.1 grade level, and his reading comprehension and math reasoning were at a 12.9 grade level. That represents a more than six-grade increase in listening comprehension, a nine-grade increase in reading comprehension, and a five-grade increase in math reasoning. Many of his left-brain skills also increased to a 12th-grade level. The point of our program is to achieve balance. Sean was in 6th grade, but many of his skills were well above his grade level, and we certainly did not want to bring those down. Sean is a truly gifted child. All of his skills when he completed his program were on average around 10th or 11th grade. Some parents are afraid that when their child does a brain balance program, the strengths or gifts that make the child special will be lost or weakened. But the opposite is true. By focusing only on the weaknesses and getting them to match their strengths, we truly bring out how special these children are and allow them to reach their full potential. We eventually rotated all foods back into Sean's diet, and there were no apparent negative reactions. His sense of smell is now normal, his eczema cleared up, and he got a cold for the first time. His primitive reflexes were all gone, and he is now clearly right-hand dominant. His pupils are equal in size, and his blood pressure is equal on both sides of his body as well. He showed significant increases in muscle tone, and all his motor skills are consistent with his age. Perhaps most important to his parents, he now has several friends and is interested in girls and dating. He has good eye contact, and his nonverbal communication is typical for his age. He expresses his emotions much more and even told his parents that he loves them. By the time he left the program, he was doing great in school and no longer needed an IEP. He is much more open to foods and often comments on the smell and taste of food. He is not concerned with texture as much. He no longer has any stims, he does not have anger outbursts, he is no longer compulsive, and he is much more flexible in his thoughts and behaviors. Follow-up blood tests also showed complete elimination of all food sensitivities, even though all of the foods were fully back in his diet. We believe this reflects the fact that many food sensitivities are a result of an imbalance in the brain, which results in an imbalance in the immune response and an imbalance in the autonomic sympathetic, parasympathetic tone, which leads to a "leaky gut." When we correct the imbalance in the brain, we also correct the immune imbalance and the leaky gut, so that the child can go back to a normal, healthy diet with no restrictions. He is now not only free of an autism diagnosis, he is functioning at his potential, and his future is forever changed.

ONGOING CARE

Brain imbalances are most likely to occur during fetal and early childhood development, because this is when the two sides of the brain have different sensitive periods of peak development. When the brain is more mature, and the two hemispheres have synchronized and formed connections, it is more difficult to "disconnect" or imbalance these areas, but it can still happen. Therefore, ongoing mental health is dependent on a healthy diet (which generally includes nutritional supplements), avoiding neurotoxicants, and an emotionally supportive home and school environment.

6

Nutrition and Children's Mental Health

Bonnie J. Kaplan and Julia J. Rucklidge

MODERN EATING HABITS

We have all seen the recommendations: "eat more fruits and vegetables," "shop around the outside aisles of your grocery store," and "avoid processed food." But the one that we think speaks most eloquently to the change in our food habits in recent history is this: "don't eat anything your grandparents would not have recognized as food." This dictum points dramatically to the changes in eating habits that have occurred in Western society, particularly since World War II.

How did our grandparents eat? For one thing, they consumed fruits and vegetables only in the season in which they grew naturally, which likely maximized their nutrient content. They might have begun to eat frozen vegetables, which Clarence Birdseye introduced in about 1930, and which became popular after the war period. The process of canning had been invented more than a century before that, but canning food was driven primarily by the need to preserve foods carried by soldiers—initially, canned food was not seen as a staple of the family diet. (An oddity associated with this fact is that the can *opener* was not invented until about 30 years after the invention of the can. There was no need for it, because soldiers used their bayonets to open their food. When the Napoleonic wars ended, canned food spread to home use, and bayonets were no longer offered an ideal for opening them.) By the mid-20th century it was generally thought that frozen and canned food had been a huge boon to nutrient intake in North America, as they diversified the average family's diet. It is important to remember that fact, as the term "processed food" is currently taking on a totally negative meaning, but 100 years ago "processed" meant canned or frozen: two inventions that likely improved many people's vegetable intake.

Another difference in how our grandparents thought about food is that they would have been completely unfamiliar with the idea of "food advertising," especially advertising directed at children. Children were expected to eat whatever the adults prepared. And of course in middle-class families, there was likely a woman at home full time who was responsible for food shopping and preparation. Long hours of preparation were typically required, because food did not arrive at the home in packages that were ready to cook: people bought their meat from the butcher who killed the animal and grew their own produce or bought it from farmers who grew it.

If we use the term "processed food" to mean packaged foods that are commercially prepared to facilitate ease of consumption, and do not include canned or frozen foods in that category, then the shift to processed foods is the single greatest change that has occurred in the lifetime of everyone reading this. The implications of this single difference are actually quite profound: having no processed food meant our ancestors ate *fresh, recently grown or butchered food, with no chemical additives or preservatives*. And for us, of course, the reverse is true.

The second major shift in eating patterns is even more recent than the postwar period. Our grandparents ate close to 100 percent of their meals in their homes. In the 1950s North Americans began eating at restaurants occasionally, and by 1967 MacDonald's had begun the fast-food craze. Nowadays, though numbers vary from survey to survey, it is clear that many people eat more meals outside the home than inside, and some people simply do not cook.

How could the current dietary pattern in Western societies be described? A recent summary in *Psychology Today*[1] reported that the top five most-consumed foods by American adults consist mostly of refined grains or sugars. In fact, refined carbohydrates, added fats, and added sugars make up over 60 percent of our diets. Vegetables and fruit hardly get noticed: amazingly, not a single one is in the top 25 foods consumed.

Another way of examining the modern diet is contained in the 2013 U.S. government report entitled "State Indicator Report on Fruits and Vegetables," which actually maps fruit and vegetable intake all across America by individual state as well as by the nation overall.[2] The results are surprisingly similar across the country, and also across ages when adults are compared to adolescents. Some 37.7 percent of adults and 36.0 percent of adolescents reported that they consumed fruits or vegetables less than once a day. The age groups diverged a bit on vegetables: 22.6 percent of adults and 37.7 percent of adolescents reported eating vegetables less than once a day. These numbers cannot, of course, be converted directly to quantity. But the low *frequency* of fruit and vegetable consumption is surely a cause for concern.

So if we are not eating many fruits or vegetables, what are we consuming? Under the subheading "Consumption of Caloric Sweeteners Hits Record High in 1999," the U.S. Department of Agriculture factbook on American food consumption states that Americans hit a record high of an average 150 pounds of added sugar per year.[3] It helps to compare this amount to historical figures, available in T. L Cleave's classic *The Saccharine Disease*.[4] According to British trade journals and government documents, in 1810 the average consumption of sugar was approximately 15 pounds/person/year; by 1970, it was approximately 120 pounds/person/year. In other words, according to the American data from 1999, we are now consuming *10 times* the amount consumed by our ancestors just 200 years ago.

What about those who do, often with considerable effort, eat 5–10 servings of fruits and vegetables every day, as recommended by our health organizations and governments? Can they be confident that they are consuming adequate nutrients? Perhaps not. There are at least three reasons that confidence in the quality of our fruits and vegetables is eroding:

- *Depletion of nutrients from our soil.* A few hundred years ago in North America, one notable custom related to food was that the native tribes in North America moved often so that their crops would have fresh soil and more nutrients. The Huron tribes of what is now Ontario moved regularly every 10–15 years, so that crops could be planted in freshly turned soil. In the ensuing 300 or so years, farming has changed dramatically. New farming methods such as crop rotation and use of fertilizers have permitted us to grow our food continuously in one location, so our "tribes" do not need to relocate every decade or so. But has there been a cost? Studies that have assessed nutrient content of fruits and vegetables over 50-year periods[5] have shown very dramatic decreases in important vitamins and minerals. To use just one example, it is difficult to escape the conclusion that the broccoli we eat now has only a fraction of the calcium that our grandparents' broccoli contained. And the same can be said of other vegetables and fruits, and of both vitamins and minerals.[6]

- *Mineral-chelating herbicides.* Agriculturalists who are concerned about feeding the hungry of the world tend to look at their success only in terms of crop yield. But what if their crops are filling hungry bellies without providing adequate nutrients to feed the brain and body? Unfortunately, that seems to be happening, especially with the development of glyphosate (e.g., Roundup), a mineral-chelating herbicide. Agricultural research has shown that crops treated with glyphosate, or genetically modified to be resistant to the glyphosate applied to adjacent weeds, sequester important minerals such as iron and zinc and also reduce availability of omega-3 fatty acids.[7]

- *Reduced mineral* content *due to increased atmospheric carbon dioxide.* There is no doubt that climate change is bringing with it an increase of CO_2 in our atmosphere. A certain amount of CO_2 increase results in enhanced plant growth, because plants "eat" CO_2 and then produce oxygen. But recently scientists have become concerned about whether CO_2 is changing the nutrient content of our food supply. This is an extremely important question, as CO_2 levels are certainly going to continue to rise. A recent meta-analysis was published to address this question, using a clever method.[8] A number of studies have grown plants in concentric circles (thereby controlling for sunlight and water), with a source of CO_2 located in the center. What the meta-analysis showed was that the *zinc* and *iron* content of the crops was significantly correlated with location of the plants with respect to the CO_2 source: they concluded that increasing CO_2 caused decreased availability of zinc and iron. Dietary zinc and iron are the two most worrisome nutrient deficiencies worldwide; it is estimated that two billion people are deficient in one or both of these important minerals, resulting in lowered IQs, impaired immune systems, and vulnerability to fatal diseases.

Elsewhere in this book (see chapters 1 and 5) concerns about rising levels of children's mental illness in our society are described in detail. In this chapter we ask: How does nutrition contribute to *brain development and children's mental health,* and how effective are nutritional interventions in treating children's psychological disturbances?

PRENATAL DEVELOPMENT: THE ROLE OF NUTRITION

Prenatal Nutrition and Fetal Brain Development

Fetal cells need vitamins, minerals, and essential fatty acids for proper growth, differentiation, and development. A wealth of research on laboratory animals demonstrates the impact of prenatal nutrition on fetal development. It is now so widely accepted that the quality of a pregnant woman's diet is of vital importance to the health of her fetus and infant, that pregnant women are routinely admonished to eat well for the baby, to "eat for two," and to take prenatal vitamins.

As recently as 10 years ago, the lay public was unfamiliar with the term "omega 3s," but although today familiarity is likely universal, there remains a great deal of confusion about the terminology. Polyunsaturated fatty acids (PUFAs), essential fatty acids (EFAs), omega-3, omega-6—these are all terms that refer to a group of compounds that are particularly critical for brain development and healthy cell walls throughout the body. The nutritional concern that was likely the greatest trigger for the change in awareness that emerged over the past decade was the new knowledge that *processed foods provide excessive amounts of omega-6s*, disturbing the optimal balance of 3:6 EFAs in our diet. There is ample data showing that humans have evolved to need approximately equal amounts of these two EFAs; that is, our ideal intake ratio should be approximately 1:1, or perhaps 2:1. However, the Western diet of processed food and very little fish is generally reported to have omega-6 to omega-3 ratios of around 15:1 or even higher. The impact on health is of great concern: these high ratios of omega-6 to omega-3 have been associated with cardiovascular disease and many forms of cancer.[9] With respect to mental health, the two omega-3 metabolites; docosahexaenoic acid (DHA) and eicosapentaenoic acid (EPA) appear to be very significant. DHA plays an especially important role in the central nervous system, particularly in building the brains of fetuses and young children.

Research has established that iron, omega-3 fatty acids, and folate play a very significant role in optimizing fetal brain development.[10] When a pregnant woman's nutritional intake is insufficient, the fetus is deprived of the raw materials that are essential for building neurons (brain cells) and the biochemical infrastructure that enable neurons to communicate with each other. In addition to structural deficiencies, inadequate supplies of prenatal nutrients can impair the brain's capacity to respond appropriately to stress. Research with both animals and humans has established that when the fetus is deficient in DHA (a metabolite of omega-3), the hypothalamic-pituitary-adrenal (HPA) axis does not function optimally. This brain-and-endocrine pathway is responsible for sensing when the "fight-or-flight" response is required, which prepares the brain and body to cope with stressful situations. Damaged HPA stress responses promote enduring mood disorders.[11] This very important finding illustrates an underlying mechanism by which insufficient amounts of a nutrient during the prenatal period could lead to long-term mental health problems.

Prenatal Nutrition and Cognitive Development

Although there is no longer any debate about the importance of prenatal vitamins for fetal health, and having women take them is an almost universal standard of practice across the world, their long-term impact on children's mental health needs to be investigated further. A recent review of research on this topic[12] examined 18 articles that met predefined screening criteria. These studies involved pregnant women from 14 countries, whose offspring were then followed from two months to nine years of age, to determine the cognitive impact of prenatal supplementation. While the evidence for long-term benefits was inconclusive, two nutritional interventions appeared to have positive value for children's cognitive development: (a) supplementation with omega-3 fatty acids and (b) supplementation with broad-spectrum (rather than single) nutrients.

The role of long chain polyunsaturated fatty acid (LCPUFA) supplementation in clinical trials is promising and is consistent with correlational data reported around the world. For instance, epidemiological studies have shown a positive association between prenatal intake of DHA and neurodevelopment in infancy and childhood.[13] The mirror image has also been demonstrated: a higher n-6:n-3 ratio during gestation was negatively associated with neurodevelopment.[14] Taken together, these studies are supportive of the value of increasing omega-3s to optimize brain development.

Our current knowledge about the impact of nutrients on fetal brain development supports the importance of improving prenatal nutrition. There is growing evidence (described previously) about the degradation in the quality of the American diet and the nutrients in our food. And since the fetus usually has preferential access to nutrients during those nine months, improved nutrition during pregnancy would benefit not only the baby but also the mother. Also, research strongly supports the vital role of key nutrients during the prenatal period, such as iron, omega-3 fatty acids, and folate, in optimal brain development and brain function during the early years of life. Undermining brain development can set children up for failure, even if subsequent nutrition is improved.

Critics of prenatal supplements generally focus on vitamin A. Although some vitamin A is critical for normal fetal development, excessive amounts can cause birth defects. However, moderate amounts of all minerals and vitamins, as well as essential fatty acids, are prudent choices for pregnant women wanting to optimize development of the fetus. Especially for pregnant women whose diet centers on processed foods, improving their diet and taking a broad-spectrum nutritional supplement (in consultation with a health professional) is warranted as a precautionary approach. Given the vital importance of maximizing brain development in the fetus and infant, it would be wise for policy makers to reconsider current guidelines for the manufacture of prenatal supplements, which contain a limited array of nutrients. Guidelines should reflect our current state of knowledge, and formulas should include broad-spectrum minerals and vitamins, as well as essential fatty acids.

Prenatal Nutrition and Mental Health Outcomes

It is very challenging to determine to what extent maternal diet influences the mental health of offspring, but there are a few studies that shed some light on this topic. Research on the Dutch Hunger Winter of

1944–1945 and a severe famine in China in the late 1950s revealed an increased risk for developing schizophrenia among individuals whose mothers were pregnant during these famines.[15] Malnutrition in the first six months of life can also serve as a risk factor for developing depression, ADHD, and personality problems 30–40 years later. Deficiencies in several micronutrients, such as folate, vitamin A, vitamin D, and iron, may contribute to the increased risk. More recently, studies show that exposure to an "unhealthy" diet (characterized by high intake of processed meat products, refined cereals, sweet drinks, and salty snacks) during pregnancy predicts behavioral issues in children, independently of other potential confounding factors and childhood diet.[16] A study conducted in the Netherlands demonstrated the protective effect of the Mediterranean diet (lots of fresh fruits and vegetables, as well as fish). The less stringently the pregnant women adhered to the Mediterranean diet, and the more they adhered to the traditional Dutch diet (high in carbohydrates and fats), the more their children were likely to engage in acting out or aggressive behaviors at 1.5, 4, and 6 years.[17] Taken together, these studies suggest that as the prenatal diet declines in nutrition, mental health problems among offspring increase.

CHILD DEVELOPMENT: THE ROLE OF NUTRITION

Childhood Nutrition and Cognitive Development

The preschool years are a crucial period in neurodevelopment, during which fundamental changes in ability result from rapid maturation of the brain, especially the prefrontal cortex.[18] Animal research has demonstrated the importance of a wide variety of nutrients for optimizing neurodevelopment in early childhood. But in research that has been conducted with human children, the studies that are the most compelling are those that focus on the importance of eating breakfast.

Dozens of studies have been reported in the past couple of decades, looking at overall breakfast habits, glycemic load of the breakfast, confounding factors such as socioeconomic status, and so on. For instance, in a study conducted in China, 1,200 six-year-old school children were divided into two groups (based on parent report): those who almost always ate breakfast and those who ate breakfast only occasionally. Even when controlling for a variety of socioeconomic and parental variables such as education, the regular breakfast eaters had significantly higher IQ scores.[19] This particular analysis was part of the China Jintan Child Cohort Study, which is following longitudinally a larger group of children to evaluate early risk factors for child neurodevelopmental problems. In the breakfast study just described, the primary report was based on eating or not eating breakfast, with no description of the type of breakfast food consumed, but secondary analyses revealed that those who skipped breakfast generally consumed fewer servings of vegetables, grains, and dairy products over the course of the day.

As in the Jintan cohort study, most of the "breakfast research" focuses on the issue of simply eating food upon awakening, not on the actual content of what is consumed. But some research with adolescents has at least indirectly included the quality of the breakfast meal, by reporting on the glycemic index (GI). The GI indicates how quickly blood glucose levels rise after a given food is consumed relative to the consumption of glucose itself, which is set at a GI of 100. So, for example, foods like simple carbohydrates that are broken down quickly and cause blood glucose to rise quickly have a high GI. In one study, adolescents who habitually skipped breakfast were evaluated with cognitive tasks before and after eating a low glycemic index (GI) breakfast, as well as before and after a morning period in which they did not eat breakfast.[20] The low-GI breakfast was associated with better subjective reports of alertness and contentment, as well as generally better performance on word recall and other tasks. Similar findings were reported in a study of 52 adolescents whose cognitive performance was measured after a low-GI breakfast, a high-GI breakfast (e.g., pancakes or processed cereal), or no breakfast.[21] Once again, the low-GI breakfast was associated with a general pattern of improved performance on learning and memory tasks. The message is clear: eat a low GI breakfast if you want to be at your sharpest that morning.

The impact of the morning meal must be considered in the context of the overall nutritional level of the population being studied, a topic for which there is a very large literature going back to the 1970s.[22] In general, studies have related overall good nutrition to improved cognitive performance on tests of learning, memory, and attention. An excellent summary regarding breakfast and its context was provided by Pollitt and Matthews: "The pooled data suggest that omitting breakfast interferes with cognition and learning, an effect that is more pronounced in nutritionally at-risk children than in well-nourished children." Roughly 15 years later, a systematic review drew the same conclusions: regularly eating breakfast was consistently associated with better academic performance.[23]

Readers may wonder what an ideal breakfast might be. The first step is to ensure that children do actually eat something before running off to school. The content of that breakfast will vary with cultural context and family preferences. But if the morning meal has to sustain a child during several hours of academic instruction, one variable to pay attention to is the GI. A low GI breakfast, typically including protein and complex carbohydrates, is most likely to enable children to concentrate and do their work. Consideration of adequate levels of minerals and vitamins, either through the food items and/or supplements, is also important. Readers seeking ideas for low GI breakfast options can find a myriad of choices by searching "low GI breakfasts" on the Internet.

Childhood Nutrition and Mental Health

There are many important nutrition-related topics that we had to selectively exclude from this chapter to arrive at a manageable topic. For instance, we are not covering the important research on gut health and inflammation. Nor are we reviewing restricted diets such as gluten-free diets, casein-free diets, or the ketogenic diet. But one interesting dichotomy we want to address briefly is the distinction between "avoiding things we perhaps should not be eating" and "consuming more foods we perhaps are not eating enough of." We have focused on the latter topic for most of this chapter, as it relates most directly to our own research.

However, it is important to acknowledge that there is a lot of research going back almost 40 years about the potential harm from ingesting artificial colors and flavors, preservatives, and so on. Recent systematic reviews and meta-analyses of the research suggest some modest benefits for children with ADHD symptoms who have been placed on diets that limit certain foods and artificial colors.[24] While these studies by no means suggest restricted diets are a magic bullet for all children with psychological challenges, there appear to be a subgroup of children who improve dramatically on restricted diets, and the impact can clearly be life-changing. The precautionary principle dictates that in consideration of public health concerns and the subgroup of children who *are* adversely affected by artificial colors and flavors, these chemicals should not be introduced into our food supply until they are proven to be universally safe. After all, these ingredients confer no healthful benefit—they are purely "aesthetic," used by food manufacturers to entice children to eat more processed food. Hence the adverse effect on a few, combined with the absence of benefit, would argue that such ingredients should be minimized in our food supply. The European Food Safety Authority (EFSA) has taken a far more progressive stance on this issue than any regulatory group in North America. Since 2009 the EFSA has been evaluating the evidence on 45 food colors; its final recommendations are due in 2015 (http:// www.efsa.europa.eu/en/faqs/faqfoodcolours.htm). In June 2013 the EFSA issued a statement expressing concern about six dyes in the category called "sulphonated mono azo dyes," or "azo dyes" for short. Although it has not been definitively confirmed that these dyes are genotoxic (damaging to DNA), this agency called for further research and established acceptable daily intake levels as an indication of their concern about overexposure.

DIETARY INTAKE AND MENTAL HEALTH

Previously in this chapter we demonstrated that the Western diet has changed dramatically in recent decades. Although it has received very little media attention, there is a wealth of research on the relationship between diet and nutrition and mental health. Large population cohorts have been studied in several countries, particularly Australia, Spain, Japan, and the United Kingdom. Researchers have consistently replicated each other's findings, which can be summarized as follows: *a dietary pattern of fast food, or processed food, with low intake of fruits and vegetables, is associated with increased rates of depression and anxiety.* Typically, groups who eat whole foods, lots of fruits and vegetables, and very few fast foods (whole food or Mediterranean diets) are compared with groups eating more typical Western diets that are high in processed foods.

Following are some of the findings that show an association between nutrition and mental health:

- In Spain, the SUN (Seguimiento University of Navarra) cohort was established in 2000 to try to determine the effect of diet on a host of physical diseases. The almost 20,000 participants, most of whom are graduates of the University of Navarra, are surveyed every two years. Various diet-health relationships have been reported over the years, particularly showing an association between a Mediterranean diet and better cardiovascular health, diabetes, and glaucoma. With respect to mental health, amounts of fast food and commercial baked goods consumed have been shown to be correlated with the probability of being diagnosed with depression.[25] A subgroup of 9,000 participants were asked to report on how many processed pastries (defined as store-bought muffins, doughnuts, croissants) and how much fast food (defined as hamburgers, sausages, pizza) they ate. They were then followed for about six years, during which time 493 cases of newly diagnosed depression were reported. Compared to those with the lowest consumption of pastries and fast food, those in the higher consumption groups had a 36–38 percent greater risk of becoming depressed.
- Research conducted in Australia established a positive correlation between the amount of processed food consumed and mood and anxiety symptoms in women.[26] The researchers then wanted to find out if dietary patterns could be shown to *precede* mental health issues in children. They assessed approximately 3,000 children ages 11–18 years over a two-year period.[27] Mental health was

measured with the Pediatric Quality of Life Inventory, and dietary patterns were evaluated with a food frequency questionnaire. The study established that changes in the quality of their diet *predicted changes in mental health* in the expected direction. This finding is of particular importance because it involved teenagers. Adolescents are at a high risk for developing mood disorders, while at the same time their parents are losing influence over their dietary intake, and pizza parties and junk food consumption are common. Dietary interventions are especially important at this vulnerable stage of development.

- A study was conducted with 97 adults who were diagnosed with mood disorders.[28] They were asked to keep detailed food records of what they ate (weighed and measured), and these records were then evaluated for actual vitamin and mineral content. Seven vitamins and seven minerals were targeted, and 13 out of 14 of these nutrients were found to be significantly correlated with mental health (sodium was the exception). This appears to be the first study in which actual nutrient intake was shown to be related to quality of mental health in a dynamic way, during a three-day period. The results strongly support the importance of healthy diet, especially among those who are diagnosed with a mental illness.

Limitations of Relying on Dietary Changes Exclusively

We explained earlier that even optimal diets may not suffice to address our nutritional needs, due to the depletion of nutrients in our soil, the impact of mineral-chelating herbicides, and the impoverishment of our food supply due to rising levels of CO_2. In addition to these environmental factors, there are some other compelling reasons why just educating people to eat better may not be sufficient to influence mental health:

- *Habits are hard to change.* This fact is obvious to anyone who has tried to improve someone else's health behaviors, especially eating habits. This pithy quote, attributed to Margaret Mead, arguably the most influential cultural anthropologist of the 20th century, encapsulates the problem most clearly: "It is easier to change a man's religion than it is to change the way he eats."

- *Individual differences.* In 1956 a University of Texas physiologist named Roger Williams published the first edition of a gem of a book, *Biochemical Individuality,*[29] in which he reviewed decades of his own research that demonstrated how unique every organism is. Studying both laboratory animals and human volunteers, he showed that huge variability in the structure of organs is to be expected (our kidneys probably look very different from yours!). And he also showed that laboratory assays of chemicals in our blood and urine vary widely across people, even in normal, healthy volunteers. In reflecting on the implications of such differences, he wondered whether *variable needs for nutrients* might explain why some people get sick and others don't. With respect to people with mental disorders, he suggested that "there is the possibility that they differ in their nutritional requirements. One may have need, in order to meet the stresses of life and keep his brain metabolism functioning, a larger amount of certain crucial nutrients than the other." This expert in human variation was ahead of his time with respect to the topic addressed in this chapter. As he wrote almost 70 years ago: "Certainly the possibility needs to be explored that nutritional supplements . . . will prevent or cure various types of mental disease."

- *Inborn errors of metabolism.* Another idea to consider is quite modern, but entirely consistent with Williams's conclusions 70 years ago. In 2002 Ames and his colleagues reviewed about 50 known genetic mutations that cause the afflicted patient to require an unusually high amount of a given vitamin to sufficiently activate critical neural pathways.[30] With each mutation, giving the patient a high dose of the vitamin in question corrects the metabolic error and alleviates symptoms. That particular review article was restricted to vitamins (no minerals) and to known mutations causing physical (not mental) symptoms. But it seems to us to be a highly plausible model for some people with mental disorders: suboptimal amounts of minerals and vitamins, which act as cofactors to enable brain enzymes to do their work, result in "sluggish" metabolic pathways in the brain. Providing higher dose minerals and vitamins in a broad-spectrum formula likely enables more of those enzymatic reactions to progress more efficiently.

- *Mitochondrial function.* The mitochondria are small organelles present in every cell and are responsible for producing energy for our bodies in the form of a chemical called adenosine triphosphate (ATP). The energy required for neurons and other cells to function properly is under the direct control of the mitochondria in those cells.[31] Brain tissue in particular requires a high level of ATP with which to manufacture neurotransmitters and remodel synapses. The production of ATP is *dependent* on the availability of nutrients such as magnesium, iron, manganese, thiamine, and riboflavin. Without them, the manufacturing process can be compromised, and indeed there are known disorders, called mitochondrial disorders, that are characterized by decreased production of cellular energy. By providing the body with the nutrients required to ensure that ATP can operate normally, these mitochondrial disorders can be corrected. Recently, some researchers have hypothesized that the manufacture of ATP may be compromised in mental illness.[32] If this is the case, at least for some people struggling with mental health issues, providing a mitochondrial cocktail of nutrients might address the source of their symptoms.[33]

- *Gastrointestinal health.* The health of the gut (gastrointestinal tract) directly affects how well nutrients are absorbed from the diet. We are not what we eat, but what we absorb. Various mental problems have been reported in celiac disease,[34] an immune-mediated disease triggered by the ingestion of gluten that results in inflammation of the small intestinal mucosa, with ensuing malabsorption. A growing body of research is now uncovering the important role that inflammation may play in the expression of psychiatric illness.[35]

In summary, inborn errors of metabolism, likely causing increased metabolic need for nutrients; mitochondrial dysfunction; and gastrointestinal inflammation and/or sensitivities all point to the role of malabsorption and/or deficiencies of vitamins and trace elements in the expression of some psychiatric symptoms. In the following section we evaluate the current research on the use of nutritional supplements for the treatment of psychological disturbances in children in light of the environmental and individual factors that make diet alone an inadequate source of essential nutrients.

NUTRITIONAL SUPPLEMENTS AND CHILDREN'S MENTAL HEALTH

Given the challenges associated with changing people's diet, as well as the possibility that those changes may still not adequately meet the nutritional needs of some children, another way forward is through supplementing the diet with additional nutrients. Based on our discussion above, it should be clear that single nutrient interventions simply could not adequately address the complex array of biochemical pathways that may be aberrant in children with psychological disturbances. Only through broad-spectrum micronutrient treatment could we adequately provide the nutrients in sufficient quantity that even enzymes with drastically reduced activity become so supersaturated with the necessary cofactors that near-normal function is restored.[36] The term *micronutrient* is usually used to refer to minerals and vitamins, and sometimes other nutrients, that we need to consume in very small amounts; the term is used in contrast to macronutrients, which are the broad categories such as fats, protein, and sugars. It is the micronutrients (mostly minerals and vitamins) that function as cofactors in brain metabolism.

Over the last decade there has been a slow increase in the number of publications on multi-ingredient micronutrient formulas for the treatment of mental illness in children (including a handful of controlled trials). With the exception of a few studies conducted with megadoses of vitamins in the 1970s and 1980s,[37] all the studies using broad-spectrum micronutrient supplementation have been conducted within the last 20 years. Two studies on juvenile delinquents are notable because of the significant impact of micronutrients on offending behaviors.

Antisocial Behaviors

The idea that nutrients can affect problem behaviors may date back to World War II, when most children were given cod-liver oil and orange juice to reduce antisocial behavior.[38] In the 1980s Schoenthaler and colleagues started publishing research trials investigating the role that sugar and other refined foods lacking micronutrients played in the expression of antisocial behaviors in children and adolescents.[39] In 1997 they published the results of a randomized controlled trial (RCT) with 62 incarcerated juveniles.[40] They found that giving children a broad array of minerals such as calcium, magnesium, and zinc alongside vitamins such as thiamine, riboflavin, and folate in doses at least equivalent to, if not higher than, the recommended daily allowance (RDA) resulted in a 28 percent greater decrease in rule violations compared with those receiving the placebo. Another RCT conducted by these same researchers showed that giving delinquent schoolchildren aged 6–12 a broad spectrum of nutrients yielded even better results.[41] The 40 children in the experimental group who were prescribed a broad spectrum of nutrients (most of them given at about 50 percent of the RDA) exhibited 47 percent fewer antisocial behaviors requiring discipline than the 40 children who received a placebo. The types of behaviors the researchers monitored included threats, fighting, vandalism, defiance, endangering others, and disorderly conduct. Other recent studies have been conducted with adult incarcerated populations,[42] with similar effects on violent behaviors within prisons. These studies compel us to appreciate that a simple intervention involving nutritional supplements could have far-reaching effects on our communities at large, whereas conventional behavioral programs with young offenders have generally had very modest success. It is disheartening that this research has been around for over a decade and has not influenced how we address aggressive and violent behavior in children and adults.

Attention-Deficit/Hyperactivity Disorder

Unfortunately, early research on the use of nutritional supplements to treat ADHD was flawed and discouraged ongoing research for close to three decades. Several studies suggested that nutrients were of no benefit to children with symptoms of ADHD, in all likelihood because the researchers used megadoses of vitamins and did not include minerals. In one study nutrients were administered at toxic levels, leading to a worsening of symptoms. The research trials were also too short to demonstrate an effect. We now know that nutrients can take a much longer time to take effect than stimulant medications.[43] Not surprisingly, a recent review concluded that megadoses of vitamins are not recommended for the treatment of ADHD.[44]

Over the past decade and a half, research that uses a much broader spectrum of nutritional supplements at more appropriate dosages has shown greater promise. For example, Harding and colleagues[45] compared methylphenidate (Ritalin) with a range of dietary supplements (taurine, glutathione, α-lipoic acid, garlic extract, glycine and other amino acids, 13 minerals, essential fatty acids and phospholipids, iodine and tyrosine, all the B vitamins, and some phytonutrients) in the treatment of ADHD symptoms in 20 children over a four-week period. They found that both groups showed significant and similar improvement in neurocognitive tests that measure auditory response control, auditory attention, visual attention, and visual response control.

Patel and his colleagues[46] conducted an observational study with an even more comprehensive approach to treatment. Ten children with dual diagnoses of autism and ADHD were treated for three to six months with vitamins, minerals, coenzyme Q10, amino acids and peptides, some essential fatty acids (EFAs), milk thistle, α-lipoic acid, digestive enzymes, and probiotic bacteria. In addition, the parents received instructions on controlling environmental factors (i.e., mites, exposure to pesticides, toxins, cleaners), organic diet, gastrointestinal support, antigen injection therapy (to address dust mite allergens, molds, foods, and chemicals), chelation therapy (to remove heavy metals and other toxicants from their bodies), and injection one to three times per week with glutathione and methylcobalamin (vitamin B_{12}). Positive changes were noted by parents in all ADHD symptoms. While it is impossible to evaluate the specific effect of the nutritional supplements on behavior change because a range of interventions was offered, the findings from this study and the previous one raise the possibility that only a multimodal treatment can effectively address all the symptoms associated with this heterogeneous disorder. Studies such as this are encouraging and warrant more rigorous follow-up.

Dose is important in effecting change in symptoms, as a more recent study demonstrates. Sinn and Bryan[47] investigated 132 children who were assigned to one of three groups in a randomized, placebo-controlled, double-blind intervention for 15 weeks: EFAs alone or EFAs plus micronutrients. One hundred and four children completed the trial. Significant treatment effects were observed, with medium to large effects on all parental measures of ADHD. However, there were no group differences between those taking the EFAs alone and those taking both the EFAs and the micronutrients, suggesting that there was no additional benefit to taking the micronutrients. In retrospect, given that there was no added benefit from the micronutrients, it is possible that the dose of the micronutrient formula that the researchers used was too low and therefore not of great benefit for the treatment of ADHD symptoms. This trial is important for establishing that dose may matter in treating clinical conditions.

A few studies have used a micronutrient formula called EMPowerplus.[48] This formula consists of 14 vitamins, 16 minerals, 3 antioxidants, and 3 amino acids in doses higher than the RDA but not even approaching toxic levels. In 2004 Kaplan and colleagues[49] conducted an open-label trial with children with a variety of psychiatric disorders, including ADHD, bipolar disorder, anxiety, oppositional behaviors, and Asperger's disorder. Six of the eleven children in the trial had ADHD, although one of these dropped out. After 16 weeks of taking EMPowerplus, parent ratings on standardized tests such as the Child Behavior Checklist revealed significant improvements in attention, anxiety, aggression, delinquency, and mood. Few adverse effects were reported, and those that did occur were mild for all except two children, who were concurrently taking psychiatric medications. Indeed, Popper[50] has warned against taking such supplements concurrently with medications because of the hypothesized potentiating effect these combination formulas can have on the medication. A database analysis of 41 children with ADHD taking this same formula found that there was a significant improvement in ADHD symptoms studied over a six-month period.[51] This research shows promise, and follow-up studies that more closely monitor placebo and expectancy effects are warranted.

A randomized controlled study conducted in 2010 by Katz and his colleagues[52] compared the effects of an herbal compound containing essential nutrients (including essential fatty acids, phospholipids, essential amino acids, B-vitamins, vitamins E and C, and minerals) with a placebo on children diagnosed with ADHD. The children who took the broad-based nutritional supplement improved significantly, whereas the children receiving a placebo showed no change in symptoms. Furthermore, these group differences were still present after four months.

There have been a few studies using RCT designs to assess the impact of micronutrient supplements on attention and concentration as measured by neuropsychological tests in children who were not diagnosed with ADHD. For example, Vazir and his colleagues[53] studied 608 schoolchildren in India, half of whom drank a beverage fortified with micronutrients, and the other half a beverage with no supplementation, over a 14-month period. Supplementation with the fortified beverage produced small but significant improvements in attention and concentration compared to the placebo group. Benton's studies on the impact of nutrients on cognition have also shown beneficial effects of micronutrients on attention and concentration[54] and time spent concentrating. Overall, these studies suggest that micronutrients support attention and lessen hyperactivity and impulsivity, and follow-up research that looks at long-term gains would be valuable.

In 2014 Rucklidge and her colleagues studied 80 adults diagnosed with ADHD, half of whom were given the broad-based supplement EMPowerplus, and the other half a placebo.[55] Those who received the micronutrient treatment reported greater improvement in attention, hyperactivity, and impulsivity than those who received the placebo. Of note, clinicians observed better functioning and greater improvement in overall psychiatric symptoms in the micronutrient group than in the placebo group. Importantly, participants who were also struggling with depression showed greater benefit from the nutrients than did the placebo group. Replication of these results in children with ADHD is warranted.

Parents currently have few options to help their children with symptoms associated with ADHD other than medications. It would be wonderful if we could definitively show that nutrients can be used to treat complex neurodevelopmental problems, and research thus far is promising. It shouldn't be surprising that a complex disorder would require a complex treatment. There are currently trials underway investigating this exact issue.

Autism Spectrum Disorders

Most of the research on the role of nutrition in autism spectrum disorders has focused on diet manipulation, minimizing toxic exposures,[56] or at best, introducing small combinations of nutrients such as magnesium with B_6.[57] There have been a few studies on the benefits of single nutrients, but very few on the value of broad-based supplementation, aside from a few case studies.[58] A pilot study conducted by Adams in 2004, using a double blind RCT design, showed some promising results using a broad-spectrum supplement called Spectrum Support.[59] Twenty children out of an initial pool of twenty-five completed the three-month study; eleven in the experimental group and nine in the placebo group. Significant improvements were noted by parents after three months in sleep and gastrointestinal problems among the children taking the micronutrients, compared to the children in the placebo group. Although the experimental group also showed some improvement in behavior, eye contact, and receptive language, the sample was too small for the difference to be statistically significant. Adams and his colleagues have since replicated his pilot study using a slightly different formulation of micronutrients, and they found positive results compared with placebo in reducing tantrums and hyperactivity as well as improving receptive language and overall functioning.[60] A psychiatrist in private practice followed 44 children in his clinic diagnosed with autism spectrum disorder, whose parents agreed to treat them with EMPowerplus. He matched these 44 children to another 44 children from his clinic, whose parents elected to follow a more conventional course of treatment involving psychiatric medication. His research showed that not only was this micronutrient formula superior in reducing symptoms associated with autism as compared with medication, but it also reduced self-injurious behaviors, changes that did not occur in the medication group.[61]

Research on the effects of nutritional supplements on symptoms associated with autism spectrum disorder is in its infancy, but it appears promising. In light of the growing research that is making connections between the integrity of the gastrointestinal system and autism,[62] it is logical to assume that micronutrients should confer some benefit.

Depression and Bipolar Disorder

There is a long history of using single nutrients for the treatment of mood disorders. (Interested readers are directed to Kaplan's review of this research.[63]) Over the last two decades there have been a number of interesting and varied studies showing the benefit of a broader-based approach to the treatment of depression. However, many of these investigated the impact of supplementation on healthy, nondepressed samples. Given how common mood disorders are among children and adolescents, and the poor overall outcomes of treating these disorders with medications, it is imperative that we explore fresh approaches and follow up this preliminary research with appropriate populations using broad-based micronutrient supplements.

There have been four published studies in which children and adolescents diagnosed with bipolar disorder were given EMPowerplus.[64] In all four trials the children showed significant improvement over at least a six-month period, with about 70–80 percent of participants showing much improvement in bipolar symptoms and a reduction in the amount of medication that was needed. In addition, two case studies (within-subject cross-over designs on-off control of their tantrums and rages) of children with mood swings and explosive rage were conducted with this same nutrient formula, and both children exhibited a significant lessening of symptoms.[65] A database analysis of 120 children diagnosed with bipolar disorder revealed that more than half of the children experienced a reduction in symptoms (defined as >50 percent decrease in symptom severity) after three months of consuming this micronutrient formula.[66] Importantly, their symptom improvement was sustained at six months, making it unlikely that placebo or expectancy effects accounted for the reported changes. In 2009 a case study was published about a child diagnosed with bipolar disorder with six years of well-documented pharmaceutical treatments for his psychiatric symptoms.[67] The child and his family chose to transition from medication onto the micronutrient formula EMPowerplus when he was twelve, resulting in a complete resolution of all psychiatric symptoms.

The consistency of findings across universities and countries suggests that EMPowerplus and other broad-based micronutrient treatments are worthy of further study using more rigorous designs. Unlike the medications typically prescribed for children with bipolar disorder—antipsychotics and mood stabilizers—whose adverse effects are well documented, micronutrient supplements *at worst* will confer general health benefits with no benefit for mental health and with no adverse effects. The research thus far certainly suggests that trial supplementation with children diagnosed with bipolar disorder may be helpful and is certainly unlikely to do any harm.

Psychotic Disorders

A case study published in 2012 of a 10-year-old boy who was suffering from hallucinations and delusions reports that micronutrients successfully treated his psychosis and other psychiatric symptoms.[68] Another study established that among youth who were at risk for becoming psychotic, treatment with EFAs for 12 weeks significantly reduced the transition to psychotic disorder in comparison with youth who were given a placebo.[69] It is imperative that research continue along this line of early prevention, in light of concerns about the use of antipsychotic medication for the long-term treatment of schizophrenia.[70]

CONCLUSION AND RECOMMENDATIONS

A wealth of studies conveys a consistent message regarding the relationship between nutrition and mental health: (1) the Western diet of primarily processed, low-nutrient foods can be harmful; (2) the Mediterranean diet of vegetables, fruits, whole grains, and fish is probably protective; and (3) broad-spectrum micronutrient formulas are benefiting children with a wide range of psychiatric symptoms. Generally, when people think about health and safety, they focus on physical health. But the point of this chapter is that brain/mental health is critically important also.

One can find many definitions of the term *precautionary principle*, but the essence of all of them in relation to the issues discussed in this chapter is this: our food supply should be protected from chemicals that have not been proven in the very long term to be safe and beneficial to humans. The policy implications of the research we have cited are that we need to press our governments to restrict genetically modified food, ban the use of mineral-chelating herbicides such as glyphosate, and order the food industry to eliminate food additives that are not proven to be safe.

What else can the ordinary family do? Optimize your brain health and that of your children. Following are some concrete suggestions that families ought to consider:

- Only eat food that your ancestors would recognize as food.
- Emphasize low GI food for your children, especially on school days.
- If your child has psychiatric symptoms, or you even have a family history that suggests vulnerability to a psychiatric disorder, think of medication as a last resort, to be used only as a temporary measure. Instead, focus on dietary intake and add broad-spectrum mineral/vitamin supplements.
- Teach your children that only rarely is food to be considered a treat. Instead, every bite of food is an opportunity to feed your brain and body what it needs to function optimally. Children are too frequently rewarded for good behavior with processed foods. Parents/teachers need to rethink whether this pairing intuitively makes sense.
- Involve your children in the kitchen from an early age to revitalize the importance of cooking from raw ingredients as part of our culture.
- If considering pregnancy, ensure your diet is enriched in nutrients, including a high intake of fruits and vegetables.
- Lobby governments to make drastic changes to food policies. A significant shift in dietary patterns is going to take a community to effect changes. A population health approach may be the only way forward to ensure primary prevention of common mental health problems.[71]

7

Concussions in Children and Youth: A Multidisciplinary Approach to Healing the Brain

Daniel Gallucci

Concussions are receiving significant media exposure. At the time of this writing, a Google search for "concussions in children" returns 3.92 million results. A recent review indicates that up to 3.8 million recreation- and sports-related concussions occur annually in the United States.[1] Concussions represent 9 percent of all high school athletic injuries, yet are underreported by pediatric and adolescent athletes.[2] Football and ice hockey have the highest concussion rates among high school males. Soccer and basketball have the highest rates in female athletes. Females have higher concussion rates than males when comparing similar sports, but there are not enough data at this time to fully understand why that is the case.

A decade or so ago a clinician could go for months without seeing a concussion patient. Now a day isn't complete without seeing a patient walk in with sunglasses when there isn't a trace of sun in the sky. This is partly because children are playing organized sports more than ever before, with schedules rivaling those of professional athletes: the greater the exposure, the greater the risk. But the main reason is awareness. The subject of concussions has permeated our society over the last decade, and we are finally beginning to take notice. Advocates such as Chris Nowinski, a college football player turned professional wrestler who was forced to retire due to postconcussion syndrome, are a big reason why. He cofounded the Sports Legacy Institute, a nonprofit organization dedicated to solving the concussion crisis through education, policy, and research. Advocacy by individuals like Chris have created a tipping point and have given concussions international attention. As I write this chapter, President Barack Obama is hosting the first-ever White House Summit on Youth Concussions to address this growing public health concern.

The volume of information beginning to emerge about concussions can be daunting for medical professionals to deal with, let alone parents. Weeding through and making sense of the information presents an enormous challenge. Our job as clinicians working the front lines of concussion care is to filter and provide patients and their families with credible information and education to facilitate the recovery process. Helmets, mouth guards, and nanotechnology supplements gliding past the blood-brain barrier in search of inflammation do not prevent concussion. However, education does. In talks I give at schools, the majority of students believe that helmets will protect them from concussion. Nothing could be further from the truth. Helmets are vital in protecting against skull fractures and lacerations, but they do not stop the brain from bouncing around inside the skull.

INTERSECTING SCIENCE AND TECHNOLOGY

Current concussion management is much too linear, often frustrating, and atrociously ineffective. Our medical community treats the concussion of a 15-year-old female soccer player and a 55-year-old male falling off a ladder in the exact same manner, using the same diagnostics, drugs, and rehabilitation. This hasn't changed since the 1970s, when the use of randomized controlled trials spawned an era of evidence-based medicine. This strategy has been invaluable for treating numerous diseases and disorders, but has not worked so well for concussions.

No longer should patients be wrangled like cattle into large-scale, cookie cutter rehabilitation programs that focus on singular rehab strategies. A paradigm shift that embraces the individuality of each and every patient must occur. We have entered a new era of technology, in which the accumulation of large amounts of patient data has never been easier. As I stated at the beginning of the chapter, 3.8 million sports and recreation concussions occur each year in the United States. If we captured data on everything from vital signs to social factors on each patient, in five years we would have an extensive database of 19 million concussion cases. Software tools can readily sift through information and identify patterns that allow clinicians to apply rehabilitation in a strategic, personalized way, while reducing treatment errors and patient costs.

Dg2 is a "high tech, high touch" integrated therapy clinic in Toronto, Canada. I founded Dg2 to open the lines of communication between clinicians and researchers and to bring large-scale data into the rehabilitation world. We utilize a network of professionals, including medical doctors, genetics researchers, radiologists, osteopaths, functional neurologists, trainers, meditation practitioners, nutritionists, neuropsychologists, and neuroscientists—all in the belief that no one person knows as much as everyone together. Technology has expanded our ability to perform research and collect data, yet the application of clinical strategies has been grossly inadequate. The Dg2 multidisciplinary approach bridges the gap between research and practice to guide patients on a personalized path of brain health. The data captured at each step along the way serve as the foundation of our daily, as well as future, rehabilitation initiatives.

I think the biggest innovations of the twenty-first century will be the intersection of biology and technology.

—Steve Jobs

THREE POUNDS OF JELLY

The human brain is a three-pound collection of 85 billion neurons (nerve cells) with a jelly-like consistency. The solidified brain showcased on television programs has been rendered tough with formaldehyde. The living brain resting comfortably in your skull is much less resilient. The brain is highly complex and greedy. It processes more information in 30 seconds than the Hubble telescope has done in 30 years. It consumes 25 percent of our oxygen supply and 30 percent of the body's glucose, just to fuel its daily demands. Each neuron is connected to between 1,000 and 10,000 other neurons. Neurons enable communication to take place within all areas of the brain and central nervous system. They are supported by a group of cells called glial cells, often referred to as "glue" cells. Glial cells outnumber neurons by almost 10:1 and play much more than just a supporting role. The brain is divided into the left and right hemispheres, each of which contains four regions, or lobes:

- The *frontal lobes*, located directly behind the forehead, make up the largest region of the brain, often referred to as the "executive brain," and differentiate humans from other animals. They are largely responsible for our higher-order thinking and unique personality.
- The *temporal lobes* are located above the ears and deal mainly with sound, speech comprehension, many aspects of memory, and emotional responses.[3]
- The *parietal lobes* are located behind the ears and can be referred to as the touch and movement lobes. These lobes interpret the feeling of walking on a sandy beach or the weight of a warm blanket on a Canadian winter night. Input from

the skin, muscles, and joints convenes here and creates an awareness of position in space, enabling efficient balance and movement.

- The *occipital lobes* are at the back of the head and process all that we see from our visually rich world. These densely connected areas interpret motion, shape, and color.

Another vital area of the brain is tucked away tightly under the occipital lobes. The cerebellum, "little brain," was our mammalian ancestors' main brain. The cerebellum takes up only 10 percent of the brain's volume, yet contains half the neurons. This master information collector maintains an active picture of the body, knows the intention of movement, constantly updates position, and then can brilliantly predict future behavior. Research has shown that the cerebellum also plays a role in cognition.[4]

Neuroplasticity

Even though American psychologist and philosopher William James presented the first theory of neuroplasticity in *Principles of Psychology* 120 years ago, the brain was regarded as a hard-wired circuit board immutable to change until the mid-20th century. Pioneers such as Donald Hebb, Jerry Konorski, Paul Bach-y-Rita, Edward Taub, and Michael Merzenich began proving otherwise. Each brain is highly unique, ever changing, and fascinatingly sensitive to its environment. In fact, the human brain is the most complex system in the universe and can be revised, strengthened, weakened, and constantly manipulated by our everyday actions. The world we live in changes at a rapid pace. Our 25,000 genes cannot quickly respond to these changes. Neuroplasticity gives us the ability to react, learn, and adjust to these changes quickly. Concussions can reduce the brain's neuroplastic ability.[5] This can lead to prolonged symptoms, decreased function, and delayed brain development.[6] In the wake of a concussion, it is essential to maximize positive neuroplastic changes while limiting negative changes.

WHAT IS A CONCUSSION?

Following is the consensus statement from the 4th International Conference on Concussion in Sport. Considered the "gold standard" within the clinical community, the consensus statement helps to illustrate the complex nature of a concussion:

Concussion is a brain injury and is defined as a complex pathophysiological process affecting the brain, induced by biomechanical forces. Several common features that incorporate clinical, pathologic and biomechanical injury constructs that may be utilized in defining the nature of a concussive head injury include:

- Concussion may be caused either by a direct blow to the head, face, neck or elsewhere on the body with an "impulsive" force transmitted to the head.
- Concussion typically results in the rapid onset of short-lived impairment of neurological function that resolves spontaneously. However, in some cases, symptoms and signs may evolve over a number of minutes to hours.
- Concussion may result in neuropathological changes, but the acute clinical symptoms largely reflect a functional disturbance rather than a structural injury and, as such, no abnormality is seen on standard structural neuroimaging studies.
- Concussion results in a graded set of clinical symptoms that may or may not involve loss of consciousness. Resolution of the clinical and cognitive symptoms typically follows a sequential course. However, it is important to note that in some cases symptoms may be prolonged.

Although concussions are classified as mild traumatic brain injuries (mTBI), at our Dg2 Integrated Therapies clinic, our multidisciplinary team of health professionals removes the term "mild." Coaches, teachers, and even parents often downplay the severity of a child's concussion because of this word. There is nothing mild about a child suffering from a brain injury with symptoms lasting for months or years. A mild knee or shoulder sprain heals within a couple weeks; a concussion may not.

Undermining the severity of a concussion puts children at risk for second impact syndrome (SIS)—a serious and potentially lethal head injury resulting from a second impact, when the initial symptoms were not fully cleared from the initial impact.[7] Research has demonstrated that SIS can result in a subdural hematoma, the most common cause of death in sports-related head injuries. Research from the National Center for Catastrophic Sports Injury Research has demonstrated that in American football, 38 percent of athletes suffering a subdural hematoma were playing while still experiencing symptoms from a prior concussion.[8] Our own informal surveillance research at Dg2 has astonishingly revealed that over 80 percent of high school athletes admitted to playing their sport while experiencing concussion symptoms! This frightening realization is what initiated our concussion education campaign.

What Happens to the Brain during a Concussion?

When a concussion occurs, the linear acceleration/deceleration and rotational forces cause the brain to shift and smack against the fixed bony ridges inside the skull. These biomechanical forces immediately disrupt the brain. Potassium leaks out from sheared neurons, and calcium rushes in. The excitatory amino acid glutamate then activates NMDA and AMPA receptors, which further exacerbates the leaking of potassium outside the cell.[9] Free radicals, the by-product of oxygen use, accumulate prolifically within the brain and cause a disruption in neuron function.[10] Microglial cells, the brain's security guards and housekeepers, are immediately called to action. The massive excitation is then followed by a wave of neuronal suppression. Researcher David Hovda at UCLA refers to this somewhat protective mechanism as "spreading depression."

In an attempt to regain balance, the brain starts consuming massive amounts of glucose. This leads to an increase in both lactate production and accumulation. Increased levels of lactate may damage neuron membranes, alter blood-brain barrier permeability, and increase brain swelling.[11] A paradoxical reaction occurs, as blood flow to the brain is decreased at a time when the brain needs it most. This leaves a person highly vulnerable to second impact syndrome and a host of other brain pathologies.

Seeing Is Believing

Neuroscientists and researchers are now able to see changes in the brain that had only been hypothesized previously. Diffusion magnetic resonance imaging (dMRI), used for research purposes (eventually to be used in a clinical setting), is demonstrating objective traumatic changes caused by concussions. Dr. Paul Echlin, a sports medicine physician in Burlington, Ontario, who specializes in concussions, published a study in the *Journal of Neurosurgery* that demonstrated that concussions could alter the structural white matter (communication portion of neuron) parts of the brain.[12] The most significant finding was that previously concussed athletes who were clear of symptoms *still* showed white matter changes at the end of a hockey season. This is a true game changer in the concussion world. Most clinicians operate on the assumption that "symptom free" equals "brain damage free"; this is not the case. Prolonged disruption of neuronal communication may have physical and psychological implications that we are only beginning to understand. And while we cannot jump to conclusions about these changes leading to long-term problems, this research gives us a clearer picture of what is happening in the brain.[13]

CONCUSSION DIAGNOSIS

At the present time, there is no physiological test for a concussion. While we have learned a great deal about the physiological consequences of concussions, and concussion biomarkers are now being studied in research settings, we do not (at the time of this writing) have a concrete test to diagnose a concussion. CT or MRI scans cannot identify the microstructural and metabolic damage seen in concussion. These scans are ordered to rule out intracerebral or structural lesions, such as a skull fracture.

A qualified health professional makes a diagnosis based on the observation of physical and cognitive signs along with a thorough patient history. The consensus statement from the 4th International Conference on Concussion in Sport states that signs and symptoms of concussion can include, but are not limited to, the following:

- Symptoms: somatic (e.g., headache), cognitive (e.g., feeling as if in a fog), and/or emotional
- Physical signs (e.g., loss of consciousness [LOC], amnesia)
- Behavioral changes (e.g., irritability)
- Cognitive impairment (e.g., slowed reaction times)
- Sleep disturbance (e.g., insomnia)

It must be stressed that any noticeable change in behavior should be viewed as a symptom. No one is going to know a child better than the parents. If parents observe or hear that their child has sustained a fall or any type of head injury and subsequently notices that their child isn't sleeping well, or has lost appetite, or has difficulty focusing at school, they should consider the possibility that their child may have a concussion. When a parent feels that something is wrong, it usually is.

At some point in the near future technology will eliminate subjectivity from concussion diagnosis. Relatively new imaging technology, such as diffusion tensor imaging (DTI), will identify dysfunction with pinpoint precision currently unavailable. Portable hand-held devices (www.brainscope.com) that measure the brain's electrical activity will enable health professionals to rapidly and objectively assess brain function. This is an example of only a few of the technologies that will enable clinicians to enhance diagnostic, preventative, and therapeutic strategies. Technology will also improve the much-needed ability to collect data on a national scale.[14]

On-Site Action

You are at a child's soccer game when two players collide and one is suspected of sustaining a concussion. What do you do?

- Quickly identify if there is a licensed health-care provider on site. If so, he or she should begin emergency medicine protocols if necessary. Special attention will be given to exclude a cervical spine (neck) injury.

- If no health-care provider is available, the player should be urgently referred to a physician after first aid issues have been addressed.

- Administer brief sideline assessment tools to assess memory function, attention, and balance. The Sports Concussion Assessment Tool 3 (SCAT3) is used to quickly assess a concussive injury. The Child version (Child SCAT3) is used for children 5–12 years of age.

  (Side note: If you have a child involved in sports, stop reading this chapter and download the SCAT3 version now! Although designed for health professionals, it includes information such as signs to watch for and how to monitor a child. Keep in mind, this is just a preliminary tool and does not replace more comprehensive professional testing.)

- Over the first few hours, have someone remain with the child at all times. Symptoms may be delayed or evolve over several hours, so it is essential to monitor for signs of an alteration or deterioration of the child's state.

Computerized Neuropsychological Testing

Neuropsychological computerized testing has become the cornerstone of concussion management in North America. It is estimated that 10 to 15 percent of U.S. high school programs now contract with ImPACT, an industry leading neurocognitive company. Neuropsychological tests are meant to determine a "normal" baseline of neurocognitive function when an individual is healthy. The test is then redone after a concussion, and the preconcussion scores are compared to the postconcussion scores. These tests measure working memory, attention span, reaction time, nonverbal problem solving, sustained and selective attention time, and response variability.

The National Football League and National Hockey League are huge proponents of the ImPACT program, despite the fact that there is insufficient evidence to support the widespread use of this form of neuropsychological testing. Test and retest reliability, test sensitivity, and test specificity are factors that must be taken into consideration. Another is brain development. It is difficult to take one child and compare his or her development to related norms. We all have different rates of development and cognitive maturation, especially rapidly growing children and adolescents.[15] If a child takes a test, suffers a concussion one year later, and takes a retest, how much of those data can be attributed to the concussion? What if the child had difficulty in school in the months leading up to the injury? What if her parents' impending divorce has taken an emotional toll? Neuropsychological testing alone is not sensitive enough to discern these factors. It's meant to be used as *a* tool in the toolbox, not the only tool.

I fear parents are being misled to believe that neuropsychological testing is the panacea of concussion management. Parents should seek out a pediatric neuropsychologist well versed in concussions to discuss neuropsychological testing. This is particularly important for children with learning disorders and/or ADHD.[16] At Dg2, children with learning or developmental disabilities are referred to a neuropsychologist, who goes beyond generic testing and performs a more comprehensive assessment, often over the course of several days. These findings are then interpreted along with the diagnostics that we perform in-house to construct individualized rehabilitation guidelines.

A computer-tells-all approach gives the illusion of doing something productive and protective without changing the beliefs that put many of the kids at the computer screen to begin with. "Complete the test and go on your way," although highly profitable, is a much too simplistic approach for the complex nature of concussion. Going to a clinic to work with specialists who spend a few thousand dollars a year to be christened as "certified," with little to no training, is like hiring a personal trainer who has only taken a weekend course. One-dimensional concussion care is not the answer. I have yet to see a singular strategy that is effective in healing the complex nature of the human brain. Parents must seek out health professionals well versed in a multidisciplinary approach, which is necessary to heal concussions. Unfortunately this is easier said than done.

Most clinics adopt a "we can fix everything" mentality. You visit a chiropractor, who tells you he can fix your child's concussion by adjusting his spine a few times a week. You cross the street and visit an osteopath, who wants to manipulate your child's abdomen. On your way home you get a call from your massage therapist, who promises to cure your child's headaches by loosening neck muscles locked in spasm. This type of knowledge bias is widely prevalent and extremely ineffective. "When all you have is a hammer, everything looks like a nail" should be the motto of these cookie-cutter concussion clinics.

CONCUSSION MANAGEMENT

After a concussion we all need rest, especially children: physical, emotional, and cognitive rest. That means no cell phone, no computer, no texting, no television, no school, no bright lights, no loud noise, and no friends. The brain is in a hyper-energetic state and needs total rest. With children, the rest stage continues until the acute symptoms are gone. You would never think of sending your child into a soccer game with a torn anterior cruciate ligament (ACL), yet parents are often sending their concussed children to take that all-important science test or math exam. The brain does not rest while learning or studying, so school is off the table. Once the child is back in school full-time, the "return to play" guidelines developed by the International Conference on Concussion in Sport can be implemented to get children back on the field of play (see table 7.1).

With this stepwise progression, the athlete should continue to proceed to the next level if he or she is asymptomatic at the current level. Generally, each step should take 24 hours, so that an athlete would take approximately one week to proceed through the full rehabilitation protocol once he or she is asymptomatic at rest and with provocative exercise. If any postconcussion symptoms occur while in the stepwise program, then the patient should drop back to the previous asymptomatic level and try to progress again after a further 24-hour period of rest has elapsed.[17]

While research shows the majority (80–90 percent) of concussions resolve in 7–10 days, keep in mind that with recent discoveries on the lingering nature of some concussions, parents must err on the side of caution when restoring their child's activity level. No chart or guidelines can replace a parent's observation. When in doubt, sit them out!

TABLE 7.1. Graduated Return to Play Protocol

Rehabilitation Stage	Functional Exercise at Each Stage of Rehabilitation	Objective of Each Stage
1. No activity	Symptom limited physical and cognitive rest	Recovery
2. Light aerobic exercise	Walking, swimming, or stationary cycling keeping intensity < 70% maximum permitted heart rate. No resistance training	Increase HR
3. Moderate aerobic exercise	Skating drills in ice hockey, running drills in soccer; no head impact activities	Add movement
4. Noncontact training drills	Progression to more complex training drills, e.g., passing drills in football and ice hockey. May start progressive resistance training	Exercise, coordination, and cognitive load
5. Full-contact practice	Following medical clearance, participation in normal training activities	Restore confidence and assess functional skills by coaching staff
6. Return to play	Normal game play	

Unfortunately many of the patients who don't resolve within 7–10 days end up developing postconcussion syndrome (PCS), which is diagnosed when concussion symptoms persist for weeks, months, or even years. The concussion rehabilitation we perform at Dg2 is designed to help those suffering from postconcussion syndrome. Therefore we typically do not see patients for rehabilitation until four weeks after the incident. Until that point in time we monitor the patient's health, advise on healing strategies, and educate whenever possible. This includes managing the patients', and their families', clinical expectations.

Orthopedic injuries like an ankle sprain follow a linear progression, with gradual improvement day after day, week after week. Concussion rehabilitation does not work that way. Patients will have good days and bad days, with no correlation to time or other variables.

Research has not provided us with all the answers, and it never will. Conducting research in a clinical concussion setting is difficult. Randomized controls are tough to implement; costs are exorbitant; and multiple variables need to be accounted for, placebo effects considered, and patient/tester bias factors accounted for—the list goes on and on. That is why it is crucial that we start collecting data on types of interventions and their effectiveness, or lack thereof, across all ages of males and females. The more data we can collect the better. Clinicians need to widen the lens through which they look at concussion rehabilitation. Open communication between disciplines, with a sharing of data, will foster the development of strategies needed to heal those suffering from a problem we are only beginning to understand.

Currently institutions operate as reductionist silos, in which the cross-fertilization of ideas and strategies is impractical and rare. The primary physician doesn't speak to the neuropsychologist, who doesn't confer with the physiotherapist, who doesn't talk to the athletic trainer. Each professional plays his or her role on the team, but there is no coach calling the plays. This disconnectedness is passed down to the patient. Parents show up at appointments with concussed children in tow looking like 16th-century explorers lost while navigating the earth.

Education and Environment

Helmets, mouth guards, and other protective devices do not prevent concussions;[18] education, awareness, and activism do. Parents must encourage their children to notify them if they are not feeling well or are experiencing symptoms attributed to an impact to the head or body. Teachers, counselors, athletic directors, coaches, trainers, and friends should all have a working knowledge of concussion awareness and care. Involving the entire social environment is empowering for everyone involved. Yes, it feels good to do something for yourself, but how much better do you feel when you do something for someone else?

I have used NHL players in clinics to work with children suffering from postconcussion syndrome. These athletes are more helpful than I could have ever imagined. Temporarily, parents may need to take back responsibilities bestowed upon increasingly independent children. Laundry duty, dog walking, and knitting with grandma will stress the healing brain as much as video games and cell phones. This needs to be done with caution, as you want to encourage healing without your child feeling vulnerable or unneeded.

Taking Control

Clinicians working the front lines of concussion care are often secondary or tertiary care providers. Eighty percent of the concussion patients I see in the clinic are referred with "postconcussion syndrome" illegibly scratched on a prescription pad. Many of the children have been removed from school and sports, have passed numerous neuropsychological evaluations, and continue to suffer on a daily basis. The parents suffer just as much. The first thing we do at our clinic is restore hope to the child and family. Regardless of a child's history, her imploding grades, or withdrawn disposition, if she comes in able to breathe, I have something to work with. The constantly evolving brain is capable of positive changes, no matter the dysfunction. Clinicians provide the therapeutic message and tools; the patients do all the healing themselves. Playing an active role in restoring one's own brain health is rewarding and empowering. Being instructed to "lie down in a dark room" when it is all the child has done for the last six months is not. Conventional clinical wisdom puts the patient at the mercy of his or her dysfunctional brain, whereas we take a proactive approach in healing it.

Functional Neurology

Functional neurology, developed by Dr. Frederick Carrick, focuses on the evolving science of neuroplasticity to modulate activity in the nervous system. The senses are used to target specific neuronal pathways in efforts to maximize the potential of one's nervous system. This is done without the use of drugs or surgical intervention. Functional neurology gives the clinician many of the tools necessary to effectively manage concussions. Dg2 uses many functional neurology principles for diagnostic and rehabilitation purposes, with specific consideration given to neuron theory.

Neuron Theory Simplified

While it is scientifically fashionable to talk about neuroplasticity, very few clinicians have an appreciation or understanding of the processes involved in neuroplastic change. To create positive, healing neuroplasticity, we need healthy functioning neurons. Healthy functioning neurons need three things: oxygen, glucose, and stimulation. Delivering adequate amounts of all three will make the brain happy and healthy. When neurons have not received adequate oxygen, glucose, or stimulation, protein manufacture is lessened (down-regulated). Proteins produce neurotransmitters, form microtubules and filaments, provide skeletal structure, and support membrane and enzyme production. Down-regulation of proteins leads to neuron degeneration.[19]

Concussion rehabilitation must ensure that neuron receptors are stimulated properly, cellular health is restored, cellular immediate early gene responses (CIEGr) are activated, neurotransmitters are produced, and up-regulation of second-order neurons leads to long-term potentiation of the NMDA/AMPA receptors. That in a nutshell is neuroplasticity! That is how your child heals his or her brain!

POSTCONCUSSION SYNDROME: A MULTIDISCIPLINARY PARADIGM

Diagnosis

The key to managing concussion rehabilitation that does not resolve quickly lies in comprehensive and multidisciplinary diagnostics that are used to create a structured, individualized program that involves many moving parts from many professionals. An integrated team that understands the brain from a single-neuron microscopic level all the way up to how we interact within our social environment gives us the best chance of revealing the issues in all of their complexity. This approach in turn gives a child the best chance at maximizing his or her recovery.

A thorough history and physical exam enables the clinician to identify where the problems (lesions) are. At Dg2 we use functional neurology to identify lesions within four areas of the nervous system:

1. Peripheral nervous system: muscles, joints, fascia, receptors, organs, efferent/ afferent nerves
2. Level of the spinal cord: cervical, thoracic, lumbar spine, and sacrum
3. Cerebellum and brain stem: anterior, posterior, and floccular cerebellum; medulla, pons, and midbrain
4. Cerebral hemispheres and cortex: right and left hemispheres and cortex

In addition, we require a complete blood count (CBC) for every patient. Is there a pituitary gland problem causing blood pressure issues? Is postconcussion syndrome responsible for the fatigue and light-headedness, or is it the low red blood cells?

Pinpointing where lesions exist is a difficult task, which is why a multidisciplinary approach is crucial. Clinicians must be concerned with seemingly "minor" (there's that ugly word again) asymmetries in function. They may be of great importance from a physiological perspective and help to establish a differential diagnosis—alternative diagnostic possibilities that must be explored.

Technologies That Aid in Diagnosis and Treatment

Videonystagmography (VNG), used mainly by functional neurologists, is the diagnostic tool of choice when identifying problems within the vestibular (balance) and oculomotor (eye movement) systems. The patient wears a pair of goggles with infrared cameras that record eye movements and vestibular information, which is then transmitted to a computer. Communication between the visual and vestibular systems is intimately connected and often disrupted with concussion. VNG measures and provides data on both reflexogenic and volitional eye movements, which is of primary importance due to differing pathways. VNG is also used for oculomotor training (eye movement training) and as a way to measure rehabilitation progress. Research conducted by Marcus Heitger and colleagues at the Van der Veer Institute for Parkinson's and Brain Research in New Zealand is demonstrating that eye movements are a more reliable indicator of postconcussion syndrome and ongoing brain impairment than neuropsychological testing.[20]

Computerized dynamic posturography (CDP) is an assessment technique used to diagnose balance disorders and postural issues. Patients stand on a horizontal force plate while steadiness, symmetry, and dynamic stability are measured. Balance is a complex process involving many central and peripheral mechanisms. The negative effect of concussion on postural stability has been theorized to occur as a result of sensory interaction problems among visual, vestibular, and somatosensory systems.[21] Collectively using VNG and CDP is standard practice among functional neurologists and is of tremendous help when pinpointing physiologic lesions within the nervous system.

Ongoing research at Dg2 has shown that patients' movement patterns are often significantly altered when suffering from postconcussion syndrome. This led us to implement numerous innovative diagnostic and rehabilitation techniques using *inertial movement devices*, which are made up of lightweight sensors placed on the body that wirelessly transmit data on postural sway, upper limb movements, lower limb movements, and postural transitions. Capturing these data in both baseline and post-concussion scenarios has given us valuable information and enables us to create effective rehabilitation guidelines.

Developed by Marty Hinz and Al Stein, *monoamine transport optimization* is used for the management of nutritional deficiencies found in association with low or inadequate levels of catecholamines (serotonin, dopamine, norepinephrine, and/or epinephrine). Urine testing of organic cation transporters (OCT2) determines catecholamine levels. Natural precursors of serotonin and dopamine, along with sulfur amino acids, are then provided to restore the nutritional deficiencies. In the clinic we use this approach in postconcussion cases that have not responded well to prior rehabilitation programs. Nutritional metabolic issues may be more of a concern than the restoration of specific neuropathways.

MOVING BEYOND DESCARTES'S DUALITY

Rene Descartes, a 17th-century French philosopher, believed that the mind and body were separate entities. This implies that the mind can exist without the body, and vice versa. Fast forward 350 years, and Descartes's duality is still the concussion management philosophy of choice. Concussion rehabilitation usually involves the head and neck only. Rarely do we see an approach that truly appreciates the connectedness of the brain and body: the understanding that a frozen shoulder is as relevant to brain function as an error in numeric recall.

Gravity is a stimulus on the body 24/7 and is resisted by our anti-gravity musculature. Muscle spindles innervate each one of our working muscles to provide for efficient, complex movement. This response to gravity supports brain health. This is why we see negative physiological changes in astronauts and people experiencing extended periods of bed rest.[22] A complete orthopedic assessment that considers joint and muscle function, biomechanics, and fascial tissue integrity gives the clinician a more complete understanding of the interconnectedness between brain and body. The skeletal muscle system is the largest sensory organ in the body, making it a valuable therapeutic target.

We are not sea squirts that permanently attach to rocks and digest our brains for food. We need our brains, because we need to move!

CONCUSSION AND MENTAL HEALTH

Research conducted at St. Michael's Hospital in Toronto, under the auspices of the Brain Under Constant Change (BUCC) program, provides the first population-based evidence demonstrating the extent of the association between concussion and poor mental health outcomes. Adolescents who have suffered a concussion are at significantly higher risk for being bullied and attempting suicide.[23] At our clinic, a mental health professional is immediately brought on board if a child is experiencing depression, anxiety, fear, erratic behavior, or other mental health–related issues.

Medications

When parents are seeking care for a child whose concussion is not resolving quickly, the question of pharmaceutical intervention will inevitably arise. An entire book could be written about the drugs prescribed to concussion patients. They are used in one of two ways:

for management of specific or prolonged symptoms (e.g., anxiety, depression, sleep disturbance) or

to target underlying physiology in hopes of repairing the system and decreasing symptoms (e.g., glutamate receptor antagonists).

In spite of these drugs' popularity, at the present time there is no evidence-based drug therapy to offer a concussed individual.[24] Most of the research has been conducted with severe brain injury patients, and this needs to be understood when discussing treatment options with a medical doctor. Adolescents are often prescribed antidepressants to ameliorate postconcussion symptoms.[25] While children suffering from concussions often experience depression, and it is of vital importance to address this, Harvard psychologist Irving Kirsch has used advanced statistical analysis to demonstrate that antidepressants are generally no better than a placebo in treating depression, so other approaches to treatment should be considered.[26]

Nutrition

Although nutrition is mentioned only briefly in this chapter, that does not undermine its importance in restoring brain function. Children typically arrive at our clinic significantly dehydrated. Water helps the central nervous system to function, strengthens the immune system, removes toxins, and performs a host of other processes. Children recovering from concussion should be drinking eight glasses a day at a minimum. We also recommend a natural whole foods diet with fresh fruits and vegetables with lots of color, protein sources free from hormones/antibiotics, and grains that have not been processed or refined. This stabilizes blood sugar and supports brain health.

It is just as important to address what not to eat. Foods that spike inflammation and autoimmune responses are harmful for the gut and the brain. Sugar and refined and processed foods promote inflammation that crosses the protective blood-brain barrier into the brain itself. This causes neuron dysfunction and ultimately neuron death. No food is a more powerful trigger of neurological issues and autoimmunity than gluten, the protein found in wheat.[27] The gluten we consume today is not the gluten of yesteryear, due to hybridization. Refined sugars, processed foods, and gluten should be avoided when restoring brain health.

Some nutrients appear to have neuroprotective and neurorestorative properties, according to research. They include the following.

Omega 3 fatty acids decrease neuroinflammation and oxidative stress, while boosting growth factors and activation of cell survival pathways.[28] Food sources include black cod, herring, mackerel, salmon, sardines, and pumpkin seeds. These are not staples in the North American diet. Supplementation of omega 3s with high DHA (docosahexaenoic acid) concentration should be done under the guidance of a health professional.

Magnesium is an essential mineral, required to perform over 300 chemical reactions in the body. In rat studies, pretreatment with magnesium led to better post-traumatic outcomes than the nontreatment group experienced.[29] This illustrates the importance of a magnesium-rich diet. Food sources include spinach, almonds, cashews, pollock, quinoa, avocado, and dark chocolate. In the clinic we supplement with magnesium glycinate or magnesium threonate. Again, this should be done under health professional supervision.

Glutathione is an antioxidant that acts like a bodyguard to protect us from damage and removes toxins from our bodies and brains.[30] The body produces its own glutathione, but stress, medication, and toxins can deplete glutathione stores. Sulfur-containing foods such as dark green vegetables can provide small amounts, but a supplement is often recommended. The body breaks down the protein when it is taken orally. We give L-cysteine, the precursor to glutathione. Liposomal glutathione creams can also be used.

Vitamin D acts like a steroid hormone and is crucial to brain health. It regulates enzymes in the brain that stimulate nerve growth and produce neurotransmitters (chemical messengers). We can get vitamin D from sunshine, coldwater fish, and mushrooms. How much vitamin D is needed is open to debate. In the clinic we use blood tests to titrate either up or down to get people into the 70–80ng/mL range.

This is a small sample of the nutritional strategies that can be used in concussion care as well as for overall health. Vegetarians and vegans make challenging brain care patients. Healing and rehabilitating from a brain injury requires substrates to build new neurons. Cholesterol is a substrate crucial to the repair process. Start with beef stock, preferably homemade from bones, twice a day for a week before introducing solid animal products.

> *Let food be thy medicine and let thy medicine be thy food.*
>
> —Hippocrates

Cognitive Training

When a child receives medical clearance, the coach gets him back in the gym to train his body. The same way a child exercises his quads, shoulders, and abs, he can exercise his memory, visual processing, and attention. While brain training is becoming more popular, it needs to be done properly to achieve the desired results. Dg2 has partnered with Brain HQ[31] (www.brainhq.com), developed by world-renowned neuroplasticity pioneer Dr. Michael Merzenich, to provide evidence-based, individualized brain training. "Return to learn" always precedes "return to play." Cognitive training precedes physical training and enables our kids to get back in the classroom willing and able to learn.

Stress Reduction

Being a child or adolescent in today's society is stressful enough. Add the roller coaster of issues and emotions related to a concussion injury, and the stress may become overwhelming. Concussed children can't attend school, hang out with their friends, or participate in the activities that often make up a large part of their identity. In addition to referring kids to the appropriate professionals, there is a lot we can do in-house. Having children take an active part in the rehabilitation process is a great stress reducer. No one wants to sit at home with nothing to do for months on end. Setting and reaching tangible goals in a rehab setting is rehabilitation in itself. Dg2 uses the NeuroSky Electroencephalogram (EEG) biosensor device to train both attentional and stress reduction techniques with children in a fun, quantitative, and innovative manner.

MULTIDISCIPLINARY DIAGNOSIS AND TREATMENT OF CONCUSSION: A CASE STUDY

Jared is a pleasant, 16-year-old male high school student diagnosed with postconcussion syndrome by his family physician. He had sustained three concussions, 4, 9, and 15 months before coming to our office with his mother. He is a highly competitive hockey player, and this is how he sustained the first and third concussions. His second concussion was sustained after hitting his head in a swimming pool. His symptoms are widespread. He described the last two months as being on a terrible decline, with increasing headaches, difficulty walking at times, and feeling unstable as a passenger in a vehicle. He was "cleared" according to his last three neuropsychological assessments and has done 25 hyperbaric treatments, with no change, at a cost of $150 a treatment. Using hyperbaric treatment without correcting the underlying neurologic dysfunction is like casting a fracture without reducing it first.

Significant Examination Findings

Jared was nervous but in good spirits despite his condition, and his mother was very supportive. His pupils were round and responsive to light, and the ophthalmic vein to artery ratio was 2:1 bilaterally. His hands were sweaty bilaterally. His nervousness diminished as we discussed the excitement of the upcoming World Cup.

With his right-sided gaze holding he had significant facial twitching, but he could maintain gaze. He showed marked slowness with optokinetic (OPK) stimulus to the left when his head was in left yaw (rotation). The leftward horizontal gaze showed hippus with gaze fixation failure. On vertical pursuits, there was consistent breakdown downward at .2 and .4hz.

His left-hand rapid alternating movement (finger to thumb) was better than the right. Jared is right handed.

An inertial movement device was used to assess his gait and demonstrated a bilateral loss of arm swing when walking. Dual tasking increased his left arm swing and the left side bend of his torso. His right-sided lower extremity stride length was shortened with dual tasking.

Computerized assessment of postural systems was performed on a perturbed (unstable) and nonperturbed (stable) surface. With his eyes open and a neutral stance on a nonperturbed surface, his stability score was 97 percent. It was 87 percent with his eyes closed on a nonperturbed surface with a posterior leftward sway.

With his head in right yaw (right rotation) on a perturbed surface, his center of pressure was posterior and leftward, with a stability score of 77.5 percent. With his head in left yaw (left rotation) on a perturbed surface, his center of pressure was posterior and leftward again, with a stability score of 84 percent.

Jared's test results were consistent with postconcussion syndrome and a centrally maintained vestibular syndrome. Previous appointments at other clinics had focused solely on neuropsychological testing, with some balance and strength exercises. That type of approach lacks the specificity, sensitivity, and data necessary to even begin to understand the complexity of concussion.

Jared was fatigued at the end of the assessment. His heart rate and blood pressure were normal, but his oxygen saturation floated around the low 90s.

Jared was excited to begin his rehabilitation program. He was just happy to be doing something other than "resting" at home and was pleased that the assessment was able to identify tangible dysfunctions that could be rehabilitated. His family doctor and previous concussion clinic had focused on "compensation" strategies—strategies to alter his life around his dysfunction. He flourished while taking on the responsibility of his rehabilitation.

Program Recommendations: To Be Completed Three Times a Day

1. Breathing exercise: 3-second inhale, 6-second exhale for improved vagal (autonomic nervous system) activity.
2. Customized rehabilitation developed by Dr. Carrick for certain eye movements using a computer, in which Jared saccades (eye jumps) from low left to up right at a specific degree/time. Pursuit activity of the eyes to the low left follows the saccade. These target both cortical and subcortical brain structures in a very unique and effective manner.
3. Head in right rotation, Jared saccades (jumps) his eyes to a right-sided target and then performs a series of YES (up/down) head movements.
4. Slow horizontal two-times viewing exercise with a pause at the end of motion.
5. Four-inch Dot drill with right saccade (jump) with YES head movement after fixation.
6. Vestibular exercise given with right chair rotation with head in slight forward pitch and eyes focused on right thumb.

The vestibulo-ocular reflex (VOR) was consistently used therapeutically for Jared. The exercises above are an example of the specificity needed to develop effective rehabilitation programs.

Osteopathic soft tissue, joint mobilizations, chiropractic adjustments, and contemporary medical acupuncture were used to improve tissue quality and joint range of motion.

Nutritional recommendations were made. Cognitive training was performed using www.brainhq.com, and EEG brainwave training was completed using NeuroSky. The program changed many times throughout his rehabilitation.

Outcome

At 12 weeks Jared was asymptomatic and returned to school on a full-time basis feeling great. He also returned to hockey, but at the high school and house league level because he decided to prioritize his schoolwork. Was the 12-week rehabilitation program completed in a linear fashion, in which Jared felt better day after day, week after week? Not at all. There were many ups and downs, and changes had to be made along the way. We used Jared's data, as well as data from other patients, to develop and alter his program. For example, our data showed that many hockey players concussed at his age perform tracking eye exercises less effectively at slower speed and more effectively at higher speeds. This is opposite to what is "normally" seen and may be due to players being conditioned to track a rapidly moving puck. We implemented specific slow-tracking exercises to correct this dysfunction. This not only helped Jared regain his health, but will help those who come after him.

PROMISING FUTURE

We are in the midst of a brain revolution. Although knowledge is allowing us to tackle the concussion epidemic, we have a long way to go. We do not have accurate concussion reporting numbers. There is little information on biomechanical or physiological triggers in children, and we don't know the epidemiological consequences of concussions as we age. But we are headed in the right direction.

National surveillance studies are being initiated to determine the incidence of concussions in youth. Data are being gathered to establish age- and sex-specific guidelines. Preexisting conditions and their relationship to concussion rehabilitation are being explored, and technology will enable us to better diagnose and manage the cumulative impact of concussions. Imaging studies such as diffused tensor imaging (DTI), functional MRI (fMRI), biomarkers S100B, neuron specific enolase (NSE), and concussion genomic sequencing capabilities are only a few of the research areas that will be closer to clinical application by the time you read this book.

Clinicians are beginning to abandon linear, reductionist dogma in favor of an integrated approach. We will go beyond static wiring diagrams and single treatment modalities to understand the dynamic and emergent nature of complex brain networks. We will embrace this marvelous complexity and realize that no one area of the brain or body can perform its function alone. In addition to the advances being made, a cultural shift must occur to protect our children. Education on all aspects of concussion needs to be implemented on a national scale. Parents, teachers, coaches, and children can change the culture surrounding this not-so-invisible injury. While these cumulative strategies will not provide all the answers, they will enable us to collect information and continue to ask the right questions.

8

The Building Blocks of Children's Mental Health: Care and Community

Sharna Olfman

Urie Bronfenbrenner, one of the leading scholars in developmental psychology, found it "sobering" to discover that after 50 years of work in the field, he was able to distill the necessary conditions for healthy child development down to two facts. In order to become fully intact human beings, he concluded, children need "the enduring, irrational involvement of one or more adults . . . [i]n short, *somebody has to [be] crazy about that kid*." And caregivers in turn "need public policies and practices that provide opportunity, status, resources, encouragement, stability, example, and above all *time* for parenthood."[1]

To state this even more simply, children need unconditional love and consistent care from their families, and families in turn need a "village" to support their efforts. These two principles capture not only the essence of Bronfenbrenner's prolific research, but also that of a number of towering figures in child psychology, including Diana Baumrind, John Bowlby, Erik Erikson, and Stanley Greenspan. In recent years, with the advent of brain imaging techniques, researcher Allan Schore and his colleagues have documented that reliable, loving care during infancy and early childhood has a profound impact on the development of regions of the brain that are critical for regulating emotions and coping with stress. And the abilities to regulate feelings and manage stress are the hallmarks of mental health.[2]

Talk of giving children "unconditional love" sounds clichéd, unless we clarify what this means within the context of parents' daily routines of feeding and carrying infants, coping with tantrums and toilet training, and juggling domestic and work schedules. It is also necessary to explicate the kind of support that parents need in order to be fully present both emotionally and physically for their children. A few generations ago, new parents expected to learn these precepts from their own parents and from hands-on experience gleaned from helping to care for younger siblings and cousins in stable family and community networks. But in recent decades technological innovation and globalization have engendered radical changes in our lifestyles—often within a single generation—and as a result, the lessons to be learned from our parents and grandparents may seem obsolete. In addition, changes in the workplace require many adults to relocate frequently, separating young parents from their families of origin. And so new parents must often sort out the challenges and complexities of parenthood for themselves.

A PORTRAIT OF CARE

Time and again over the past half century, a veritable army of researchers has demonstrated that a relationship with at least one loving, responsive, and dependable caregiver is essential for a child's present and future psychological well-being. The quality of this relationship extends well beyond the mere provision of food and shelter and impacts intellectual, language, personality, social, emotional, and brain development. This caregiver-infant relationship is called "attachment."[3] It is not essential that the caregiver in the attachment relationship be the biological mother. Any adult—who in Bronfenbrenner's inimitable words is "crazy about that kid"—can serve as an attachment figure, and in fact it is better for the child to have more than one caregiver to rely on.

As psychologist Robert Karen explains in *Becoming Attached*:

"The concept of "attachment," born in British psychoanalysis some forty years ago and nurtured to near maturity in the developmental psychology departments of American universities . . . encompasses both the quality and strength of the parent-child bond, the ways in which it forms and develops, how it can be damaged and repaired, and the long-term impact of separations, losses, wounds, and deprivations. Beyond that, *it is a theory of love and its central place in human life*."[4]

Attachment: An Anthropological Perspective

Beyond the immediate pleasure that tender loving care might give an infant or young child, why does its presence or absence have profound psychological consequences that reverberate throughout our lives? In *Childhood Lost*, anthropologist Meredith Small helps us to understand why the attachment between parent and child is of such central importance. Small explains:

"Humans, like all primates, are designed to be involved with the upbringing of their offspring for many years, but as we will see, particular evolutionary pressures have rendered the human caregiver-child relationship especially intense and long-lasting. About four million years ago . . . when early humans stood up and started to walk on two legs, that type of locomotion required an increase in the gluteus maximus and minimus muscles which in turn pushed for a short and broad bony pelvic shape. As a result, the pelvic opening, or birth canal, also changed; the opening became essential ovoid instead of round with the sacrum tilted inward forming a bowl. This change in pelvic architecture was not a problem at first because our earliest ancestors still had small brains—comparable in size to the brains of modern chimpanzees—and infants could easily navigate the birth canal. The real crisis came about 1.5 million years ago when there was intense pressure for brain growth in the human lineage and suddenly babies had much bigger heads relative to the size of the pelvic opening. At this point, evolution had to make a compromise because there is only so far you can push the width of the pelvis to accommodate infant head size; if the human pelvis were any wider, women would not be able to walk.

Instead, Natural Selection opted for another route; human infants are born too soon—neurologically unfinished compared to other primates. As a result they are physically and emotionally very dependent. But this level of dependence could not have appeared if there hadn't been some corresponding evolutionary shift in parental behavior that facilitated the capacity to respond to infant needs. And so, there must have been a "co-evolution" of dependent infants and responding adults for human infants to have survived. A human newborn, therefore, is designed by evolution to be "entwined" with an adult of its species. In other words, human infants have evolved to be "attached" both emotionally and physically to their caregivers and when that attachment is denied, the infant is at risk.[5]

Small also reminds us that for 95 percent of our human history, we were all hunter-gatherers. And it was in this physical and social milieu that our species evolved. Studying the few extant hunter-gatherer tribes in modern history provides us with a window on the conditions in which we first evolved as a species and the way that we are designed to live and raise our children. Today, most people on Earth practice a subsistence form of farming called small plot horticulture, so it is instructive to examine the parenting practices of these societies as well. Why? *Because in spite of the headlong pace of technological change, which repeatedly reshapes our social, cultural, and economic lives, children's irreducible needs endure.* Therefore, parents cannot simply adjust themselves and their children to prevailing conditions. They must also seek to adjust conditions to address their—and their children's—real human needs.

A survey of different hunter-gatherer and horticultural groups reveals the rich diversity of beliefs, values, and lifestyles that is typical of our species. But despite these variations, a common pattern emerges: in the preindustrial milieu, infants are in almost constant skin contact with their caregivers, who respond immediately to their needs and never leave them to cry. This style of infant care is also standard practice in technologically advanced countries like Japan. In fact, even today it is typical of the vast majority of human societies. *And this style of care is precisely what a half-century of "attachment" research tells us infants need for optimal psychological and neurological development.*

The Premature Push for Independence

It is striking that the United States—where so much attachment research is conducted—is one of the few countries in which parents do not routinely care for their infants in these physically responsive ways that are optimal for psychological and neurological development. Why is this so? As Small suggests:

The primary goal of Western—that is North American and European parents, but especially American parents—is independence and self-reliance for children. This push for independence is most striking in infancy when babies are expected to sleep alone and are fed on a schedule. Western parents also expect infants to "self comfort" when they cry so many parents delay responses to crying or do not respond at all but believe in a policy of letting the infant "cry it out."

This caretaking style results in many hours during which infants are not held and are not part of a social group. Western babies are held 50% less than in all other cultures, spend 60% of day time alone, and the West is the only culture in which babies are expected to sleep alone.[6]

Paradoxically, though, infants who are in constant physical contact with their caregivers and never left to cry—as opposed to infants who are "trained" to be independent by being left alone to "cry it out" several hours a day—are much more likely to become confident, independent children. This is not too difficult to understand when we place ourselves in comparable circumstances. Imagine that you are alone in your bedroom. You have fallen and broken your ankle, or perhaps you have awakened with a high fever, or from a terrifying dream. Your spouse is in the next room. You call out in anguish, and he pops his head in, smiles benevolently, and suggests that you settle down and go to sleep. You cry out to him repeatedly, but he does not return. The familiar sounds of the household—conversation, music, laughter—surround you, but you are alone, too incapacitated to move, and unable to effectively communicate how desperately ill or frightened or sad you feel. Eventually you fall silent because your efforts to reach out to your loved one are fruitless. Over the coming weeks you are routinely ignored by your spouse. But you are a competent adult with many personal and interpersonal resources. If your relationship with your husband does not improve, you are free to leave and seek out a more gratifying relationship.

An infant, on the other hand, does not have these competencies or freedoms. She is utterly dependent on her caregivers. When left for hours to cry herself to sleep, day after day, week after week, she will eventually stop crying and become "well-behaved." But inwardly, she may be paralyzed with fear, seething with anger, or overwhelmed with sadness. And in the process, she is acquiring an overarching orientation of mistrust—of herself, of others, of her world. While learning to self-comfort and not to cry, other important lessons are being learned as well: that her needs and feelings are insignificant, that she can't rely on others to help her when she is in pain, that how she feels is not particularly informative, that how she communicates is not particularly effective. By contrast, the infant who is in continual contact with her caregivers, who take seriously and respond quickly to her needs as they arise, builds up an image of herself as competent, of her family as loving, and of her world as safe. And it is this infant who will acquire the confidence with which to exercise true independence.

The Dance of Attachment

Given how vital attachment is to the infant's survival, it should not come as a surprise that human infants are born with a number of characteristics and instinctive behaviors that help to "woo" the parent into a loving relationship. Research has shown that infants' physical characteristics—their round faces and eyes, soft skin, gentle grasp, the way they mold their bodies when held, their radiant smiles, coos, and babbles—are deeply appealing to adults. In addition, from birth the infant is attracted to the smell of his mother's breast milk, the sound of her voice, the rhythm of her heartbeat, the touch of her skin.[7] Daniel Stern's analysis of videos of infants and mothers revealed that quite unconsciously, they engage in a synchronous dance as first one and then the other gazes, touches, and communicates with the other verbally and nonverbally.[8] Infants are so attuned to and dependent on this dance of attachment that they become distressed when a beloved caregiver does not return their smile. Touch is a key element in the attachment relationship. Research has shown that when premature infants are held and stroked each day, they show more rapid neural and physical development than those who receive standard hospital care.[9]

Born Too Soon

Because babies are "born too soon"—neurologically unfinished—during the first several months of life, human infants are not yet capable of regulating their bodies. Therefore, the attachment or entwined relationship is one of physiological and not just emotional dependency. Sleep expert James McKenna has demonstrated that when nursing mothers and their infants share sleep, their heart rates, brain waves, breathing patterns, and sleep cycles become synchronized.[10]

Breast-feeding also helps to regulate and augment their physiological processes. Over and above the nourishing proteins, minerals, vitamins, fats, and sugars, breast milk also supplies antibodies to assist the infant's immature immune system; growth factors that help in tissue development and maturation; and a variety of hormones, neuropeptides, and natural opioids subtly shape brain development and behavior. The breast has been described as the "external counterpart of the placenta, picking up where [it] left off the task of ushering the infant toward physical and neurological completion."[11]

Learning to Feel

The attachment relationship helps infants to modulate, interpret, and communicate emotions. Sue Gerhardt describes this process in *Why Love Matters: How Affection Shapes a Baby's Brain*:

To become fully human, the baby's basic responses need to be elaborated and developed into more specific and complex feelings. With parental guidance, the basic state of "feeling bad" can get differentiated into a range of feelings like irritation, disappointment, anger, annoyance and hurt. Again, the baby or toddler can't make these distinctions without help from those in the know. The parent must also help the baby to become aware of his own feelings and this is done by holding up a virtual mirror to the baby, talking in baby talk and emphasizing and exaggerating words and gestures so that the baby can realize that this is not mum or dad just expressing themselves, this is them "showing" me my feelings. It is a kind of "psychofeedback" which provides the introduction to a human culture in which we can interpret both our own and others' feelings and thoughts. Parents bring the baby into this more sophisticated emotional world by identifying feelings and labeling them clearly. Usually this teaching happens quite unselfconsciously.[12]

Brain Development

In recent years, with the help of brain imaging technologies, Allan Schore and his colleagues at the UCLA School of Medicine have documented that brain development in the first few years of life is dependent on the social and sensory stimulation that is part and parcel of the attachment relationship.[13] Despite a growth industry in flash cards, videos, toys, and software, which boasts that it can turn your baby into the next Einstein, it is human rather than electronic stimulation that grows a baby's brain. The human touch, voice, gaze, and smile trigger a complex cascade of neurochemicals that catalyze growth in regions of the brain that play a critical role in our ability to empathize, control our impulses, and develop a sense of self. One of the most vital brain regions to develop as an outgrowth of attachment relationships is the orbitofrontal cortex.

The orbitofrontal cortex plays a key role in emotional life. It enables us to empathize with others and to control our emotional responses. Although social emotions such as the pain of separation from a loved one and shame originate in the amygdala and hypothalamus, the orbitofrontal cortex serves to control our impulses and express ourselves in socially appropriate and reflective ways. It is very significant that the prefrontal cortex in general and the orbitofrontal cortex in particular has a growth spurt between 6 and 12 months of age, corresponding exactly with when the attachment bond is being consolidated. There is a second growth spurt in early toddlerhood, around the time the child begins to walk, which is also a period of intense pleasure between parent and child.[14]

In a study conducted with Romanian orphans who had no opportunity to form attachments with caregivers during infancy and early childhood, brain imaging revealed a black hole where the orbitofrontal cortex should be. People who sustain damage to the orbitofrontal cortex become insensitive to social and emotional cues. They may also be prone to dissociation or even to sociopathy.[15]

After the orbitofrontal cortex has matured, other areas of the social-emotional brain begin to mature, including the anterior cingulate, which helps us to tune into our feelings. Soon thereafter the dorsolateral prefrontal cortex—the primary site of working memory—begins to develop. Together, the anterior cingulate and dorsolateral cortex facilitate verbal and nonverbal communication of feelings. During the third year of life the hippocampus, which plays a key role in long-term memory, begins to mature and becomes strongly linked to the anterior cingulate and the dorsolateral prefrontal cortex. The hippocampus enables the child to create a personal narrative with a past and a future, and so for the first time, she has an enduring sense of self and no longer lives just in the moment. *This sequence of postnatal brain development is largely dependent on the sensory, intellectual, and emotional stimulation that is integral to the attachment relationship.*[16]

Beyond Attachment

The style of parenting that fosters attachment is ideal during infancy and early toddlerhood. But what then? Although space constraints prevent me from exploring their work at length, the parenting research of Diana Baumrind and Erik Erikson's psychosocial theory of development provides excellent guidelines beyond the intense early months of "attachment" parenting.

Authoritative Parenting

In the 1970s Diana Baumrind conducted research to discern what style of parenting is optimal for psychological development. She discovered that an approach to parenting that she named "authoritative" has the best long-term outcomes for children. In the decades since then, her research has been replicated and elaborated, and there is now wide consensus among parenting experts that this approach fosters healthy development.[17]

Authoritative parents are warm, attentive, and sensitive to their child's needs. At the same time, they consistently assert age-appropriate expectations and responsibilities. So, for example, their young children know that they are not to eat cookies before dinner, and that they must do their homework, complete household tasks, and treat others with respect. When making their expectations known, these parents provide their children with a cogent rationale. As a result, over time their children internalize their parents' underlying motives and values, so that they don't remain dependent on authority figures to "do the right thing." As children get older, authoritative parents grant them increasing autonomy over decisions that affect them, thereby gently ushering them along their journey toward adulthood.

Authoritative parenting has been linked to a variety of positive outcomes. During the preschool years, children of authoritative parents are happier, they have better impulse control, they persevere at challenging tasks, and they are more cooperative at school. Older children have higher self-esteem, are more socially and morally mature, and perform better at school.[18]

Psychosocial Stages

Psychoanalyst Erik Erikson's theory of psychosocial development describes the central psychological challenges that confront all human beings at different stages of the life cycle.[19] The central psychological challenge of infancy is the acquisition of *trust*. Securely attached infants whose caregivers consistently respond to their needs in a loving and timely fashion come to approach life with optimism. Children who are imbued with trust find it easier to acquire *autonomy* in toddlerhood. Toddlers have a burgeoning sense of self that is ushered in by an explosion of new intellectual, linguistic, and motor skills. Suddenly they are walking, talking, climbing, and exploring. Parents who allow their toddlers to "do for themselves," whether it be climbing the stairs, putting on their own shirts, or feeding themselves, without providing absolute freedom on the one hand—which would be unsafe—or too little freedom on the other hand—which conveys a message of incompetence—provide optimal support during toddlers' bid for autonomy. During the preschool years children need time for unstructured imaginative play in natural settings in order to develop *initiative*. Psychologically healthy school-age children feel a natural desire to develop the capacity for *industry*. When children find their passion, whether it be tennis, literature, or woodwork, they will work with great diligence toward mastery when parents and teachers facilitate their efforts as mentors and guides.

The predominant psychological challenge of adolescence is to acquire a coherent and meaningful sense of *identity*. Adolescents who begin their search for identity with a healthy sense of trust, autonomy, initiative, and industry are greatly advantaged. And when they enter adulthood knowing who they are, what they believe in and value, and where they are going in life, they are more capable of achieving the central tasks of adulthood: the capacity for enduring *intimacy* and *generativity*. Generativity refers to our desire to nurture the next generation. While parents and "helping professionals" such as teachers and therapists may nurture children in direct ways, everyone, whether artists, managers, environmentalists, or politicians, can make "generative" choices that inspire or secure the safety and prospects of the next generation.

And now we come full circle. Adults who were securely attached infants with authoritative parents who helped them to successfully negotiate the central psychological challenges of childhood will acquire a healthy sense of identity, which is a precursor for intimacy and generativity. The capacity to sustain intimacy and act generatively are in turn necessary to successfully parent one's own children. In other words, adults who lack trust, autonomy, initiative, industry, and a strong sense of identity will be greatly compromised in their ability to offer intimate and altruistic care to their children.

PORTRAIT OF COMMUNITY

As anthropologist Meredith Small reminds us, there is an evolutionary push toward an "entwined" or "attachment" relationship with our children that is as old as our primate history. But our potential for intimacy and generativity will not be actualized unless we ourselves have been the recipients of responsive and responsible care from our own parents. Harlow's research with monkeys revealed that infant monkeys who were separated from their mothers at birth were incapable of nurturing their own offspring.[20] But even when we have been well parented ourselves, our natural desire to parent must be augmented by direct experience with child care, as well as a healthy dose of intelligence and energy. And still these circumstances do not suffice. In Bronfenbrenner's evocative words: *The heart of our social system is the family. If we are to maintain the health of our society, we must discover the best means of nurturing that heart.*[21] In other words, parents must be supported in myriad ways by their communities and the wider culture.

What Parents Need

If adults are to have the time, resources, and physical and emotional health necessary to parent their children, they need

- family, friends, and neighbors who can provide practical and emotional support;
- health care for themselves and their children that is affordable, comprehensive, and not contingent on the whims of an employer;
- affordable housing in safe neighborhoods with amenities that support family life, such as parks, community centers, libraries, and grocery stores;
- paid parental and child sick leave that is generous enough to enable parents to form secure attachments with their children and that never obligates them to choose between nursing a sick child or paying the rent;
- day care that is affordable and of the highest quality;
- a living wage so that their "second shift" can be at home with their children;
- flexible work arrangements that allow them to complete work at home or share a position without forsaking essential benefits such as health care or permanently compromising opportunities for career advancement;
- public schools that are safe, with small teacher-child ratios, and that utilize developmentally sensitive approaches to education;
- media regulation so that their children are no longer relentlessly exposed to violence, pornography, sexism, racism, and commercials for products that undermine their health; and
- clean air, soil, and water.

American parents who read this "wish" list may dismiss it as utopian, yet it describes the status quo in many industrialized nations. In fact the conditions listed above should be regarded as fundamental human rights, because they are the preconditions for fostering attachments and authoritative parenting, which in turn are essential for healthy psychological and neurological development.

WHEN CARE AND COMMUNITY BREAK DOWN

How can a mother who must return to work only days after giving birth—while placing her newborn in substandard care—establish a secure attachment with her infant? If a single mother must work two or three low-wage jobs to make ends meet, while her children return to an empty home, how can she scaffold their arduous journey toward adulthood? And how can she protect them from the tidal wave of violence, hatred, racism, sexism, and pornography that pervade the media? And if this mother is the second or third generation to have raised children under these compromised circumstances, how will she herself have acquired the psychological maturity and wisdom to relate lovingly and responsibly to her children? These are precisely the conditions under which millions of American parents are obliged to raise their children. As Bronfenbrenner has lamented, *"the comparative lack of family support systems in the United States is so extreme as to make it unique among modern nations."*[22]

Sadly, it appears that support for families in the United States continues to deteriorate in lockstep with the rise in psychiatric disturbances. Psychologist Laura Berk described this downward spiral in *Childhood Lost*:

American children and adolescents of all walks of life are experiencing more stress than their counterparts of the previous generation. An examination of hundreds of studies of nine- to seventeen-year-olds carried out between the 1950s and the 1990s revealed a steady, large increase in anxiety over this period. A combination of reduced social connectedness and increased environmental dangers (crime, violent media, fear of war, etc.) appeared responsible. . . . Interestingly, whereas societal indicators of diminished social connectedness . . . showed strong associations with children's rising anxiety, economic conditions such as poverty and unemployment had comparatively little influence. *A child's well-being, it appears, is less responsive to whether the family has enough money than to whether it promotes close, supportive bonds with others.* Other changes in the American family also point to a withering of social connectedness. For example, Americans are less likely to visit friends, join community organizations, and volunteer in their communities than they once were. [P]arents and children converse and share leisure time less often than they did in the past.

Simultaneously, young people's sense of trust in others has weakened. In 1992 only 18.3 percent of high school seniors agreed that one can usually trust people, compared with 34.5 percent in 1975. Young people's increased anxiety is a natural response to lower quality relationships. *As social connectedness in the United States declined, youth suicide rates rose.* Between the 1950s and 1970s, they rose by 300 percent for fifteen–twenty-five-year olds; and between 1980 and 1997, by 109 percent for ten- to fourteen-year-olds.[23]

CONCLUSION

The current and ongoing breakdown in caregiving and community support plays a significant role in the epidemic of psychiatric disturbances that we are now witnessing among children in the United States. That view is not very popular, however, because policy-based efforts to heal communities, empower parents, and regulate industry do not generate profits for the pharmaceutical or genetic technology industries. And stellar careers in research are not built on promoting practices that many of our grandmothers and great-grandmothers knew intuitively to be good. In contrast, the claim that mental health or illness is encoded in our genes is so widespread that social psychologist Carol Travis apparently had no qualms about including the following statement as part of a list of false assumptions that have been *"resoundingly disproved by research"*: *"The way that parents treat a child in the first five years (three yeas) (one year) (five minutes) of life is crucial to the child's later intellectual and emotional success."*[24] This statement was published in *The Chronicle of Higher Education*, one of the most widely read and respected newspapers in academic circles.

As a result of our skewed emphasis on the heritability of mental illness, we spend untold millions of dollars looking for genetic markers. Meanwhile, and in spite of all the bipartisan talk about "family values," we are not providing adequate support to families, which is what we *must* do if we are to address the root cause of children's psychological disturbances. Environments that enable caregivers to form healthy attachments to their children in turn support healthy genetic expression and brain maturation. I close with a quote from Bronfenbrenner:

One telling criterion of the worth of a society—a criterion that stands the test of history—is the concern of one generation for the next. As we enter our third century, we Americans, compared to other industrialized societies, appear to be abandoning that criterion. . . . It would appear that the process of making human beings human is breaking down in American society. To make it work again, we must reweave the unraveling social fabric and revitalize the human bonds essential to sustaining the well-being and development of both present and future generations.[25]

Series Afterword: Childhood in America

Sharna Olfman, PhD, Series Editor

The rich diversity of cultures created by humankind is a testament to our ability to develop and adapt in diverse ways. But however varied different cultures may be, children are not endlessly malleable; they all share basic psychological and physical needs that must be met to ensure healthy development. The Childhood in America series examines the extent to which U.S. culture meets children's irreducible needs. Without question, many children growing up in the United States lead privileged lives. They have been spared the ravages of war, poverty, malnourishment, sexism, and racism. However, despite our nation's resources, not all children share these privileges. In addition, values that are central to American culture, such as self-reliance, individualism, privacy of family life, and consumerism, have created a climate in which parenting has become intolerably labor intensive, and children are being taxed beyond their capacity for healthy adaptation. Record levels of psychiatric disturbance, violence, poverty, apathy, and despair among our children speak to our current cultural crisis.

   Although our elected officials profess their commitment to "family values," policies that support family life are woefully lacking and are inferior to those in other industrialized nations. American families are burdened by inadequate parental leave, a health-care system that does not provide universal coverage for children, a minimum wage that is not a living wage, "welfare to work" policies that require parents to leave their children for long stretches of time, unregulated and inadequately subsidized day care, an unregulated entertainment industry that exposes children to sex and violence, and a two-tiered public education system that delivers inferior education to poor children and frequently ignores individual differences in learning styles and profiles of intelligence. As a result, many families are taxed to the breaking point. In addition, our fascination with technological innovation is creating a family lifestyle that is dominated by screen rather than human interaction.

The Childhood in America series seeks out leading childhood experts from across the disciplines to promote dialogue, research, and understanding regarding how best to raise and educate psychologically healthy children, to ensure that they will acquire the wisdom, heart, and courage needed to make choices for the betterment of society.

Notes and References

CHAPTER 1

1. C. A. Boyle, P. Decoufle, and M. Yeargin-Alsopp, "Prevalence and Health Impact of Developmental Disabilities in US Children." *Pediatrics* 93 (1994): 399–403.

2. S. Olfman, ed., *All Work and No Play: How Educational Reforms Are Harming Our Preschoolers* (Santa Barbara, CA: Praeger, 2003); S. Olfman, ed., *Childhood Lost* (Santa Barbara, CA: Praeger, 2005).

3. T. Insel, "Director's Blog: Transforming Diagnosis," *My Blog* (blog), NIMH: National Institute of Mental Health, April 29, 2013, http://www.nimh.nih.gov/about/director/2013/transforming-diagnosis.shtml (accessed Jun 1, 2014).

4. A. Frances, *Saving Normal* (New York: HarperCollins, 2013).

5. A. Schore, *The Science of the Art of Psychotherapy* (New York: W.W. Norton, 2012).

6. M. Small, *Our Babies, Ourselves: How Biology and Culture Shape the Way We Parent* (New York: Anchor, 1999).

7. T. Insel and A. Lieberman, "DSM-5 and RDoC: Shared Interests" (press release), NIH: National Institute of Mental Health, May 13, 2013, http://www.nimh.nih.gov/news/science-news/2013/dsm-5-and-rdoc-shared-interests.shtml (accessed June 1, 2014) (emphasis added).

8. SSRI antidepressants increase the availability of serotonin in the brain.

9. I. Kirsch, *The Emperor's New Drugs: Exploding the Antidepressant Myth* (New York: Basic Books, 2010).

10. S. Olfman, Introduction to *Drugging Our Children: How Profiteers Are Pushing Antipsychotics on Our Youngest, and What We Can Do about It*, ed. S. Olfman and B. Robbins (Santa Barbara, CA: Praeger, 2012), ix–xvii.

11. R. Whitaker, "Weighing the Evidence: What Science Has to Say about Prescribing Atypical Antipsychotics to Children," in *Drugging Our Children: How*

Profiteers Are Pushing Antipsychotics on Our Youngest, and What We Can Do about It, ed. S. Olfman and B. Robbins (Santa Barbara, CA: Praeger, 2012), 3–16.

12. S. Olfman, ed., *No Child Left Different* (Santa Barbara, CA: Praeger, 2006); S. Olfman, ed., *Bipolar Children: Cutting Edge Controversy, Insights and Research* (Santa Barbara, CA: Praeger, 2007); Olfman and Robbins, *Drugging Our Children*.

CHAPTER 2

1. B. Pescosolido, "A Disease Like Any Other?" *American Journal of Psychiatry* 167 (2010): 1321–1330; see table 1, 1324.

2. J. Swazey, *Chlorpromazine in Psychiatry* (Cambridge, MA: MIT Press, 1974), 78.

3. Ibid, 79.

4. Ibid, 105.

5. N. Winkelman Jr., "Chlorpromazine in the Treatment of Neuropsychiatric Disorders," *JAMA* 155 (1954): 18–21.

6. "TB Drug Is Tried in Mental Cases." *New York Times*, April 7, 1957, 86.

7. "Wonder Drug of 1954?" *Time*, June 14, 1954.

8. "Wonder Drugs: New Cure for Mental Ills?" *U.S. News and World Report*, June 17, 1955.

9. "Pills for the Mind." *Time*, March 7, 1955.

10. The National Institute of Mental Health Psychopharmacology Service Center Collaborative Study Group, "Phenothiazine Treatment in Acute Schizophrenia," *Archives of General Psychiatry* 10 (1964): 246–261.

11. E. Valenstein, *Blaming the Brain* (New York: The Free Press, 1998), 38.

12. "Drugs and Depression." *New York Times*, September 6, 1959.

13. H. Himwich, "Psychopharmacologic Drugs," *Science* 127 (1958): 59–72.

14. J. Schildkraut, "The Catecholamine Hypothesis of Affective Disorders," *American Journal of Psychiatry* 122 (1965): 509–522.

15. A. Baumeister, "Historical Development of the Dopamine Hypothesis of Schizophrenia," *Journal of the History of the Neurosciences* 11 (2002): 265–277.

16. M. Bowers, "Cerebrospinal Fluid 5-hydroxyindoleacetic Acid and Homovanillic Acid in Psychiatric Patients," *International Journal of Neuropharmacology* 8 (1969): 255–262.

17. R. Papeschi, "Homovanillic and 5-hydroxyindoleacetic Acid in Cerebrospinal Fluid of Depressed Patients," *Archives of General Psychiatry* 25 (1971): 354–358.

18. M. Bowers, "Lumbar CSF 5-hydroxyindoleacetic acid and Homovanillic Acid in Affective Syndromes," *Journal of Nervous and Mental Disorders* 158 (1974): 325–330.

19. J. Mendels, "Brain Biogenic Amine Depletion and Mood," *Archives of General Psychiatry* 30 (1974): 447–451.

20. M. Asberg, "Serotonin Depression: A Biochemical Subgroup within the Affective Disorders?" *Science* 191 (1976): 478–480; M. Asberg, "5-HIAA in the Cerebrospinal Fluid," *Archives of General Psychiatry* 33 (1976): 1193–1197.

21. J. Maas, "Pretreatment Neurotransmitter Metabolite Levels and Response to Tricyclic Antidepressant Drugs," *American Journal of Psychiatry* 141 (1984): 1159–1171.

22. J. Lacasse. "Serotonin and Depression: A Disconnect between the Advertisements and the Scientific Literature," *PloS Medicine* 2 (2005): 1211–1216.

23. V. Krishnan, "Linking Molecules to Mood," *American Journal of Psychiatry* 167 (2010): 1305–1320.

24. M. Bowers, "Central Dopamine Turnover in Schizophrenic Syndromes," *Archives of General Psychiatry* 31 (1974): 50–54.

25. R. Post, "Cerebrospinal Fluid Amine Metabolites in Acute Schizophrenia," *Archives of General Psychiatry* 32 (1975): 1063–1068.

26. T. Lee, "Binding of ^{3}H-neuroleptics and ^{3}H-apomorphine in Schizophrenic Brains," *Nature* 374 (1978): 897–900.

27. D. Burt, "Antischizophrenic Drugs: Chronic Treatment Elevates Dopamine Receptor Binding in Brain," *Science* 196 (1977): 326–327.

28. A. MacKay, "Increased Brain Dopamine and Dopamine Receptors in Schizophrenia," *Archives of General Psychiatry* 39 (1982): 991–997.

29. J. Martinot, "Striatal D_2 Dopaminergic Receptors Assessed with Positron Emission Tomography and Bromospiperone in Untreated Schizophrenic Patients," *American Journal of Psychiatry* 147 (1990): 44–50; L. Farde, "D_2 Dopamine Receptors in Neuroleptic-Naïve Schizophrenic Patients," *Archives of General Psychiatry* 47 (1990): 213–219; J. Hietala, "Striatal D_2 Dopamine Receptor Characteristics in Neuroleptic-Naïve Schizophrenic Patients Studied with Positron Emission Tomography," *Archives of General Psychiatry* 51 (1994): 116–123.

30. P. Deniker, "The Neuroleptics: A Historical Survey," *Acta Psychiatrica Scandinavica* 82, suppl. 358 (1990): 83–87. See also "From Chlorpromazine to Tardive Dyskinesia," *Psychiatric Journal of the University of Ottawa* 14 (1989): 253–259.

31. E. Nestler and S. Hyman, *Molecular Neuropharmacology* (New York: McGraw-Hill, 2002), 392.

32. The Balanced Mind Parent Network, "Fact Sheet: Facts About Teenage Depression," November 27, 2009, www.thebalancedmind.org/learn/library /facts-about-teenage-depression (accessed June 29, 2014).

33. Depression and Bipolar Support Alliance, "Coping with Mood Changes Later in Life," www.dbsalliance.org/site/PageServer?pagename=education_brochures _coping_mood_changes (accessed June 29, 2014).

34. NAMI, "Major Depression Fact Sheet," www.nami.org/Content /Microsites270/NAMI_Howard_County/Home258/Mental_Illness_Information1 /Depression.pdf (accessed June 29, 2014).

35. T. Insel, "Director's Blog: Mental Illness Defined as Disruption in Neural Circuits," *My Blog* (blog), NIMH: National Institute of Mental Health, August 12, 2011, http://www.nimh.nih.gov/about/director/2011/mental-illness-defined-as -disruption-in-neural-circuits.shtml.

36. National Public Radio, "When It Comes to Depression, Serotonin Isn't the Whole Story," January 23, 2012.

37. R. Pies, "Psychiatry's New Brain-Mind and the Legend of the 'Chemical Imbalance'," *Psychiatric Times*, July 11, 2011, http://www.psychiatrictimes.com/ blogs/couch-crisis/psychiatry-new-brain-mind-and-legend-chemical-imbalance.

CHAPTER 3

Notes

1. Francis, 2011.
2. Martin & Zhang, 2005.

3. Stein et al., 1972; Ravelli et al., 1976.
4. Hoch, 1998.
5. Tobi et al., 2009.
6. E.g., Haggarty, 2011.
7. See, e.g., Jackson et al., 2011.
8. Schanen, 2006.
9. Crews & Gore, 2012.
10. Barros & Offenbacher, 2009.
11. Francis, 1992.
12. Virtanen et al., 2005.
13. Skinner et al., 2010.
14. Seckl, 2008.
15. Kapoor et al., 2008.
16. Francis, 2011; Francis et al., 1999.
17. Francis, Champagne, & Meaney, 2000.
18. Francis et al., 1999; Francis & Meaney, 1999.
19. Liu et al., 1997.
20. Champagne et al., 2006.
21. Champagne et al., 2006.
22. Harlow et al., 1971.
23. Ruppenthal et al., 1976 (for a review).
24. Denenberg and Rosenberg, 1967.
25. McGowan et al., 2009.
26. See, e.g., Patton et al., 2001; Paul & Joyce, 2003.
27. Jablonka and Raz, 2009.
28. Martin et al., 2008.
29. Morgan et al., 1999.
30. Wolff et al., 1998; Dolinoy et al., 2006.
31. Rakyan et al., 2003.
32. See Francis, 2011, ch. 9.
33. Rideout et al., 2001.
34. Anway et al., 2005.
35. Marczylo et al., 2012.
36. Weaver et al., 2005.
37. Francis et al., 2002.
38. Csoka & Szyf, 2009.

References

Anway, M. D., Cupp, A. S., Uzumcu, M., & Skinner, M. K. (2005). Epigenetic trans-generational actions of endocrine disruptors and male fertility. *Science, 308*(5727), 1466–1469.

Barros, S., & Offenbacher, S. (2009). Epigenetics: Connecting environment and genotype to phenotype and disease. *Journal of Dental Research, 88*(5), 400–408.

Champagne, F. A., Weaver, I. C., Diorio, J., Dymov, S., Szyf, M., & Meaney, M. J. (2006). Maternal care associated with methylation of the estrogen receptor-α1b promoter and estrogen receptor-α expression in the medial preoptic area of female offspring. *Endocrinology, 147*(6), 2909–2915.

Crews, D., & Gore, A. C. (2012). Epigenetic synthesis: A need for a new paradigm for evolution in a contaminated world. *F1000 Biology Reports, 4*.

Csoka, A. B., & Szyf, M. (2009). Epigenetic side-effects of common pharmaceuticals: A potential new field in medicine and pharmacology. *Medical Hypotheses, 73*(5), 770–780.

Denenberg, V. H., & Rosenberg, K. M. (1967). Nongenetic transmission of information. *Nature, 216*(5115), 549–550.

Dolinoy, D. C., Weidman, J. R., Waterland, R. A., & Jirtle, R. L. (2006). Maternal genistein alters coat color and protects A vy mouse offspring from obesity by modifying the fetal epigenome. *Environmental Health Perspectives*, 567–572.

Francis, D., Diorio, J., Liu, D., & Meaney, M. J. (1999). Nongenomic transmission across generations of maternal behavior and stress responses in the rat. *Science, 286*, 1155–1158.

Francis, D. D., Champagne, F. C., & Meaney, M. J. (2000). Variations in maternal behaviour are associated with differences in oxytocin receptor levels in the rat. *Journal of Neuroendocrinology, 12*(12), 1145–1148.

Francis, D. D., Diorio, J., Plotsky, P. M., & Meaney, M. J. (2002). Environmental enrichment reverses the effects of maternal separation on stress reactivity. *The Journal of Neuroscience, 22*(18), 7840–7843.

Francis, D. D., & Meaney, M. J. (1999). Maternal care and the development of stress responses. *Current Opinion in Neurobiology, 9*(1), 128–134.

Francis, R. C. (1992). Sexual lability in teleosts: Developmental factors. *The Quarterly Review of Biology, 67*(1), 1–18.

Francis, R. C. (2011). *Epigenetics: How Environment Shapes Our Genes*. WW Norton & Company.

Haggarty, P. (2011). Nutrition and the epigenome. *Progress in Molecular Biology and Translational Science, 108*, 427–446.

Harlow, H. F., Harlow, M. K., & Suomi, S. J. (1971). From thought to therapy: lessons from a primate laboratory. *American Scientist, 50*, 538–549.

Hoch, S. L. (1998). Famine, disease, and mortality patterns in the parish of Borshevka, Russia, 1830–1912. *Population Studies, 52*(3), 357–368.

Jablonka, E., & Raz, G. (2009). Transgenerational epigenetic inheritance: Prevalence, mechanisms, and implications for the study of heredity and evolution. *The Quarterly Review of Biology, 84*(2), 131–176.

Jackson, A. A., Burdge, G. C., & Lillicrop, K. (2011). Diet, nutrition and modulation of genomic expression in fetal origins of adult disease. *Journal of Nutrigenetics and Nutrigenomics, 3*(4-6), 192–208.

Kapoor, A., Petropoulos, S., & Matthews, S. G. (2008). Fetal programming of hypothalamic-pituitary-adrenal (HPA) axis function and behavior by synthetic glucocorticoids. *Brain Research Reviews, 57*(2), 586–595.

Liu, D., Diorio, J., Tannenbuam, B., Caldji, C., Francis, D., Freedman, A., . . . Meaney, M. (1997). Hypothalamic-pituitary-adrenal response to stress. *Science, 277*, 1659–1662.

Marczylo, E. L., Amoako, A. A., Konje, J. C., Gant, T. W., & Marczylo, T. H. (2012). Smoking induces differential miRNA expression in human spermatozoa: A potential transgenerational epigenetic concern? *Epigenetics, 7*(5), 432–439.

Martin, C., & Zhang, Y. (2005). The diverse functions of histone lysine methylation. *Nature Reviews Molecular Cell Biology, 6*(11), 838–849.

Martin, D. I., Cropley, J. E., & Suter, C. M. (2008). Environmental influence on epigenetic inheritance at the Avy allele. *Nutrition Reviews, 66*(s1), S12–S14.

McGowan, P. O., Sasaki, A., D'Alessio, A. C., Dymov, S., Labonté, B., Szyf, M., . . . Meaney, M. J. (2009). Epigenetic regulation of the glucocorticoid receptor in human brain associates with childhood abuse. *Nature Neuroscience, 12*(3), 342–348.

Morgan, H., Sutherland, H., Martin, D., & Whitelaw, E. (1999). Epigenetic inheritance at the agouti locus in the mouse. *Nature Genetics, 23*, 314–318.

Patton, G. C., Coffey, C., Posterino, M., Carlin, J., & Wolfe, R. (2001). Parental "affectionless control" in adolescent depressive disorder. *Social Psychiatry and Psychiatric Epidemiology, 36*(10), 475–480.

Paul, N., & Joyce, G. (2003). Self-replication. *Current Biology, 13*, R46.

Rakyan, V. K., Chong, S., Champ, M. E., Cuthbert, P. C., Morgan, H. D., Luu, K. V., & Whitelaw, E. (2003). Transgenerational inheritance of epigenetic states at the murine Axin(Fu) allele occurs after maternal and paternal transmission. *Proceedings of the National Academy of Science U S A, 100*(5), 2538–2543.

Ravelli, G.-P., Stein, Z. A., & Susser, M. W. (1976). Obesity in young men after famine exposure in utero and early infancy. *New England Journal of Medicine, 295*(7), 349–353.

Rideout, W., Eggan, K., & Jaensch, R. (2001). Nuclear cloning and epigenetic reprogramming of the genome. *Science, 293*, 1093–1097.

Ruppenthal, G. C., Arling, G. L., Harlow, H. F., Sackett, G. P., & Suomi, S. J. (1976). A 10-year perspective of motherless-mother monkey behavior. *Journal of Abnormal Psychology, 85*(4), 341.

Schanen, N. C. (2006). Epigenetics of autism spectrum disorders. *Human Molecular Genetics, 15*(s2), R138–150. doi: 10.1093/hmg/ddl213

Seckl, J. R. (2008). SecklGlucocorticoids, developmental "programming" and the risk of affective dysfunction. *Progress in Brain Research, 167*, 17–34.

Skinner, M. K., Manikkam, M., & Guerrero-Bosagna, C. (2010). Epigenetic transgenerational actions of environmental factors in disease etiology. *Trends in Endocrinology & Metabolism, 21*(4), 214–222.

Stein, Z., Susser, M., Saenger, G., & Marolla, F. (1972). Nutrition and mental performance. *Science, 178*(62), 708–713.

Tobi, E. W., Lumey, L. H., Talens, R. P., Kremer, D., Putter, H., Stein, A. D., . . . Heijmans, B. T. (2009). DNA methylation differences after exposure to prenatal famine are common and timing- and sex-specific. *Human Molecular Genetics, 18*(21), 4046–4053. doi: 10.1093/hmg/ddp353

Virtanen, H., Rajpert-De Meyts, E., Main, K., Skakkebaek, N., & Toppari, J. (2005). Testicular dysgenesis syndrome and the development and occurrence of male reproductive disorders. *Toxicology and Applied Pharmacology, 207*(2), 501–505.

Weaver, I. C., Champagne, F. A., Brown, S. E., Dymov, S., Sharma, S., Meaney, M. J., & Szyf, M. (2005). Reversal of maternal programming of stress responses in adult offspring through methyl supplementation: Altering epigenetic marking later in life. *Journal of Neuroscience, 25*(47), 11045–11054.

Wolff, G. L., Kodell, R. L., Moore, S. R., & Cooney, C. A. (1998). Maternal epigenetics and methyl supplements affect agouti gene expression in Avy/a mice. *FASEB Journal, 12*(11), 949–957.

CHAPTER 4

1. This chapter is inspired by the seminal research of Philip Landrigan and Phillipe Grandjean and the visionary journalism of Varda Burstyn.

2. P. Grandjean and P. Landrigan, "Neurobehavioral Effects of Developmental Toxicity." *The Lancet Neurology* 14 (2014): 330–338.

3. Environmental Working Group, "The Pollution in Newborns: A Benchmark Investigation of Industrial Chemicals, Pollutants and Pesticides in Umbilical Cord Blood," 2005, http://www.ewg.org/research/body-burden-pollution-newborns (accessed July 8, 2014).

4. S. Steingraber, *Having Faith: An Ecologist's Journey to Motherhood* (New York: Berkley Books, 2001), 262.

5. This anecdote was first told to me by child advocate and children's troubadour Raffi Cavoukian, who introduced me to the work of Philip Landrigan and Sandra Steingraber while we were working on *Child Honoring: Turn This World Around* in 2005.

6. Steingraber, *Having Faith*, 251.

7. Environmental health experts still generally agree that the health benefits of breast-feeding outweigh the risks. Nonetheless, as Grandjean points out in *Only One Chance*, women in the German state of Schleswig-Holstein have the legal right to have their breast milk assessed for toxic chemicals so that they can make an informed decision about its safety.

8. V. Burstyn and G. Sampson, "Techno-Environmental Assaults on Childhood in America," in *Childhood Lost: How American Culture Is Failing Our Kids*, ed. S. Olfman (Westport, CT: Praeger Publishers, 2005), 155–183.

9. Grandjean and Landrigan, "Neurobehavioral Effects of Developmental Toxicity."

10. P. Grandjean, *Only One Chance: How Environmental Pollution Impairs Brain Development—and How to Protect the Brains of the Next Generation* (Oxford: Oxford University Press, 2013).

11. Grandjean and Landrigan, "Neurobehavioral Effects of Developmental Toxicity."

12. Grandjean and Landrigan, "Neurobehavioral Effects of Developmental Toxicity."

13. Grandjean and Landrigan, "Neurobehavioral Effects of Developmental Toxicity"; V. Burstyn and D. Fenton, "Toxic World, Troubled Minds," in *No Child Left Different*, ed. S. Olfman (New York: Rowman & Littlefield Education, 2006), 49–71.

14. P. Grandjean and P. Landrigan, "Developmental Neurotoxicity of Industrial Chemicals," *The Lancet Neurology* (November 8, 2006), doi:10.1016/50140-6736 (06)69665-7

15. Burstyn and Fenton, "Toxic World, Troubled Minds."

16. Grandjean and Landrigan, "Developmental Neurotoxicity of Industrial Chemicals"; Grandjean and Landrigan, "Neurobehavioral Effects of Developmental Toxicity."

17. Grandjean and Landrigan, "Developmental Neurotoxicity of Industrial Chemicals"; Grandjean and Landrigan, "Neurobehavioral Effects of Developmental Toxicity."

18. Grandjean, *Only One Chance*.

19. Grandjean and Landrigan, "Neurobehavioral Effects of Developmental Toxicity," 335.

20. R. Whitaker, "Weighing the Evidence: What Science Has to Say about Prescribing Atypical Antipsychotics to Children," in *Drugging Our Children: How*

Profiteers Are Pushing Antipsychotics on Our Youngest and What We Can Do to Stop It, ed. S. Olfman and B. Robbins (Westport, CT: Praeger Publishers, 2012), 3–16.

21. Grandjean and Landrigan, "Neurobehavioral Effects of Developmental Toxicity"; Grandjean, *Only One Chance*.

22. An independent ethics committee formed by institutions engaged in human research.

23. Grandjean, *Only One Chance*.

24. The National Children's Study, "About the Study," www.nationalchildrenss tudy.gov/about/Pages/default.aspx (last updated April 2, 2012; accessed July 8, 2014). After completing this chapter, I learned from Dr. Philip Landrigan that the National Children's Study is on hold due to funding issues.

25. Grandjean and Landrigan, "Neurobehavioral Effects of Developmental Toxicity."

26. Grandjean, *Only One Chance*.

27. Grandjean, *Only One Chance*.

28. R. Carson, *Silent Spring* (New York: Houghton Mifflin, 1962).

29. Pesticide Action Network, "The DDT Story," http://www.panna.org /issues/persistent-poisons/the-ddt-story (accessed July 8, 2014).

30. M. Grunwald, "Monsanto Hid PCB Pollution for Decades," Organic Consumer's Association, 2002, http://www.organicconsumers.org/monsanto /pcbs010702.cfm (accessed July 8, 2014).

31. Grandjean, *Only One Chance*; S. Steingraber, *Having Faith*, 251.

32. Stockholm Convention, "The New POPs Under the Stockholm Convention," 2008, http://chm.pops.int/TheConvention/ThePOPs/TheNewPOPs /tabid/2511/Default.aspx (accessed July 8, 2014); Grandjean, *Only One Chance*; Grandjean and Landrigan, "Neurobehavioral Effects of Developmental Toxicity."

33. Grandjean, *Only One Chance*; U.S. Environmental Protection Agency, "2006–2007 Pesticide Market Estimates: Usage," http://www.epa.gov/opp00001 /pestsales/07pestsales/table_of_contents2007.htm (last updated July 2, 2013; accessed July 8, 2014).

34. Grandjean, *Only One Chance*.

35. Grandjean, *Only One Chance*.

36. K. Than, "Organophosphates: A Common But Deadly Pesticide," *National Geographic Daily News*, July 18, 2013, http://news.nationalgeographic.com /news/2013/07/130718-organophosphates-pesticides-indian-food-poisoning /#(accessed July 8, 2014).

37. Pesticide Action Network, "Dow Corporate Profile," August 2010, http:// www.panna.org/resources/corporate-accountability/profiles/dow   (accessed July 8, 2014).

38. Grandjean and Landrigan, "Neurobehavioral Effects of Developmental Toxicity."

39. Centers for Disease Control and Prevention, "Biomonitoring Summary," http://www.cdc.gov/biomonitoring/op-dpm_biomonitoringsummary.html (accessed July 8, 2014).

40. Grandjean, *Only One Chance*.

41. Grandjean, *Only One Chance*; E. J. Kopras, "Dr. Robert Kehoe, Cars, Lead and Smoke," Society of Toxicology, 2014, http://www.toxicology.org/gp/gp _kehoe.asp (accessed July 8, 2014).

42. Grandjean, *Only One Chance*.

43. U.S. Environmental Protection Agency, "Summary of the Reduction of Lead in Drinking Water Act and Frequently Asked Questions," October 2013, http://water.epa.gov/drink/info/lead/upload/epa815s13001.pdf (accessed July 8, 2014).

44. Grandjean, *Only One Chance*; Grandjean and Landrigan, "Neurobehavioral Effects of Developmental Toxicity."

45. Methylmercury is a highly toxic industrial by-product of mercury that readily bioaccumulates.

46. Grandjean, *Only One Chance*; Grandjean and Landrigan, "Neurobehavioral Effects of Developmental Toxicity."

47. Grandjean, *Only One Chance*.

48. Burstyn and Sampson, "Techno-Environmental Assaults on Childhood in America."

49. Burstyn and Sampson, "Techno-Environmental Assaults on Childhood in America."

50. Grandjean, *Only One Chance*; Grandjean and Landrigan, "Neurobehavioral Effects of Developmental Toxicity."

51. K. Q. Seelye, "Arsenic Standard for Water Is Too Lax, Study Concludes," *New York Times*, September 11, 2001, http://www.nytimes.com/2001/09/11/us/arsenic-standard-for-water-is-too-lax-study-concludes.html (accessed July 8, 2014).

52. Grandjean, *Only One Chance*.

53. Fluoride Action Network, 2012, http://fluoridealert.org/ (accessed July 8, 2014).

54. Grandjean, *Only One Chance*; B. C. Henn et al., "Manganese Heightens Lead's Effects on Children," *Environmental Health News*, November 4, 2011, http://www.environmentalhealthnews.org/ehs/newscience/2011/09/2011-1101-lead-manganese-child-development/ (accessed July 8, 2014).

55. Grandjean, *Only One Chance*; Grandjean and Landrigan, "Neurobehavioral Effects of Developmental Toxicity."

56. Grandjean, *Only One Chance*; Grandjean and Landrigan, "Neurobehavioral Effects of Developmental Toxicity"; F. Pele et al., "Occupational Solvent Exposure During Pregnancy and Child Behavior at Age 2," *Occupational and Environmental Medicine* 70, no. 2 (2013): 114–119.

57. Grandjean, *Only One Chance*; "EPA Polybrominated Diphenyl Ethers (PBDEs) Action Plan Summary," http://www.epa.gov/oppt/existingchemicals/pubs/actionplans/pbde.html (last updated January 29, 2014; accessed July 8, 2014).

58. Grandjean, *Only One Chance*.

59. Healthy Child Healthy World, "Avoid Phthalates: Find Phthalate Free Products Instead," January 30, 2013, http://healthychild.org/easy-steps/avoid-phthalates-find-phthalate-free-products-instead%E2%80%A8%E2%80%A8/ (accessed July 8, 2014).

60. Healthy Child Healthy World, "Avoid Phthalates."

61. S. Steingraber, "Girls Gone Grown-Up: Why Are U.S. Girls Reaching Puberty Earlier and Earlier?" in *The Sexualization of Childhood*, ed. S. Olfman (Westport, CT: Praeger Publishers, 2008), 51–62.

62. Grandjean and Landrigan, "Neurobehavioral Effects of Developmental Toxicity," 335.

63. Grandjean and Landrigan, "Developmental Neurotoxicity of Industrial Chemicals"; Grandjean and Landrigan, "Neurobehavioral Effects of Developmental Toxicity."

64. Burstyn, and Fenton, "Toxic World, Troubled Minds."

65. Grandjean and Landrigan, "Neurobehavioral Effects of Developmental Toxicity," 336.

CHAPTER 5

Notes

1. Rutter, 2005.
2. Murphy, 2014.
3. Melillo, 2013.
4. Wilson, 2009.
5. Melillo & Leisman, 2009.
6. Melillo & Leisman, 2010.
7. Leisman et al., 2013.
8. Damasio & Damasio, 1989.
9. Puccetti, 1981.
10. Broca, 1861.
11. Gazzaniga, 2005; Chanraud et al., 2010.
12. Geschwind 1965a, 1965b.
13. Double, 2006.
14. Von Heisenberg, 1927.
15. Zilles et al., 1989.
16. Cooper et al., 1996.
17. Melillo & Leisman, 2010.
18. Sherman et al., 2002.
19. Sherman et al., 2002.
20. Krahe et al., 2004.
21. Melillo & Leisman, 2010.
22. Contreras et al., 1997.
23. Leisman, 1976; Leisman & Melillo, 2013; Melillo & Leisman, 2009, 2010.
24. Semrud-Clikeman, 2005.
25. Hebb, 2002.
26. Geschwind, 1982, 20, 32.
27. Coben & Myers, 2008; Uddin et al., 2013.
28. Just et al., 2007.
29. Wada et al., 1975.
30. Leisman et al., 2012.
31. Chugani, 1998.
32. Yellow, 2014; Russ, 2014.
33. Stoner et al., 2014.
34. Chiron et al., 1997.
35. Del Giudice, 2011.
36. Gerhardt & Abrams, 1996.
37. Lindell, 2006.
38. Dawes, 1984.

39. Baron-Cohen et al., 2005.
40. Geary, 1998.
41. Baron-Cohen et al., 2005.
42. Charil et al., 2010.
43. Weinstock, 2007.
44. Melillo & Leisman, 2010.
45. Kolevzon et al., 2007.
46. Melillo & Leisman, 2010.
47. Buie et al., 2010.
48. Henriques & Davidson, 1991.
49. Teicher, 2000.
50. Carmona et al., 2007.
51. See Kang et al., 1991; Neveu, 1993; Melillo & Leisman, 2010.
52. Blonder et al., 1991.
53. Phillips et al., 2003.
54. Kohler et al., 2002.
55. Goldberg et al., 1994.
56. Spinella, 2002.
57. Heining et al., 2003.
58. Eherenfried et al., 2003.
59. Dieterich et al., 2003.
60. Leitner et al., 2007; Buderath et al., 2009.
61. Ghaziuddin & Butler, 1998.
62. Newman et al., 2007.
63. Geschwind & Behan, 1984.
64. Melillo & Leisman, 2009.
65. Offner et al., 2006.
66. Snider & Swedo, 2004.
67. Leisman & Melillo, 2013.
68. Melillo & Leisman, 2010; Leisman & Melillo, 2013.

References

Ayres, A. J. (1979). *Sensory integration and the child*. Los Angeles: Western Psychological Services.

Baron-Cohen, S., Knickmeyer, R. C., & Belmonte, M. K. (2005). Sex differences in the brain: Implications for explaining autism. *Science, 310*(5749), 819–823.

Blonder, L. X., Bowers, D., & Heilman, K. M. (1991). The role of the right hemisphere in emotional communication. *Brain, 114*(3), 1115–1127.

Broca, P. (1861). [Remarque sur le siege de la faculté du language articulé, suivie d'une observation d'aphé mie (perte de la parole]. *Bulletin de la société anatomique de Paris, 36*, 330–356.

Buderath, P., Gärtner, K., Frings, M., Christiansen, H., Schoch, B., Konczak, J., . . . Timmann, D. (2009). Postural and gait performance in children with attention deficit/hyperactivity disorder. *Gait & Posture, 29*(2), 249–254.

Buie, T., Campbell, D. B., Fuchs, G. J., Furuta, G. T., Levy, J., VandeWater, J., & Winter, H. (2010). Evaluation, diagnosis, and treatment of gastrointestinal disorders in individuals with ASDs: A consensus report. *Pediatrics, 125*(supp. 1), S1–S18.

Carmona, S., Bassas, N., Rovira, M., Gispert, J. D., Soliva, J. C., Prado, M., & Vilarroya, O. (2007). Pediatric OCD structural brain deficits in conflict monitoring circuits: A voxel-based morphometry study. *Neuroscience Letters, 421*(3), 218–223.

Chanraud, S., Zahr, N., Sullivan, E. V., & Pfefferbaum, A. (2010). MR diffusion tensor imaging: A window into white matter integrity of the working brain. *Neuropsychology Review, 20*(2): 209–225.

Charil, A., Laplante, D. P., Vaillancourt, C., & King, S. (2010). Prenatal stress and brain development. *Brain Research Reviews, 65*(1), 56–79.

Chiron, C., Jambaque, I., Nabbout, R., Lounes, R., Syrota, A., & Dulac, O. (1997). The right brain hemisphere is dominant in human infants. *Brain, 120*(6), 1057–1065.

Chugani, H. T. (1998). A critical period of brain development: Studies of cerebral glucose utilization with PET. *Preventive Medicine, 27*(2), 184–188.

Coben, R., & Myers, T. E. (2008). Connectivity theory of autism: Use of connectivity measures in assessing and treating autistic disorders. *Journal of Neurotherapy, 12*(2–3), 161–179.

Contreras, D., Destexhe, A., Sejnowski, T. J., & Steriade, M. (1997). Spatiotemporal patterns of spindle oscillations in cortex and thalamus. *Journal of Neuroscience, 17*(3), 1179–1196.

Cooper, J. R., Bloom, F. E., & Roth, R. H. (1996). Dopamine. In *The biochemical basis of neuropharmacology* (pp. 293–351). New York: Oxford University Press.

Cunningham, M. W. (2012). Streptococcus and rheumatic fever. *Current Opinion in Rheumatology, 24*(4), 408.

Damasio, H., & Damasio, A. R. (1989). *Lesion analysis in neuropsychology*. New York: Oxford University Press.

Dawes, G. S. (1984). The central control of fetal breathing and skeletal muscle movements. *Journal of Physiology, 346*(1), 1–18.

Del Giudice, M. (2011). Alone in the dark? Modeling the conditions for visual experience in human fetuses. *Developmental Psychobiology, 53*(2), 214–219.

Dieterich, M., Bense, S., Lutz, S., Drzezga, A., Stephan, T., Bartenstein, P., & Brandt, T. (2003). Dominance for vestibular cortical function in the non-dominant hemisphere. *Cerebral Cortex, 13*(9), 994–1007.

Double, D. B. (2006). *Critical psychiatry: The limits of madness*. New York: Palgrave Macmillan.

Ehrenfried, T., Guerraz, M., Thilo, K. V., Yardley, L., & Gresty, M. A. (2003). Posture and mental task performance when viewing a moving visual field. *Cognitive Brain Research, 17*(1), 140–153.

Gazzaniga, M. S. (2005). Forty-five years of split-brain research and still going strong. *Nature Reviews Neuroscience, 6*(8), 653–659.

Geary, D. C. (1998). *Male, female: The evolution of human sex differences*. Washington, D.C.: American Psychological Association.

Gerhardt, K. J., & Abrams, R. M. (1996, February). Fetal hearing: Characterization of the stimulus and response. *Seminars in Perinatology, 20*(1), 11–20.

Geschwind, N. (1965a). Disconnexion syndromes in animals and man: I. *Brain, 88*(2), 237–294.

Geschwind, N. (1965b). Disconnexion syndromes in animals and man: II. *Brain, 88*(3), 585–644.

Geschwind, N. (1982). Why Orton was right. *Annals of Dyslexia, 32*(1), 13–30.

Geschwind, N., & Behan, P. O. (1984). Laterality, hormones, and immunity. In N. Geschwind & A. M. Galaburda (Eds.), *Cerebral dominance: The biological foundations* (pp. 211–224). n.p.: n.p.

Ghaziuddin, M., & Butler, E. (1998). Clumsiness in autism and Asperger syndrome: A further report. *Journal of Intellectual Disability Research, 42*(pt. 1), 43–48.

Goldberg, E., Podell, K., & Lovell, M. (1994). Lateralization of frontal lobe functions and cognitive novelty. *Journal of Neuropsychiatry and Clinical Neurosciences, 6*(4), 371–378.

Grandin, T. (1992). An inside view of autism. In Eric Schopler & Gary B. Mesibov (Eds.), *High-functioning individuals with autism* (pp. 105–126). New York: Springer US.

Hebb, D. O. (2002). *The organization of behavior: A neuropsychological theory.* Hove, UK: Psychology Press.

Heining, M., Young, A. W., Ioannou, G., Andrew, C. M., Brammer, M. J., Gray, J. A., & Phillips, M. L. (2003). Disgusting smells activate human anterior insula and ventral striatum. *Annals of the New York Academy of Sciences, 1000*(1), 380–384.

Henriques, J. B., & Davidson, R. J. (1991). Left frontal hypoactivation in depression. *Journal of Abnormal Psychology, 100*(4), 535.

Just, M. A., Cherkassky, V. L., Keller, T. A., Kana, R. K., & Minshew, N. J. (2007). Functional and anatomical cortical underconnectivity in autism: Evidence from an FMRI study of an executive function task and corpus callosum morphometry. *Cerebral Cortex, 17*(4), 951–961.

Kang, D. H., Davidson, R. J., Coe, C. L., Wheeler, R. E., Tomarken, A. J., & Ershler, W. B. (1991). Frontal brain asymmetry and immune function. *Behavioral Neuroscience, 105*(6), 860.

Kanner, L. (1943). Autistic disturbances of affective contact. *Nervous Child, 2*(3), 217–250.

Kohler, E., Keysers, C., Umilta, M. A., Fogassi, L., Gallese, V., & Rizzolatti, G. (2002). Hearing sounds, understanding actions: Action representation in mirror neurons. *Science, 297*(5582), 846–848.

Kolevzon, A., Gross, R., & Reichenberg, A. (2007). Prenatal and perinatal risk factors for autism: A review and integration of findings. *Archives of Pediatrics & Adolescent Medicine, 161*(4), 326–333.

Krahe, Rüdiger, and Fabrizio Gabbiani. (2004). "Burst firing in sensory systems." *Nature Reviews Neuroscience, 5*(1), 13–23.

Leisman, G. (1976). The role of visual processes in attention and its disorders. In Gerald Leisman (Ed.), *Basic visual processes and learning disability* (pp. 7–123). Springfield, IL: Charles C. Thomas,

Leisman, G., Machado, C., Melillo, R., & Mualem, R. (2012). Intentionality and "free-will" from a neurodevelopmental perspective. *Frontiers in integrative neuroscience, 6.* http://journal.frontiersin.org/Journal/10.3389/fnint.2012.00036/full

Leisman, G., & Melillo, R. (2013). The basal ganglia: Motor and cognitive relationships in a clinical neurobehavioral context. *Reviews in the Neurosciences, 24*(1), 9–25.

Leisman, G., Mualem, R., & Machado, C. (2013). The integration of the neurosciences, child public health, and education practice: Hemisphere-specific remediation strategies as a discipline partnered rehabilitation tool in ADD/ADHD. *Frontiers in Public Health, 1.* doi: 10.3389/fpubh.2013.00022

Leitner, Y., Barak, R., Giladi, N., Peretz, C., Eshel, R., Gruendlinger, L., & Hausdorff, J. M. (2007). Gait in attention deficit hyperactivity disorder. *Journal of Neurology, 254*(10), 1330–1338.

Lindell, Annukka K. (2006). "In your right mind: Right hemisphere contributions to language processing and production." *Neuropsychology Review, 16*(3), 131–148.

Liotti, M., & Tucker, D. M. (1996). Emotion in asymmetric corticolimbic networks. In Richard J. Davidson & Kenneth Hugdahl (Eds.), *Brain Asymmetry* (pp. 389–423). Cambridge, MA: MIT Press.

Melillo, R. (2013). *Autism: The scientific truth about preventing, diagnosing, and treating autism spectrum disorders—and what parents can do now.* New York: Penguin.

Melillo, R., & Leisman, G. (2009). "Autistic spectrum disorders as functional disconnection syndrome." *Reviews in the Neurosciences, 20*(2), 111–132.

Melillo, R., & Leisman, G. (2010). *Neurobehavioral disorders of childhood: An evolutionary perspective.* New York City, NY: Springer.

Murphy, S. K. (2014). Obesity: Paternal obesity—a risk factor for autism? *National Reviews Endocrinology, 10*(7), 389–390.

Neveu, P. J. (1993). Brain lateralization and immunomodulation. *International Journal of Neuroscience, 70*(1–2), 135–143.

Newman, T. M., Macomber, D., Naples, A. J., Babitz, T., Volkmar, F., & Grigorenko, E. L. (2007). Hyperlexia in children with autism spectrum disorders. *Journal of Autism and Developmental Disorders, 37*(4), 760–774.

Offner, H., Subramanian, S., Parker, S. M., Wang, C., Afentoulis, M. E., Lewis, A., . . . Hurn, P. D. (2006). "Splenic atrophy in experimental stroke is accompanied by increased regulatory T cells and circulating macrophages." *Journal of Immunology, 176*(11), 6523–6531.

Phillips, M. L., Drevets, W. C., Rauch, S. L., & Lane, R. (2003). Neurobiology of emotion perception I: The neural basis of normal emotion perception. *Biological Psychiatry, 54*(5), 504–514.

Puccetti, R. (1981). "The case for mental duality: Evidence from split-brain data and other considerations. *Behavioral and Brain Sciences 4*, 51–91.

Russ, K. (2014). Protecting pregnancy, protecting future generations. In *142nd APHA annual meeting and exposition (November 15–November 19, 2014).* New Orleans, LA: APHA.

Rutter, M. (2005). Incidence of autism spectrum disorders: Changes over time and their meaning. *Acta Paediatrica, 94*(1), 2–15.

Semrud-Clikeman, M. (2005). Neuropsychological aspects for evaluating learning disabilities. *Journal of Learning Disabilities, 38*(6), 563–568.

Sherman, S. M., & Guillery, R. W. (2002). "The role of the thalamus in the flow of information to the cortex." *Philosophical Transactions of the Royal Society of London. Series B: Biological Sciences, 357*(1428), 1695–1708.

Snider, L. A., & Swedo, S. E. (2004). PANDAS: Current status and directions for research. *Molecular Psychiatry, 9*(10), 900–907.

Spinella, M. (2002). A relationship between smell identification and empathy. *International Journal of Neuroscience, 112*(6), 605–612.

Stoner, R., Chow, M. L., Boyle, M. P., Sunkin, S. M., Mouton, P. R., Roy, S., & Courchesne, E. (2014). Patches of disorganization in the neocortex of children with autism. *New England Journal of Medicine, 370*(13), 1209–1219.

Teicher, M. H. (2000). Wounds that time won't heal: The neurobiology of child abuse. *Cerebrum, 2*(4), 50–67.

Uddin, L. Q., Supekar, K., & Menon, V. (2013). Reconceptualizing functional brain connectivity in autism from a developmental perspective. *Frontiers in Human Neuroscience, 7.* http://journal.frontiersin.org/Journal/10.3389/fnhum.2013.00458

Von Heisenberg, W. (1927). Über den anschaulichen Inhalt der quantentheoretischen Kinematik und Mechanik. *Zeitschrift für Physik, 43*(3–4), 172–198.

Wada, J. A., Clarke, R., & Hamm, A. (1975). Cerebral hemispheric asymmetry in humans: Cortical speech zones in 100 adult and 100 infant brains. *Archives of Neurology, 32*(4), 239–246.

Weinstock, M. (2007). Gender differences in the effects of prenatal stress on brain development and behaviour. *Neurochemical Research, 32*(10), 1730–1740.

Wilson, D. J. (2009). *Polio.* Santa Barbara, CA: ABC-CLIO.

Yellow, J. (2014). Environment, genetics may contribute equally to autism risk. *Autism, 27.*

Zilles, K., Schröder, H., Schröder, U., Horvath, E., Werner, L., Luiten, P. G. M., . . . Strosberg, A. D. (1989). Distribution of cholinergic receptors in the rat and human neocortex. In *Central cholinergic synaptic transmission* (pp. 212–228). n.p.: Birkhäuser Basel.

CHAPTER 6

Notes

1. Avena, 2013.
2. National Center for Chronic Disease Prevention, 2013.
3. USDA, 2013.
4. Cleave, 1974.
5. Mayer, 1997.
6. Mayer, 1997.
7. Bellaloui et al., 2009; Zobiole et al., 2010.
8. Myers et al., 2014.
9. Janssen & Kiliaan, 2014.
10. Georgieff, 2007; Bourre, 2006a, 2006b.
11. Chen & Su, 2013.
12. Leung et al., 2011.
13. Oken et al., 2008; Jacobson et al., 2008; Hibbeln et al., 2007.
14. Bernard et al., 2013.
15. Brown & Susser, 2008.
16. Jacka et al., 2013.
17. Steenweg de-Graaff et al., 2014.
18. Smith & Smith, 2010; Halfon et al., 2012.
19. Liu et al., 2013.
20. Defeyter & Russo, 2013.
21. Cooper et al., 2012.
22. Pollitt & Matthews, 1998.
23. Adolphus et al., 2013.
24. Stevenson et al. 2014; Sonuga-Barker et al., 2013.
25. Sánchez-Villegas et al., 2012.
26. Jacka, Pasco, et al., 2010.
27. Jacka, Kremer, et al., 2010.

28. Davison & Kaplan, 2012.

29. Williams, 1998.

30. Ames et al., 2002.

31. McNally et al., 2008.

32. Young, 2007; Russell et al., 2006; Gardner & Boles, 2005.

33. Huskisson et al., 2007.

34. Jackson et al., 2012.

35. McNally et al., 2008.

36. Ames et al., 2002.

37. Arnold et al., 1978; Haslam et al., 1984.

38. Gesch et al., 2002.

39. Schoenthaler, 1982.

40. Schoenthaler et al., 1997.

41. Schoenthaler & Bier, 2000.

42. Gesch et al., 2002; Zaalberg et al., 2010.

43. Arnold, 1999.

44. Hurt et al., 2011.

45. Harding et al., 2003.

46. Patel & Curtis, 2007.

47. Sinn & Bryan, 2007.

48. Neither author has ever had any financial relationship with Truehope Nutritional Support, the company that developed EMPowerplus, or the variations such as the one sold by Nutratek (Daily Essential Nutrients).

49. Kaplan et al., 2004.

50. Popper, 2001.

51. Rucklidge et al., 2010.

52. Katz et al., 2010.

53. Vazir et al., 2006.

54. Benton, 1988.

55. Rucklidge et al., 2014.

56. Curtis & Patel, 2008.

57. See Rossignol, 2009.

58. Adams & Conn, 1997; Xia, 2011.

59. Adams & Holloway, 2004.

60. Adams et al., 2011.

61. Mehl-Madrona et al., 2010.

62. MacFabe et al., 2011.

63. Kaplan et al., 2007.

64. Kaplan et al., 2004; Popper, 2001; Kaplan et al., 2001; Simmons, 2003; Frazier et al., 2012; Frazier et al., 2013.

65. Kaplan et al., 2002.

66. Rucklidge et al., 2010.

67. Frazier et al., 2009.

68. Rodway et al., 2012.

69. Amminger et al., 2010.

70. McIntyre & Jerrell, 2008.

71. Jacka et al., 2012.

References

Adams, J. B., Audhya, T., McDonough-Means, S., Rubin, R. A., Quig, D., Geis, E., et al. (2011). Effect of a vitamin/mineral supplement on children and adults with autism. *BMC Pediatrics, 11*, 111. doi: 10.1186/1471-2431-11-111

Adams, J. B., & Holloway, C. (2004). Pilot study of a moderate dose multivitamin/mineral supplement for children with autism spectrum disorder. *Journal of Alternative & Complementary Medicine, 10*(6), 1033–1039.

Adams, L., & Conn, S. (1997). Nutrition and its relationship to autism. *Focus on Autism and Other Developmental Disabilities, 12*(1), 53–58.

Adolphus, K., Lawton, C. L., & Dye, L. (2013). The effects of breakfast on behavior and academic performance in children and adolescents. *Frontiers in Human Neuroscience, 7*: 425.

Ames, B. N., Elson-Schwab, I., & Silver, E. (2002). High-dose vitamin therapy stimulates variant enzymes with decreased coenzyme binding affinity (increased Km), Relevance to genetic disease and polymorphisms. *American Journal of Clinical Nutrition, 75*: 616–658.

Amminger, G. P., Schäfer, M. R., Papageorgiou, K., Klier, C. M., Cotton, S. M., Harrigan, S. M., et al. (2010). Long-chain omega-3 fatty acids for indicated prevention of psychotic disorders: A randomized, placebo-controlled trial. *Archives of General Psychiatry, 67*(2), 146–154.

Arnold, L. E. (1999). Treatment alternatives for attention-deficit/hyperactivity disorder (ADHD). *Journal of Attention Disorders, 3*(1), 30–48.

Arnold, L. E., Christopher, J., Huestis, R. D., & Smeltzer, D. J. (1978). Megavitamins for minimal brain dysfunction: A placebo-controlled study. *JAMA, 240*(24), 2642–2643.

Avena, N. (2013, August 19). The American diet. *Psychology Today*. Retrieved from http://www.psychologytoday.com/blog/food-junkie/201308/the-american-diet.

Bellaloui, N., Reddy, K. N., Zablotowicz, R. M., Abbas, H. K., & Abel, C. A. (2009). Effects of glyphosate application on seed iron and root ferric (III) reductase in soybean cultivars. *Journal of Agricultural and Food Chemistry, 57*(20), 9569–9574.

Benton, D. (1988). Vitamin/mineral supplementation and non-verbal intelligence. *Lancet, 1*: 407–409.

Bernard, J. Y., De Agostini, M., Forhan, A., de Lauzon-Guillain, B., Charles, M. A., & Heude, B. (2013). The dietary n6:n3 fatty acid ratio during pregnancy is inversely associated with child neurodevelopment in the EDEN mother-child cohort. *Journal of Nutrition, 143*(9), 1481–1488.

Bourre, J. M. (2006a). Effects of nutrients (in food) on the structure and function of the nervous system: Update on dietary requirements for the brain. Part 1: micronutrients. *Journal of Nutrition, Health and Aging, 10*(5), 377–385.

Bourre, J. M. (2006b). Effects of nutrients (in food) on the structure and function of the nervous system: Update on dietary requirements for the brain. Part 2 : macronutrients. *Journal of Nutrition, Health and Aging, 10*(5), 386–399.

Brown, A. S., & Susser, E. S. (2008). Prenatal nutritional deficiency and risk of adult schizophrenia. *Schizophrenia Bulletin, 34*(6), 1054–1063.

Chen, H. F., & Su, H. M. (2013). Exposure to a maternal n-3 fatty acid-deficient diet during brain development provokes excessive hypothalamic-pituitary-adrenal axis responses to stress and behavioral indices of depression and anxiety in male rat offspring later in life. *Journal of Nutritional Biochemistry, 24*(1), 70–80.

Cleave. T. L. (1974). *The saccharine disease: Conditions caused by the taking of refined carbohydrates, such as sugar and white flour.* Bristol: John Write and Sons Ltd.

Cooper, S. B., Bandelow, S., Nute, M. L., Morris, J. G., & Nevill, M. E. (2012). Breakfast glycaemic index and cognitive function in adolescent school children. *British Journal of Nutrition, 107*(12), 1823–1832.

Curtis, L. T., & Patel, K. (2008). Nutritional and environmental approaches to preventing and treating autism and attention deficit hyperactivity disorder (ADHD): A review. *Journal of Alternative and Complementary Medicine, 14*(1), 79–85.

Davison, K. M., & Kaplan, B. J. (2012). Nutrient intakes are correlated with overall psychiatric functioning in adults with mood disorders. *Canadian Journal of Psychiatry, 57*(2), 85–92.

Defeyter, M. A., & Russo, R. (2013). The effect of breakfast cereal consumption on adolescents' cognitive performance and mood. *Frontiers of Human Neuroscience, 7*, 789.

Frazier, E., Fristad, M. A., & Arnold, L. E. (2009). Multinutrient supplement as treatment: Literature review and case report of a 12-year-old boy with bipolar disorder. *Journal of Child and Adolescent Psychopharmacology, 19*(4), 453–460.

Frazier, E. A., Fristad, M. A., & Arnold, L. E. (2012). Feasibility of a nutritional supplement as treatment for pediatric bipolar spectrum disorders. *Journal of Alternative and Complementary Medicine, 18*(7), 678–685.

Frazier, E. A., Gracious, B., Arnold, L. E., Failla, M., Chitchumroonchokchai, C., Habash, D., et al. (2013). Nutritional and safety outcomes from an open-label micronutrient intervention for pediatric bipolar spectrum disorders. *Journal of Child and Adolescent Psychopharmacology, 23*(8), 558–567.

Gardner, A., & Boles, R. G. (2005). Is a "mitochondrial psychiatry" in the future? A review. *Current Psychiatry Reviews, 1*, 255–271.

Georgieff, M. K. (2007). Nutrition and the developing brain: Nutrient priorities and measurement. *American Journal of Clinical Nutrition, 85*(2), 614S–620S.

Gesch, B., Hammond, S., Hampson, S., Eves, A., & Crowder, M. J. (2002). Influence of supplementary vitamins, minerals and essential fatty acids on the antisocial behaviour of young adult prisoners. *British Journal of Psychiatry, 181*, 22–28.

Halfon, N., Houtrow, A., Larson, K., & Newacheck, P. W. (2012). The changing landscape of disability in childhood. *Future of Children, 22*(1), 13–42.

Harding, K. L., Judah, R. D., & Gant, C. (2003). Outcome-based comparison of Ritalin versus food-supplement treated children with AD/HD. *Alternative Medicine Review, 8*(3), 319–330.

Haslam, R. H. A., Dalby, J. T., & Rademaker, A. W. (1984). Effects of megavitamin therapy on children with attention deficit disorders. *Pediatrics, 74*(1), 103–111.

Hibbeln, J. R., Davis, J. M., Steer, C., Emmett, P., Rogers, I., Williams, C., et al. (2007). Maternal seafood consumption in pregnancy and neurodevelopmental outcomes in childhood (ALSPAC study): An observational cohort study. *Lancet, 369*(9561), 578–585.

Hurt, E. A., Arnold, L. E., & Lofthouse, N. (2011). Dietary and nutritional treatments for attention-deficit/hyperactivity disorder: Current research support and recommendations for practitioners. *Current Psychiatry Reports, 13*, 323–332.

Huskisson E., Maggini S., & Ruf, M. (2007). The influence of micronutrients on cognitive function and performance. *Journal of International Medical Research, 35*(1), 1–19.

Jacka, F. N., Kremer, P. J., Leslie, E. R., Berk, M., Patton, G. C., Toumbourou, J.W., et al. (2010). Associations between diet quality and depressed mood in adolescents: Results from the Australian Healthy Neighbourhoods Study. *Australia and New Zealand Journal of Psychiatry, 44*(5), 435–442.

Jacka, F. N., Mykletun, A., & Berk, M. (2012). Moving towards a population health approach to the primary prevention of common mental disorders. *BMC Medicine, 10*(1), 149.

Jacka, F. N., Pasco, J. A., Mykletun, A., Williams, L. J., Hodge, A. M., O'Reilly, S. L., et al. (2010). Association of Western and traditional diets with depression and anxiety in women. *American Journal of Psychiatry, 167*, 305–311.

Jacka, F. N., Ystrom, E., Brantsaeter, A. L., Karevold, E., Roth, C., Haugen. M., et al. (2013). Maternal and early postnatal nutrition and mental health of offspring by age 5 years: A prospective cohort study. *Journal of the American Academy of Child and Adolescent Psychiatry, 52*(10), 1038–1047.

Jackson, J., Eaton, W., Cascella, N., Fasano, A., & Kelly, D. (2012). Neurologic and psychiatric manifestations of celiac disease and gluten sensitivity. *Psychiatry Quarterly, 83*(1), 91–102.

Jacobson, J. L., Jacobson, S. W., Muckle, G., Kaplan-Estrin, M., Ayotte, P., & Dewailly, E. (2008). Beneficial effects of a polyunsaturated fatty acid on infant development: Evidence from the Inuit of arctic Quebec. *Journal of Pediatrics, 152*(3), 356–364.

Janssen, C. I., & Kiliaan, A. J. (2014). Long-chain polyunsaturated fatty acids (LCPUFA) from genesis to senescence: The influence of LCPUFA on neural development, aging, and neurodegeneration. *Progress in Lipid Research, 53*, 1–17.

Kaplan, B. J., Crawford, S. G., Field, C. J., & Simpson, J. S. (2007). Vitamins, minerals, and mood. *Psycholical Bulletin, 133*(5), 747–760.

Kaplan, B. J., Crawford, S. G., Gardner, B., & Farrelly, G. (2002). Treatment of mood lability and explosive rage with minerals and vitamins: Two case studies in children. *Journal of Child and Adolescent Psychopharmacology, 12*(3), 205–219.

Kaplan, B. J., Fisher, J. E., Crawford, S. G., Field, C. J., & Kolb, B. (2004). Improved mood and behavior during treatment with a mineral-vitamin supplement: An open-label case series of children. *Journal of Child and Adolescent Psychopharmacology, 14*(1), 115–122.

Kaplan, B. J., Simpson, J. S. A., Ferre, R. C., Gorman, C. P., McMullen, D. M., and Crawford, S. G. (2001). Effective mood stabilization with a chelated mineral supplement: An open-label trial in bipolar disorder. *Journal of Clinical Psychiatry, 62*(12), 936–944.

Katz M., Levine, A. A., Kol-Degani, H., & Kav-Venaki, L. (2010). A compound herbal preparation (CHP) in the treatment of children with ADHD: A randomized controlled trial. *Journal of Attention Disorders, 14*(3), 281–291.

Leung, B. M., Wiens, K. P., & Kaplan, B. J. (2011). Does prenatal micronutrient supplementation improve children's mental development? A systematic review. *BMC Pregnancy and Childbirth, 11*, 12.

Liu J., Hwang, W. T., Dickerman, B., & Compher, C. (2013). Regular breakfast consumption is associated with increased IQ in kindergarten children. *Early Human Development, 89*(4), 257–262.

MacFabe, D. F., Cain, N. E., Boon, F., Ossenkopp, K. P., & Cain, D. P. (2011). Effects of the enteric bacterial metabolic product propionic acid on object-directed behavior, social behavior, cognition, and neuroinflammation in adolescent rats: Relevance to autism spectrum disorder. *Behavioral and Brain Research, 217*(1), 47–54.

Mayer, A. B. (1997). Historical changes in the mineral content of fruits and vegetables. *British Journal of Food, 99,* 207–211.

McIntyre, R. S., & Jerrell, J. M. (2008). Metabolic and cardiovascular adverse events associated with antipsychotic treatment in children and adolescents. *Archives of Pediatric and Adolescent Medicine, 162,* 929–935.

McNally, L., Bhagwagar, Z., & Hannestad, J.(2008). Inflammation, glutamate, and glia in depression: A literature review. *CNS Spectrum, 13*(6), 501–510.

Mehl-Madrona, L., Leung, B., Kennedy, C., Paul, S., & Kaplan, B. J. (2010). A naturalistic case-control study of micronutrients versus standard medication management in autism. *Journal of Child and Adolescent Psychopharmacology, 20*(2), 95–103.

Myers, S. S., Zanobetti, A., Kloog, I., Huybers, P., Leakey, A. D., Bloom, A. J., et al. (2014). Increasing CO_2 threatens human nutrition. *Nature.* doi: 10.1038/nautre 13179

National Center for Chronic Disease Prevention and Health Promotion. (2013). State indicator report on fruits and vegetables. In Control CfD (Ed.), Centers for Disease Control and Prevention. *State Indicators Report on Fruits and Vegetables,* 2013. Atlanta, GA: Centers for Disease and Control and Prevention, U.S. Department of Health and Human Services.

Oken E., Radesky, J. S., Wright, R. O., Bellinger, D. C., Amarasiriwardena, C. J., Kleinman, K. P., et al. (2008). Maternal fish intake during pregnancy, blood mercury levels, and child cognition at age 3 years in a US cohort. *American Journal of Epidemiology, 167*(10), 1171–1181.

Patel, K., & Curtis, L. T. (2007). Comprehensive approach to treating autism and attention-deficit hyperactivity disorder: A prepilot study. *Journal of Alternative and Complementary Medicine, 13*(10), 1091–1097.

Pollitt, E., & Mathews, R. (1998). Breakfast and cognition: An integrative summary. *American Journal of Clinical Nutrition, 67*(4), 804S–8013S.

Popper, C. W. (2001). Do vitamins or minerals (apart from lithium) have mood-stabilising effects? *Journal of Clinical Psychiatry, 62*(12), 933–935.

Rodway M., Vance, A., Watters, A., Lee, H., Bos, E., & Kaplan, B. J. (2012). Efficacy and cost of micronutrient treatment of childhood psychosis. *BMJ Case Reports, 2012.* doi: 10.1136/bcr-2012-007213

Rossignol, D. (2009). Novel and emerging treatments for autism spectrum disorders: A systematic review. *Annals of Clinical Psychiatry, 21*(4), 213–236.

Rucklidge, J. J., Frampton, C. M., Gorman, B., & Boggis, A. (2014). Vitamin-mineral treatment of ADHD in adults: A double-blind, randomized, placebo controlled trial. *British Journal of Psychiatry, 204,* 306–315.

Rucklidge, J. J., Gately, D., & Kaplan, B. J. (2010). Database analysis of children and adolescents with bipolar disorder consuming a multinutrient formula. *BMC: Psychiatry, 74*(10). doi: 10.1186/471-244X-10-74

Russell, V. A., Oades, R. D., Tannock, R., Killeen, P. R., Auerbach, J. G., Johansen, E. B., et al. (2006). Response variability in attention-deficit/hyperactivity disorder: A neuronal and glial energetics hypothesis. *Behavioral and Brain Functions, 2*(30), 23.

Sánchez-Villegas, A., Toledo, E., de Irala, J., Ruiz-Canela, M., Pla-Vidal, J., & Martínez-González, M. A. (2012). Fast-food and commercial baked goods consumption and the risk of depression. *Public Health and Nutrition 15*(03), 424–432.

Schoenthaler, S. J. (1982). The effect of sugar on the treatment and control of antisocial behavior: A double-blind study of an incarcerated juvenile population. *International Journal of Biosocial Research, 3*(1), 1–9.

Schoenthaler, S. J. (1983). Diet and crime: An empirical examination of the value of nutrition in the control and treatment of incarcerated juvenile offenders. *International Journal of Biosocial Research, 4*(1), 25–39.

Schoenthaler, S. J., Amos, S. P., Doraz, W. E., Kelly, M. A., Muedeking, G. D., & Wakefield, J. A. (1997). The effect of randomized vitamin-mineral supplementation on violent and non-violent antisocial behavior among incarcerated juveniles. *Journal of Nutritional and Environmental Medicine, 7*, 343–352.

Schoenthaler, S. J., & Bier, I. D. (2000). The effect of vitamin-mineral supplementation on juvenile delinquency among American schoolchildren: A randomized, double-blind placebo-controlled trial. *Journal of Alternative and Complementary Medicine, 6*(1), 7–17.

Simmons, M. (2003). Nutritional approach to bipolar disorder. *Journal of Clinical Psychiatry, 64*(3), 338.

Sinn, N., & Bryan, J. (2007). Effect of supplementation with polyunsaturated fatty acids and micronutrients on learning and behavior problems associated with child ADHD. *Journal of Developmental & Behavioral Pediatrics, 28*(2), 82–91.

Smith, J. P., & Smith, G. C. (2010). Long-term economic costs of psychological problems during childhood. *Social Science & Medicine, 71*(1), 110–115.

Sonuga-Barke, E. J., Brandeis, D., Cortese, S., Daley, D., Ferrin, M., Holtmann, M., et al. (2013). Nonpharmacological interventions for ADHD: Systematic review and meta-analyses of randomized controlled trials of dietary and psychological treatments. *American Journal of Psychiatry, 170*(3), 279–289.

Steenweg-de Graaff, J., Tiemeier, H., Steegers-Theunissen, R. P., Hofman, A., Jaddoe, V. W., Verhulst, F. C., et al. (2014). Maternal dietary patterns during pregnancy and child internalising and externalising problems: The Generation R Study. *Clinical Nutrition, 33*(1), 115–121.

Stevenson, J., Buitelaar, J., Cortese, S., Ferrin, M., Konofal, E., Lecendreux, M., et al. (2014). Research review: The role of diet in the treatment of attention-deficit/ hyperactivity disorder—an appraisal of the evidence on efficacy and recommendations on the design of future studies. *Journal of Child Psychology and Psychiatry, 55*(5), 416–427.

U.S. Department of Agriculture. (2013). *Profiling food consumption in America.* Washington, DC: USDA.

Vazir, S., Nagalla, B., Thangiah, V., Kamasamudram, V., & Bhattiprolu, S. (2006). Effect of micronutrient supplement on health and nutritional status of schoolchildren: Mental function. *Nutrition, 22*(1, supp.), S26–S32.

Williams, R. J. (1998). *Biochemical individuality: The basis for the genetotrophic concept.* New Canaan, CT: Keats.

Xia, R. R. (2011). Effectiveness of nutritional supplements for reducing symptoms in autism-spectrum disorder: A case report. *Journal of Alternative and Complementary Medicine, 17*(3), 271–274.

Young, L. T. (2007). Is bipolar disorder a mitochondrial disease? *Journal of Psychiatry and Neuroscience, 32*(3), 160–161.

Zaalberg, A., Nijman, H., Bulten, E., Stroosma, L., & van der Staak, C. (2010). Effects of nutritional supplements on aggression, rule-breaking, and psychopathology among young adult prisoners. *Aggressive Behavior, 36*(2), 117–126.

Zobiole, L. H., Oliveira, R. S., Visentainer, J. V., Kremer, R. J., Bellaloui N., & Yamada T. (2010). Glyphosate affects seed composition in glyphosate-resistant soybean. *Journal of Agricultural and Food Chemistry, 58*(7), 4517–4522.

CHAPTER 7

1. M. Halstead and K. Walter, "Sport-Related Concussion in Children and Adolescents," *Pediatrics* 126, no. 3 (2010): 597–615.

2. Halstead and Walter, "Sport-Related Concussion in Children and Adolescents."

3. Emotions are generated primarily in a collective structure known as the limbic system, which contains the thalamus (relay station and central information hub), hypothalamus and pituitary gland (keeps us adapted to our environment), hippocampus (essential for memory formation), and amygdala (fear processing and approach/avoidance behavior).

4. J. D. Schmahmann and D. Caplan, "Cognition, Emotion and the Cerebellum," *Brain* 129 (2006): 290–292.

5. S. Bashir, M. Vernet, and A. Pascual-Leone, "Changes in Cortical Plasticity after Mild Traumatic Brain Injury," *Restorative Neurology and Neuroscience* 30, no. 4 (2012): 277–282.

6. N. Li et al., "Evidence for Impaired Plasticity after Traumatic Brain Injury in the Developing Brain," *Journal of Neurotrauma* 31, no. 4 (2014): 395–403.

7. R. C. Cantu, "Second- impact Syndrome," *Clinical Sports Medicine* 17, no. 1 (1998): 37–44.

8. B. Boden et al., "Catastrophic Head Injuries in High School and College Football Players," *American Journal of Sports Medicine* 35 (2000): 1–7.

9. D. Hovda and C. Giza, "The Neurometabolic Cascade of Concussion," *Journal of Athletic Training* 36, no. 3 (2001): 228–235.

10. L. Theodore et al., "Transcranial Amelioration of Inflammation and Cell Death after Brain Injury," *Nature* 10 (2013): 10–38.

11. D. Hovda and C. Giza, "The Neurometabolic Cascade of Concussion," *Journal of Athletic Training* 36, no. 3 (2001): 228–235.

12. P. Echlin et al., "Microstructural White Matter Alterations in Concussed Hockey Players," *Journal of Neurosurgery* 120 (2014): 873–881.

13. P. Echlin et al., "Microstructural White Matter Alterations in Concussed Hockey Players," *Journal of Neurosurgery* 120, no. 4 (2014): 873–881.

14. R. Graham et al., *Sports-Related Concussions in Youth: Improving the Science Changing the Culture* (Washington, DC: Institute of Medicine and National Research Council, 2013).

15. J. Cavanaugh, K. Guskiewicz, and N. Stergiou, "A Nonlinear Dynamic Approach for Evaluation Postural Control," *Sports Medicine* 35 (2005): 935–950.

16. P. McCrory, A. Collie, and V. Anderson, "Can We Manage Sport Related Concussion in Children the Same as in Adults?" *British Journal of Sports Medicine* 38 (2004): 516–519.

17. "Consensus Statement on Concussion in Sport: The 4th International Conference on Concussion in Sport," *British Journal of Sports Medicine* 47 (2012): 250–258.

18. M. Gammons, "Helmets in Sport: Fact and Fallacy," *Current Sports Medicine Reports* 6 (2013): 377–380.

19. R. Beck, *Functional Neurology for Manual Practitioners* (Auckland, NZ: Elsevier Books, 2008).

20. M. Heitger et al., "Impaired Eye Movements in Post-concussion Syndrome Indicate Suboptimal Brain Function Beyond the Influence of Depression, Malingering or Intellectual Ability," *Brain* 132 (2009): 2850–2870.

21. C. Ingersoll and C. Armstrong, "The Effects of Closed-Head Injury on Postural Sway," *Medical Science and Sports Exercise* 7 (1992): 24–25.

22. G. Kessler, "Cognitive Performance in Space and Antigravity Environments," *International Journal of Cognitive Ergonomics* n.v. (1999): 352–353.

23. G. Ilie et al., "Suicidality, Bullying and Other Conduct and Mental Health Correlates of Traumatic Brain Injury in Adolescents," *PlosOne* 9 (2014): 4–5.

24. P. McCrory, "Should We Treat Concussions Pharmacologically?" *British Journal of Sports Medicine* 36 (2002): 3–5.

25. W. Mittenberg et al., "Treatment of Post Concussion Syndrome Following Mild Head Injury," *Journal of Clinical Experimental Neuropsychology* 6 (2001): 829–836.

26. I. Kirsch, *The Emperor's New Drugs: Exploding the Antidepressant Myth* (New York: Basic Books, 2010).

27. D. Kharrazian, *Why Isn't My Brain Working?* (Carlsbad, CA: Elephant Press Books, 2013).

28. A. Michael-Titus and J. Priestly, "Omega-3 Fatty Acids and Traumatic Neurological Injury," *Trends in Neuroscience* 1 (2014): 30–38.

29. T. McIntosh et al., "Magnesium Deficiency Exacerbates and Pretreatment Improves Outcome Following Traumatic Brain Injury in Rats," *Journal of Neurotrauma* 1 (1988): 17–31.

30. C. Sanfeliu and J. Sebastia, "Methylmercury Neurotoxicity in Cultures of Human Neurons, Astrocytes, Neuroblatoma Cells," *Journal of Neurotoxicology* 3 (2001): 317–327.

31. The author has no business affiliation with Brain Hq.

CHAPTER 8

An earlier version of this chapter first appeared in *No Child Left Different*.

1. U. Bronfenbrenner, "Strengthening Family Systems," in *The Parental Leave Crisis: Toward a National Policy*, ed. E. F. Zigler and M. Frank (New Haven, CT: Yale University Press, 1988), 143–160.

2. A. Schore, *Affect Dysregulation and Disorders of the Self* (New York: Norton, 2003).

3. R. Karen, *Becoming Attached: First Relationships and How They Shape Our Capacity to Love* (New York: Oxford University Press, 1998).

4. Karen, *Becoming Attached*, 3.

5. M. Small, "The Natural History of Children," in *Childhood Lost: How American Culture Is Failing Our Kids*, ed. S. Olfman (Westport, CT: Praeger, 2004), 3–18.

6. Small, "Natural History of Children."

7. Karen, *Becoming Attached*, 3; Small, "Natural History of Children."

8. D. Stern, *The Interpersonal World of the Infant* (New York: Basic Books, 1985).

9. R. S. Rice, "Neurophysiological Development in Premature Infants Following Stimulation," *Developmental Psychology* 13 (1997): 69–76; J. L. White, and R. C. Labarba,

"The Effects of Tactile and Kinesthetic Stimulation on Neonatal Development in the Premature Infant," *Developmental Psychobiology* (1976): 569–577.

10. J. J. McKenna, S. S. Mosko, C. Richard, S. Drummond, L. Hunt, M. B. Cetel, and J. Arpaia, "Experimental Studies of Infant-Parent Co-sleeping: Mutual Physiological and Behavioral Influences and Their Relevance to SIDS (Sudden Infant Death Syndrome)," *Early Human Development* 38 (1994): 187–201.

11. N. Angier, "Mother's Milk Found to Be Potent Cocktail of Hormones," *New York Times*, May 24, 1994, B5.

12. S. Gerhardt, *Why Love Matters: How Affection Shapes a Baby's Brain* (New York: Brunner-Routledge, 2004).

13. Schore, *Affect Dysregulation and Disorders of the Self*.

14. Gerhardt, *Why Love Matters*.

15. Gerhardt, *Why Love Matters*.

16. Gerhardt, *Why Love Matters*.

17. D. Baumrind, "Current Patterns of Parental Authority," *Developmental Psychology Monograph* 4, no. 1 (1971): pt. 2; L. Kuczynski and S. Lollis, "Four Foundations for a Dynamic Model of Parenting," in *Dynamics of Parenting*, ed. J. R. M. Gerris (Hillsdale, NJ: Erlbaum, 2002); A. Russell, J. Mize, and K. Bissaker, "Parent-Child Relationships," in *Handbook of Childhood Social Development*, ed. P. K. Smith and C. Hart (Oxford: Blackwell, 2002).

18. L. E. Berk, *Infants, Children and Adolescents* (Boston: Pearson & Allyn and Bacon, 2005).

19. E. H. Erikson, *Childhood and Society* (New York: Norton, 1950).

20. H. F. Harlow and R. Zimmerman, "Affectional Responses in the Infant Monkey," *Science* 130 (1959): 421–432; M. F. Small, *Our Babies, Ourselves: How Biology and Culture Shape the Way We Parent* (New York: Anchor Books, 1999).

21. Bronfenbrenner, "Strengthening Family Systems" (emphasis added).

22. U. Bronfenbrenner, "Child Care in the Anglo-Saxon Mode," in *Child Care in Context*, ed. M. E. Lamb, J. J. Sternberg, C. P. Hwang, and A. G. Broberg (Hillsdale, NJ: Lawrence Erlbaum, 1992), 281–291 (emphasis added).

23. L. Berk, "Why Parenting Matters," in *Childhood Lost*, ed. S. Olfman (Westport CT: Praeger, 2004), 19–53 (emphasis added).

24. Berk, "Why Parenting Matters" (emphasis added).

25. U. Bronfenbrenner, "The Future of Childhood," in *Children: Needs and Rights*, ed. V. Greaney (Irvington Publishers, 1985): 167–186.

About the Editor and Contributors

EDITOR

Sharna Olfman is a professor of clinical and developmental psychology at Point Park University and a psychologist in private practice. She is the editor/author of the Childhood in America book series for Praeger Publishers. Her books include *Drugging Our Children* (coedited with Brent Robbins, 2012), *The Sexualization of Childhood* (2008), *Bipolar Children* (2007), *No Child Left Different* (2006), *Child Honoring: How to Turn This World Around* (coedited with Raffi Cavoukian, 2006), *Childhood Lost* (2005), and *All Work and No Play* (2003). Dr. Olfman has written and lectured internationally on the subjects of children's mental health and parenting. She was the founder and director of the annual Childhood and Society Symposium, a multidisciplinary think tank on childhood advocacy, from 2001 to 2008.

CONTRIBUTORS

Richard C. Francis is a freelance science writer. He received his PhD in neurobiology and behavior from Stony Brook University and was a recipient of the National Research Science Award from the National Institute of Mental Health. He is the author of *Why Men Won't Ask for Directions* and *Epigenetics: How Environment Shapes Our Genes*. Before becoming a freelance writer, he conducted widely published postdoctoral research in evolutionary neurobiology and sexual development at the University of California, Berkeley, and Stanford University.

Daniel Gallucci is a postgraduate student and a clinical and research fellow under Dr. Frederick R. Carrick at the Carrick Institute, with a focus on traumatic brain injury/vestibular rehabilitation. He is the founder of Dg2 (www.dgallucci.com), a neurological therapy clinic in Toronto, Canada, with a "high tech, high touch" approach to rehabilitation and performance. Dg2 utilizes an integrated network of health professionals and data sets to unlock the secrets of the brain and guide patients on a path of personalized recovery, health, and performance. Research projects currently underway include (1) collecting longitudinal movement/posture data on postconcussion patients to establish links between postconcussion syndrome and neurodegenerative disease/dysfunction and (2) the impact of postconcussion syndrome on catecholamine levels.

Bonnie J. Kaplan completed her undergraduate degree in psychology at the University of Chicago, and her master's degree and PhD in physiological psychology at Brandeis University in Waltham, Massachusetts. She completed postdoctoral training in neurophysiology and physiological psychology at the Neuropsychology Laboratory of the West Haven (Connecticut) VA Hospital, and at the Neurology Department, Yale University Medical School, New Haven, Connecticut. She then remained in Yale's Neurology Department for two years as a basic researcher in neurophysiology. In 1979 Dr. Kaplan moved to Calgary, Alberta, Canada, to establish a behavioral research unit at the Alberta Children's Hospital, where she remains to this day. As a professor in the faculty of medicine at the University of Calgary, her primary research interest is the relationship between nutrition and brain *development* (pregnancy cohort study; www.ApronStudy.ca) and brain *function* (the use of broad spectrum micronutrients to treat mental disorders). She has published well over a hundred peer-reviewed studies and is a sought-after speaker on nutrition and mental health. Her research can be found at http://research4kids.ucalgary.ca/members /kaplan_full.

Gerry Leisman is an Israeli neuroscientist with a doctorate in neuroscience and biomedical engineering from Union University. He previously held the position of professor of rehabilitation sciences at Leeds Metropolitan University in the United Kingdom and concurrently at the University of Haifa in Israel. He is currently the director of the National Institute for Brain and Rehabilitation Sciences in Nazareth, Israel; professor of biomedical and rehabilitation engineering in the Department of Mechanical Engineering at O.R.T.-Braude College of Engineering in Karmiel, Israel; and professor of brain and rehabilitation sciences at the Universidad de Ciencias Médicas de la Habana Facultad Manuel Fajardo in Havana, Cuba. He is editor-in-chief of the journal *Functional Neurology, Rehabilitation, and Ergonomics*.

Dr. Leisman's scientific career has focused on two broad areas of endeavor. First, he has been active since the early 1970s in the promotion of consciousness as a scientifically tractable problem and has been particularly influential in arguing that a fundamental understanding of consciousness can be approached using the modern tools of neurobiology and understood by mechanisms of theoretical physics, having developed biomedical applications of continuum theory. He has also been influential in examining mechanisms of self-organizing systems in the brain and nervous system applied to cognitive functions, exemplified by his work in memory, kinesiology, optimization, consciousness, death, and autism. He has likewise applied optimization strategies to movement and gait, cognition, and coma recovery. It is in this context that in the early 1970s he was one of the first to identify functional disconnectivities in the brain and nervous system. He was elected a fellow of the Association for Psychological Science in 1990, a senior member of the Engineering in Medicine and Biology Society of IEEE in 1986, a life fellow of the American Association for Forensic Examination-International in Forensic Engineering in 1994, and a life fellow of the International Association of Functional Neurology and Rehabilitation in 2010, having received its Lifetime Achievement Award in 2011. He is the coauthor of a text with Dr. Robert Melillo on neurobehavioral disorders of childhood from an evolutionary perspective. He has published hundreds of papers in the neurosciences, engineering, and systems sciences literature and is the holder of patents.

Robert Melillo has been an active clinician for over 25 years and is one of the world's most respected specialists in childhood neurological disorders. His areas of expertise include autism spectrum disorders, ADD and ADHD; dyslexia; Asperger's syndrome; Tourette's syndrome; bipolar disorder; and other attention, behavioral, and learning disorders. He also specializes in neuroimmune disorders in children and adolescents, such as PANDAS and PANS and focuses on preconception programs for adults. He has been working with children with neurological disabilities for more than 20 years.

His work as a university professor and a cutting-edge brain researcher and his success with over a thousand children in his private program led to the creation of Brain Balance Achievement Centers. The centers use a medicine-free, multimodal curriculum focused on correcting the primary issue inherent in most neurological developmental disorders: a functional disconnection in the brain in which one side of the brain is growing too slow or too fast, preventing the two sides from integrating and working in harmony.

Dr. Melillo and his research partner, Dr. Gerry Leisman, are considered two of the world's leading experts on and pioneers in functional disconnection and its relationship to neuro-behavioral disorders. Since they introduced the concept, functional disconnection has become the leading theory as the key issue related to autism, ADHD, dyslexia, and other similar conditions. Their work is leading the way to understanding the underlying nature of these disorders and their causes. Their lab is focused on developing effective treatments.

Dr. Melillo wrote a working-theory textbook on development disabilities called *Neurobehavioral Disorders of Childhood: An Evolutionary Perspective*, which was published in 2004. In 2009 Perigee published his first book for a lay audience, *Disconnected Kids*. Greeted by an overwhelmingly positive response, the book serves as the foundation for the work being done at the 100 Brain Balance Achievement Centers around the country. His second book, *Reconnected Kids*, was published by Perigee in 2011 and has also been a best seller since its release. Dr. Melillo's third book, *Autism: The Scientific Truth about Preventing, Diagnosing, and Treating Autism Spectrum Disorders and What Parents Can Do Now*, was published by Penguin in January 2013. It takes on the question of what causes autism and how it can be prevented. He describes in the book a cutting-edge preconception program for parents that lowers the risk of having a child with autism or other developmental disabilities.

Dr. Melillo's leadership in the field, as well as his personal dedication to helping children with neurological disorders, have made him one of the most sought-after speakers on the subject, both in the United States and abroad. His optimistic and straightforward approach to overcoming childhood brain disabilities has given hope to countless families throughout the world. He has made dozens of national and local television appearances and has been interviewed on hundreds of radio programs. He frequently appears as an expert commentator on Fox News and NBC.

Dr. Melillo is an affiliate professor of rehabilitation sciences at Nazareth Academic Institute and a senior research fellow with the National Institute for Brain and Rehabilitation Sciences. He is a postgraduate professor of childhood developmental disabilities. He holds a master's degree in neuroscience and a master's degree in clinical rehabilitation neuropsychology and is completing his doctorate in the same subjects. He holds a doctorate in chiropractic, a diplomate in neurology, a fellowship with the American College of Functional Neurology, and a fellowship with the American Board of Childhood Developmental Disabilities, and is the executive director of the FR

Carrick Research Institute and The Children's Autism Hope Project. He is also president of the International Association of Functional Neurology and Rehabilitation and the coeditor-in-chief of the professional journal *Functional Neurology, Rehabilitation and Ergonomics*. He has published numerous scientific papers and contributed chapters to seven professional books. He has also made hundreds of conference presentations. He maintains a private practice in New York City and Atlanta, Georgia, and lives in Rockville Centre, New York, with his wife and three children.

Julia J. Rucklidge is a professor of clinical psychology in the Department of Psychology at the University of Canterbury, Christchurch, New Zealand. Originally from Toronto, Canada, she did her undergraduate training in neurobiology at McGill University in Montreal. She then completed a master's degree and a PhD at the University of Calgary in clinical psychology, where she studied the psychological profiles of women with ADHD. She went on to the Hospital for Sick Children in Toronto to complete a two-year postdoctoral fellowship investigating gender differences in ADHD adolescents. In 2000 she and her husband moved to Christchurch, New Zealand, where she secured a position at the University of Canterbury in the Department of Psychology. She teaches child and family psychology in the Clinical Psychology Programme and more recently has introduced the topic of mental health and nutrition into the wider psychology program. Her interests in nutrition and mental illness grew out of her own research showing poor outcomes for children with significant psychiatric illness despite receiving conventional treatments for their conditions. In the last decade, she has been running clinical trials investigating the role of broad-spectrum micronutrients in the expression of mental illness, specifically ADHD, bipolar disorder, anxiety, and more recently stress and PTSD associated with the Canterbury earthquakes. She is also studying the effect of probiotics on depression. Julia has done more than 70 peer-reviewed studies and is passionate about helping people find alternative treatments to medications for their psychiatric symptoms. Her current research interests can be found at http://www.psyc.canterbury.ac.nz/people/rucklidge.shtml.

Robert Whitaker is the author of four books, two of which tell about the history of psychiatry. His first, *Mad in America: Bad Science, Bad Medicine and the Enduring Mistreatment of the Mentally Ill*, was named by *Discover* magazine as one of the best science books of 2002. His newest book on this topic, *Anatomy of an Epidemic: Magic Bullets, Psychiatric Drugs, and the Astonishing Rise of Mental Illness in America*, won the

Investigative Reporters and Editors book award for best investigative journalism in 2010. Prior to writing books, he worked as the science and medical reporter at the *Albany Times Union* newspaper in New York for a number of years.

Index